AI Governance in Irish Finance: A Practical Guide for Compliance and Innovation by Joe Houghton

First published in Ireland – May 2025
First edition – May 2025

Website: https://houghton.consulting
Email: joe@houghtonphoto.com
LinkedIn: https://www.linkedin.com/in/joehoughton/

ISBN: 978-1-916579-05-7 (paperback 1st edition)
ISBN: 978-1-916579-06-4 (hardback 1st edition)

Table of Contents

1 WHY YOU SHOULD READ THIS BOOK 9
1.1 How I wrote the book 10
1.2 How to contact me 12
1.3 My other books 13

2 INTRODUCTION 16
2.1 AI and Society 17
2.2 Glossary of Terms 18

3 FAIRNESS & NON-DISCRIMINATION 22
3.1 Ensuring Fairness in AI Systems 24
3.2 Non-Discrimination in AI 27
3.2.1 Explainable AI in Financial Services 28
3.2.2 AI Regulations and Guidelines in Ireland 30
3.2.3 AI in Irish Enterprise 32
3.2.4 AI Serving the Public 32
3.2.5 Research and Innovation 33
3.2.6 AI Education and Skills 35
3.2.7 Infrastructure for AI 35
3.2.8 AI Applications in Irish Financial Institutions 36
3.2.9 Potential examples of AI Discrimination 39
3.3 Challenges to AI Adoption in Ireland 40
3.4 Conclusion 41
3.5 References 43

4 TRANSPARENCY & EXPLAINABILITY 46
4.1 Transparency in AI for Financial Services 47
4.1.1 Dimensions of Transparency 48
4.1.2 Benefits of Transparency 49
4.2 Explainability in AI for Financial Services 51
4.2.1 Methods for Achieving Explainability 53
4.2.2 Benefits of Explainability 54
4.2.3 Irish Context and Practical Examples 56
4.3 Applying Transparency and Explainability in the Irish Context 63
4.4 Open Banking and AI 64
4.5 Practical Considerations for Staff in Irish Financial Institutions 65
4.5.1 Practical Guidance for Staff 66
4.5.2 Training and Education 67
4.6 Implementation Framework and Roadmap 68
4.6.1 Risk Management Lifecycle for AI 70
4.6.2 Third-Party AI Providers 71
4.7 Case Studies 72
4.8 Synthesis and Recommendations 73
4.9 References 75

5 PRIVACY & DATA PROTECTION.. 77
5.1 The Imperative of Privacy & Data Protection 78
5.2 The Evolving Regulatory Landscape for AI and Data Protection 81
5.2.1 General Data Protection Regulation (GDPR) 81
5.2.2 EU Artificial Intelligence Act (AI Act) 83
5.2.3 Irish Regulatory Authorities 86
5.3 AI Applications and Associated Privacy Risks 89
5.3.1 Fraud Detection and Prevention 89
5.3.2 Credit Scoring and Risk Assessment 90
5.3.3 Customer Service Chatbots and Virtual Assistants 91
5.3.4 Algorithmic Trading and Investment Strategies 92
5.3.5 Other AI Applications and the Importance of Privacy by Design 93
5.4 Key Privacy and Data Protection Considerations for Responsible AI 95
5.4.1 Effective Consent Management 95
5.4.2 Adherence to Data Minimization and Purpose Limitation 96
5.4.3 Transparency and Explainability 97
5.4.4 Mitigation of Algorithmic Bias 98
5.4.5 Robust Cybersecurity Measures 99
5.4.6 Human Oversight and Intervention 100
5.5 Practical Implications and Recommendations 102
5.5.1 Develop Robust AI Governance Frameworks 102
5.5.2 Conduct Thorough Data Protection Impact Assessments (DPIAs) 104
5.5.3 Implement Staff Training and Awareness Programs 105
5.5.4 Ensure Ongoing Regulatory Compliance 105
5.5.5 Implement Best Practices for Third-Party Vendor Management 107
5.6 Case Studies of Privacy and Data Protection in AI 109
5.6.1 An Post Money 109
5.6.2 "BIG Bank" (Anonymized Case Study) 110
5.6.3 Finclude 111
5.7 The Future of AI and Data Protection 112
5.8 Conclusion: Fostering Trust and Responsibility in the Age of AI 114
5.9 References 116

6 ACCOUNTABILITY & RESPONSIBILITY.. 125
6.1 Introduction 126
6.1.1 Background on AI Adoption 126
6.1.2 Importance of Accountability and Responsibility 127
6.1.3 Scope and Objectives 128
6.2 Defining Accountability and Responsibility 130
6.2.1 Defining Accountability 130
6.2.2 Defining Responsibility 131
6.3 Accountability and Responsibility in Literature and Industry Reports 133
6.3.1 Academic Perspectives on Accountability 133
6.3.2 Industry Perspectives on Accountability and Responsibility 134
6.4 The Irish Regulatory Landscape for AI in Financial Services 135
6.4.1 Central Bank of Ireland's Stance 135

6.4.2 Other Relevant Irish Regulatory Bodies 137
6.4.3 Implications of the EU AI Act 138
6.5 Analysis of Accountability in AI Applications 139
6.5.1 Conceptualizing Accountability in AI Use Cases 139
6.5.2 Mechanisms for Ensuring Accountability 140
6.6 Analysis of Responsibility in AI Applications 141
6.6.1 Defining and Assigning Responsibility 141
6.6.2 Ethical Considerations and Responsibility 142
6.7 Recommendations from Irish Regulatory Guidelines 143
6.7.1 Central Bank of Ireland's Requirements 143
6.7.2 EU AI Act Obligations for Irish Firms 144
6.7.3 Table of Key Requirements and Recommendations 146
6.8 Comparing Perspectives on Accountability and Responsibility 149
6.8.1 Convergence and Divergence 149
6.8.2 Potential Gaps or Inconsistencies 150
6.9 Conclusion and Recommendations 152
6.9.1 Summary of Key Findings 152
6.9.2 Comprehensive Recommendations for Financial Institutions 153
6.10 References 155

7 GOVERNANCE 164
7.1 Defining AI Governance 167
7.2 Core Principles of AI Governance 169
7.3 Specific Importance for Financial Institutions 175
7.4 Regulatory and Supervisory Landscape in Ireland 179
7.4.1 The EU AI Act and its Implications for Irish Finance 179
7.4.2 Central Bank of Ireland: Guidance and Expectations 188
7.4.3 Irish Data Protection Law (GDPR) and AI Systems 191
7.5 AI Applications in Irish Financial Institutions 194
7.5.1 Common Use Cases (Current and Emerging) 194
7.6 Analysing Key AI Risks in Irish Financial Services 199
7.6.1 Algorithmic Bias and Fairness Concerns 199
7.6.2 Transparency and Explainability Challenges 201
7.6.3 Data Privacy and Security Vulnerabilities 202
7.6.4 Model Risk and Reliability 204
7.6.5 Cybersecurity Threats Amplified by AI 206
7.6.6 Operational and Third-Party Risks 207
7.7 AI Governance Frameworks and Best Practices 210
7.7.1 Overview of Relevant Frameworks and Standards 210
7.7.2 Best Practices for Implementing AI Governance: 213
7.7.3 Aligning Frameworks with Risk Mitigation 215
7.8 Ethical Considerations for AI in Irish Finance 219
7.8.1 Consumer Protection Issues 219
7.8.2 Ensuring Fairness and Non-Discrimination 221
7.8.3 Accountability in AI-Driven Decisions 222
7.8.4 Promoting Responsible AI Principles 223

7.9 Practical Implementation Challenges 225
7.9.1 Resource Constraints and Skills Gaps 225
7.9.2 Integrating Governance into Existing Processes 225
7.9.3 Navigating Regulatory Interpretation 226
7.9.4 Data Management and Quality Issues 227
7.9.5 Other Challenges 227
7.10 Conclusion 230
7.11 References 232
7.11.1 Works cited 239

8 BIAS... 250
8.1 Why Addressing Bias is Critical 252
8.2 Unpacking AI Bias: Types, Sources, and Manifestations 255
8.2.1 A Taxonomy of Bias in Financial AI 255
8.2.2 Tracing the Roots: How Bias Enters the AI Lifecycle 261
8.2.3 Real-World Examples 263
8.3 The Regulatory Imperative: Navigating Irish and EU Rules 266
8.3.1 The Central Bank's Expectations for AI Fairness and Responsibility 266
8.3.2 Decoding the EU AI Act for Financial Services 269
8.3.3 Interplay with GDPR and the Consumer Protection Code 273
8.4 Consequences of AI Bias in Ireland 275
8.4.1 Impacts on Irish Consumers and Society 275
8.4.2 Risks and Liabilities for Financial Institutions 278
8.5 A Toolkit for Mitigation: Practical Strategies and Techniques 280
8.5.1 Proactive Measures: Data Governance and Feature Engineering 280
8.5.2 During Development: Fairness-Aware Modelling and Testing 283
8.5.3 Detection and Monitoring: Fairness Metrics and Auditing Tools 285
8.5.4 Essential Pillars: Transparency, Explainability (XAI), and Human Oversight 287
8.5.5 Organisational Measures 289
8.5.6 Mitigation Techniques Mapped to AI Lifecycle Stages 290
8.6 Addressing AI Bias in Practice 292
8.6.1 Case Study: AIB's Initiative on Algorithmic Fairness 292
8.6.2 Case Study: Central Bank & Academia Collaboration on Responsible AI 294
8.6.3 Case Study: Industry Commitments (e.g., Insurance Ireland) 295
8.6.4 Other Relevant Irish Context/Examples 296
8.7 Building a Foundation: An Implementation Framework for Irish Firms 298
8.7.1 Key Pillars of a Responsible AI Framework 298
8.7.2 Developing a Tailored Roadmap 302
8.7.3 Assigning Roles and Responsibilities 304
8.7.4 Implementation Framework Summary 305
8.8 Your Role in Ensuring Fairness: A Practical Guide for Staff 307
8.8.1 Recognising Potential Bias in Day-to-Day Work (Role-Specific Examples) 307
8.8.2 Following Internal Procedures and Best Practices 310
8.8.3 Raising Concerns and Contributing to Solutions 311
8.8.4 Conclusion: Fostering a Culture of Responsible AI 311
8.9 References 313

9 MICROSOFT COPILOT IN THE ENTERPRISE 322
9.1 AI and Copilot in the Irish Enterprise 324
9.1.1 Understanding Microsoft Copilot Offerings 325
9.1.2 Overview of the Copilot Ecosystem 325
9.1.3 Standard Copilot (Free Tier) 326
9.1.4 Copilot Pro (Premium Consumer/Individual Tier) 327
9.1.5 Copilot for Microsoft 365 (Enterprise Integration) 328
9.1.6 Microsoft Copilot Studio (Customisation and Agent Building) 329
9.1.7 Underlying Technologies 331
9.1.8 Table 1: Comparison of Microsoft Copilot Versions 332
9.2 The Regulatory and Ethical Framework for AI in Ireland 335
9.2.1 EU AI Act 335
9.2.2 General Data Protection Regulation (GDPR) 337
9.2.3 Irish Regulatory Guidance 339
9.2.4 Microsoft's Responsible AI Standard 341
9.3 Practical Applications of Copilot Across the Irish Enterprise 344
9.3.1 Enhancing Productivity and Collaboration 344
9.3.2 Role-Specific Use Cases 345
9.4 Navigating Responsible and Ethical AI Considerations with Copilot 350
9.4.1 Data Privacy and Security: Leveraging Organisational Data Safely 350
9.4.2 Mitigating Bias in Inputs and Outputs 351
9.4.3 Ensuring Transparency and Explainability 353
9.4.4 Establishing Accountability for AI-Assisted Decisions 354
9.5 Validating Accuracy and Reliability of Copilot Outputs 355
9.5.1 Addressing Potential Misuse and Overreliance 355
9.5.2 Implementing Robust Mitigation Strategies and Governance 357
9.5.3 Developing Clear AI Usage Policies and Guidelines 357
9.6 Strengthening Data Governance and Access Controls 359
9.6.1 Establishing Procedures for Verification and Human Oversight 360
9.6.2 Comprehensive Employee Training Programs 361
9.6.3 Defining Roles, Responsibilities, and Accountability 362
9.6.4 Table 2: Checklist for Responsible AI Controls for Copilot Deployment 364
10.1 Microsoft Copilot in Action: Irish Case Studies 367
10.1.1 Introduction to Case Examples 367
10.1.2 Case Study 1: Musgrave Group (Retail) 368
10.1.3 Case Study 2: KPMG Ireland (Professional Services / Advisory Role) 369
10.1.4 Case Study 3: Other Relevant Irish Examples & Partner Activity 371
10.1.5 Synthesis of Learnings from Irish Context 373
10.2 A Practical Implementation Framework for Irish Organisations 374
10.2.1 Phase 1: Assessment and Planning 375
10.2.2 Phase 2: Policy Development and Governance Setup 377
10.2.3 Phase 3: Pilot Programs and Testing 378
10.2.4 Phase 4: Technical Integration and Security Configuration 379
10.2.5 Phase 5: Training and Change Management 380
10.2.6 Phase 6: Monitoring, Auditing, and Continuous Improvement 381
10.3 Conclusion and Recommendations 383

10.4 References 386

11 GLOSSARY OF TERMS 402

12 INDEX 430

1 Why you should read this book

Since ChatGPT first hit the public consciousness at the end of 2022, businesses and individuals have been trying to make sense of the fastest growing technological disruption to occur in any of our lifetimes – AI, or artificial intelligence.

Using AI is not an option – it's an imperative, but with the power of this tech comes great responsibility, especially for financial institutions and their staff. Ethically, and in order to comply with legislation such as the EU AI Act – financial institutions of all sizes have to get this right – for the company, for the customers, for their staff.

I've separated the book into chapters covering each of the key topics within the overarching topic of responsible use of AI as follows:

- Fairness & non-discrimination (page 22)
- Transparency & explainability (page 46)
- Privacy & data protection (page 77)
- Accountability & responsibility (page 125)
- Governance (page 164)
- Bias (page 250)
- MS Copilot in the Enterprise (page 250)

There's a comprehensive set of sources used in compiling the material in a References sub-section at the end of each chapter.

At the end is a Glossary of terms and a comprehensive Index.

1.1 How I wrote the book

One of my passions is technology, and I've always loved gadgetry, tech and computers in general. I started my professional career as a computer programmer and have been scratching that itch ever since!

This book was written on a MacBook Pro with an M4 processor – one of the most significant jumps in computer power I'd ever come across in my many years of using personal devices. It's set in 11-point Aptos font and produced in Microsoft Word.

My editing setup is to have the MacBook on the desk with a small stand and then I have it hooked up to a second screen mounted on the wall – a whopping 42" 4k TV that gives me loads of room for opening lots of windows as I do my research.

And for this book, given the recent emergence of a slew of new artificial intelligence tools, I've been playing with Perplexity, Claude, CoPilot, ChatGPT, Gemini, NotebookLM and others to help structure and offer up ideas for the materials within. The tools are amazing even in their early form – generating lists of points instantly that can then be reviewed and expanded upon.

I teach a module for the Institute of Bankers on the responsible use of AI in Irish financial services, and for each session I produced a primer document – using various Deep Research AI tools such as Google Gemini, ChatGPT, Perplexity and others. These primers have formed the basis for most of the main chapters of the book, with an additional final chapter on how to approach implementing Microsoft Copilot into your organisation if you haven't yet done so. I think that Copilot is going to be the default for most medium and larger organisations as it has all the security built in.

Using these AI tools definitely sped up the process of creating this little tome! Month by month all the tools we have at our fingertips are getting better and better. As Conor Grennan says "*The AI we are using today are the worst one's we'll ever use*".

I hope you enjoy reading it as much as I enjoyed writing it – this book was a really fun exploration into emerging technologies whilst writing about a subject I love – doesn't get much better than that!

1.2 How to contact me

I'm based in Lucan, Dublin in Ireland, and these days mostly offer online services. If I can help you or you'd like to discuss an idea for training, coaching or programme development of any kind do get in touch through any of the channels below – I'm always happy to discuss new opportunities!

- Connect with me on LinkedIn at https://www.linkedin.com/in/joehoughton/
- Email me at joe.houghton@gmail.com
- Call me on +353 86 384 3670 – I'm in Dublin, Ireland
- Book me for an AI seminar or series, consulting, coaching or training at www.houghton.consulting

1.3 My other books

In Feb 2023 I published the first of the Plus One Education series:

- "Innovative teaching with AI: Creative approaches to enhancing learning in education"

Amazon link: https://amzn.to/40M1O2n

The second book in the Plus One Education series (April 2023):

- "Project management made easy... the ECCSR approach

Amazon link:
https://amzn.to/4bjKS8o

The third in the Plus One Education series (Sept 2023):

- Applying artificial intelligence to close the accessibility gap – a practical handbook for educators and students

Amazon link:
https://amzn.to/45N8iSz

The fourth book in the Plus One education series (July 2024):

- "Study Smart with AI – 150 essential apps"

Amazon link: https://amzn.to/3YluASX

I've also published 3 books in the Houghton Photography Guides series to date with more in the pipeline:

1. "*Streets of Dublin*" – a guide to street photography
2. "*Take your time*" – the art and craft of long exposure photography
3. "*Picture perfect*" – a beginners guide to digital photography

Streets of Dublin

A guide to street photography

Take your time

The art & craft of long exposure photography

Picture Perfect

A beginnner's guide to photography

All these books are available around the world on Amazon – my author page has links to all the books and can be accessed at: https://www.amazon.co.uk/Joe-Houghton/e/B07XWQRNJQ/ref=dp_byline_cont_book_1 or via this QR code.

2 Introduction

Artificial intelligence (AI) is rapidly transforming the financial services landscape, offering opportunities to improve efficiency, customer experience, and decision-making [1].
However, the use of AI in finance also raises ethical concerns, particularly regarding fairness and non-discrimination.

This is especially important in the Irish context, where there is a strong emphasis on public trust and responsible technology adoption.

The Irish government actively promotes trustworthy AI through initiatives like the appointment of Dr. Patricia Scanlon as AI ambassador and the establishment of the AI Advisory Council to guide AI policy and engage with the public [2].

This guide explores fairness and non-discrimination in detail, providing examples and relating the discussion to practical uses and considerations for staff in Irish financial institutions.

2.1 AI and Society

The increasing use of AI in various sectors has a significant impact on society, raising questions about trust, ethics, and the potential for unintended consequences. In Ireland, the government recognizes the importance of public trust in AI adoption and is committed to raising awareness about trustworthy AI [2]. This includes promoting AI literacy as part of the national literacy, numeracy, and digital literacy strategy to ensure that citizens understand the implications of AI and can engage in informed discussions about its use [2].

AI can also affect consumer behaviour and expectations in financial services. As AI-powered tools become more prevalent, consumers may expect faster, more personalized services, but they also need to be protected from potential risks, such as biased algorithms or discriminatory outcomes [3].

The emergence of the "algorithmic consumer," who interacts with financial services primarily through AI-powered platforms, raises new challenges for financial consumer protection and requires regulators and financial institutions to adapt their approaches to ensure fairness and transparency [3].

2.2 Glossary of Terms

Artificial Intelligence (AI)

AI refers to the simulation of human intelligence in machines that are programmed to think and learn like humans. It is rapidly transforming various sectors, including financial services, to improve efficiency, customer experience, and decision-making.

AI Advisory Council

A council established by the Irish government to guide AI policy and engage with the public on the use of AI and its implications.

AI Ambassador

An appointed representative responsible for promoting trustworthy AI and raising awareness about its implications. In Ireland, Dr. Patricia Scanlon serves as the AI ambassador.

Algorithmic Consumer

A consumer who interacts with financial services primarily through AI-powered platforms, presenting new challenges for financial consumer protection.

Bias

A tendency for an AI system to produce prejudiced results due to erroneous assumptions or data patterns that reflect existing prejudices.

Counterfactual Fairness

A term referring to ensuring that an AI system's decisions would remain the same even if certain variables, such as race or gender, were altered.

Digital Literacy

The ability to effectively and critically navigate, evaluate, and create information using a range of digital technologies.

Discriminatory Outcomes

Results produced by AI systems that unfairly disadvantage certain groups or individuals based on race, gender, age, or other protected characteristics.

Explainable AI (XAI)

AI systems designed to provide clear, understandable explanations of their processes and decisions, ensuring that users and stakeholders can comprehend how outcomes are achieved. This transparency helps build trust and allows for better oversight and mitigation of biases.

Fairness in AI

The principle that AI systems should treat all individuals and groups equitably, ensuring that they do not produce discriminatory outcomes or perpetuate existing biases.

Financial Consumer Protection

Measures and regulations designed to protect consumers from unfair, deceptive, or harmful practices by financial institutions, especially as AI becomes more prevalent in financial services.

Group Fairness

Ensuring that different groups are treated equally or proportionally by an AI system. For example, an AI system for loan approvals should have similar approval rates for different demographic groups, provided they meet the relevant criteria.

Individual Fairness

Ensuring that similar individuals are treated similarly by an AI system, regardless of their group membership. For instance, two individuals with similar financial profiles should receive similar credit scores, regardless of their race or gender.

Public Trust

The confidence that the public has in the fairness, transparency, and accountability of AI systems and their outcomes.

AI

Trustworthy AI

AI systems that are designed and implemented in a manner that ensures fairness, transparency, accountability, and respect for human rights and values.

Unintended Consequences

Unexpected and potentially harmful outcomes resulting from the deployment of AI systems, often due to biases in data or algorithm design.

XAI – see Explainable AI

3 Fairness & Non-Discrimination

Fairness in AI generally refers to ensuring that AI systems do not produce discriminatory outcomes or perpetuate existing biases. This means that AI systems should treat all individuals and groups equitably, regardless of their race, gender, age, or other protected characteristics. In the context of financial services, this is particularly important, as AI is increasingly used in credit scoring, loan approvals, insurance pricing, and other critical decisions that can have a significant impact on people's lives.

Type of Fairness	Definition	Example
Group fairness	Ensuring that different groups are treated equally or proportionally.	An AI system for loan approvals should have similar approval rates for different demographic groups, provided they meet the relevant criteria.
Individual fairness	Ensuring that similar individuals are treated similarly, regardless of group membership.	Two individuals with similar financial profiles should receive similar credit scores, regardless of their race or gender.
Counterfactual fairness	Ensuring that AI systems are fair even in hypothetical scenarios.	An AI system for insurance pricing should not produce different quotes for individuals with the same risk profile if their

		gender or ethnicity were different.
Procedural fairness	Ensuring that the decision-making process is fair and transparent.	An AI system used for credit scoring should provide clear explanations for its decisions, allowing individuals to understand the factors that influenced their score.

It is important to note that these different types of fairness may overlap or even conflict in practice. Therefore, financial institutions need to carefully consider which fairness criteria are most relevant to their specific AI applications and develop strategies to ensure that their systems meet those criteria.

3.1 Ensuring Fairness in AI Systems

Ensuring fairness in AI systems is a complex challenge that requires a multi-faceted approach. Financial institutions need to take proactive steps throughout the AI lifecycle, from data collection and algorithm design to deployment and monitoring.

Step	Explanation	Example
Know the data	Understand the sources of data used to train AI systems and identify potential biases.	A financial institution should carefully examine the data used to train its credit scoring system, considering whether it includes a representative sample of applicants from different demographic groups and whether it reflects any historical biases in lending practices.
Test for bias	Regularly evaluate AI systems for bias using fairness metrics and testing methodologies.	A financial institution could use fairness metrics, such as statistical parity difference or equal opportunity difference, to assess whether its loan approval system is treating applicants fairly across different demographic groups.
Analyse results	Systematically investigate and	If bias testing reveals that a credit scoring system is

	study the results of bias testing to identify key risk areas.	unfairly penalizing applicants from a particular demographic group, the financial institution should investigate the reasons for this disparity and take steps to address the underlying bias.
Step	Explanation	Example
Independently verify	Engage third-party organizations to assess AI systems for fairness and compliance.	A financial institution could hire an independent auditor to review its AI systems for fairness, ensuring that they meet regulatory requirements and ethical standards.
Use synthetic data	Consider using synthetic data to improve model strength and reduce bias.	A financial institution could use synthetic data to augment its training data for a loan approval system, ensuring that the system is exposed to a wider range of scenarios and reducing the risk of bias.
Promote transparency	Make the AI decision-making process clear and understandable to users.	When an AI system rejects a loan application, it should provide a clear explanation of the factors that influenced the decision, allowing the applicant to understand

		the reasons for the outcome.
Establish accountability	Define clear lines of responsibility for AI decision-making.	A financial institution should have clear policies and procedures in place to ensure that there is accountability for AI-driven decisions, including mechanisms for human review and oversight.
Provide training	Educate staff on the ethical considerations of AI and how to identify and mitigate bias.	Financial institutions should provide training to their staff on responsible AI practices, including how to identify and mitigate bias in AI systems, ensuring that they are used fairly and ethically.

In addition to these steps, it is crucial to foster a culture of responsibility and ethical awareness within financial institutions. This includes promoting open discussions about AI ethics, encouraging staff to raise concerns about potential biases, and providing channels for feedback and continuous improvement.

3.2 Non-Discrimination in AI

Non-discrimination in AI refers to the principle that AI systems should not discriminate against individuals or groups based on protected characteristics. This principle is enshrined in various anti-discrimination laws, such as the Equal Credit Opportunity Act (ECOA) and the Fair Housing Act [5].

Discrimination can occur in AI systems in two main ways:

- **Disparate treatment:** This occurs when an AI system intentionally treats individuals differently based on a protected characteristic. For example, an AI system used for loan approvals might automatically reject applications from individuals living in certain neighbourhoods, even if they meet the financial criteria.
- **Disparate impact:** This occurs when an AI system has an adverse effect on a particular group, even if it was not designed with the intent to discriminate. For example, an AI system used for credit scoring might unintentionally penalize applicants from certain demographics if the training data reflects historical biases in lending practices [5].

Financial institutions need to be vigilant in identifying and mitigating both types of discrimination in their AI systems. This requires a comprehensive approach that includes careful data selection, algorithm design, and ongoing monitoring.

3.2.1 Explainable AI in Financial Services

Explainable AI (XAI) is a critical component of responsible AI in finance. It refers to AI systems that can provide clear explanations for their decisions, making the reasoning behind AI-driven outcomes understandable to humans [12].
XAI is essential for building trust in AI systems and ensuring that they are used fairly and responsibly. In the financial sector, XAI can help:

- **Protect from bias:** By revealing the factors that influence AI decisions, XAI can help identify and mitigate potential biases. For example, in a loan approval scenario, XAI can show which variables, such as income, credit history, or employment status, were most influential in the decision, allowing reviewers to assess whether any protected characteristics unfairly influenced the outcome [12].
- **Reveal feature importance:** XAI can help understand which features or variables are most important in driving AI decisions. This can be valuable for model validation and improvement, ensuring that AI systems are focusing on the most relevant factors and not inadvertently relying on biased or discriminatory features [12].
- **Allow decision traceability:** XAI enables the tracking of AI decision-making processes, making it easier to identify and address errors or biases. This can be particularly important in complex AI systems with multiple layers of processing, where it can be challenging to understand how the system arrived at a particular decision [12].

Real-world applications of XAI in financial services include:

- **Loan Approvals and Credit Scoring:** XAI can provide clear explanations for credit scores and loan approval decisions, helping customers understand the factors that influenced the outcome and enabling financial institutions to demonstrate fairness and transparency.

- **Fraud Detection:** XAI can help fraud analysts understand why an AI system flagged a particular transaction as suspicious, providing insights into the underlying patterns and anomalies that triggered the alert.
- **Risk Assessment:** XAI can help risk analysts interpret complex models by breaking down the factors that contribute to risk scores, such as economic indicators, market trends, and asset performance [13].

By adopting XAI, financial institutions can enhance trust, improve decision-making, and ensure that their AI systems are used ethically and responsibly.

3.2.2 AI Regulations and Guidelines in Ireland

The regulatory landscape for AI in Ireland is evolving rapidly. The EU AI Act, which entered into force in August 2024, establishes a risk-based framework for AI systems [7]. The Act prohibits certain AI practices that pose unacceptable risks, such as social scoring and manipulative uses of AI, while imposing strict requirements on high-risk AI systems [7].

Under the AI Act, AI systems used in financial services, such as those for credit scoring and insurance pricing, are categorized as high-risk and are subject to strict requirements, including:

- **Risk management systems:** Financial institutions must implement robust risk management systems to identify and mitigate potential risks associated with their AI systems.
- **Data governance:** Appropriate data governance practices are essential to ensure that the data used to train and operate AI systems is accurate, reliable, and free from bias.
- **Technical documentation:** Comprehensive technical documentation is required to demonstrate compliance with the AI Act and to provide transparency about the design and operation of AI systems.
- **Human oversight:** Human oversight is crucial to ensure that AI systems are used responsibly and ethically, with mechanisms in place for human review and intervention when necessary [7].

It's important to note that the AI Act has a phased implementation, with different timelines for various provisions. While the general provisions of the Act came into force in August 2024, the specific requirements for high-risk AI systems, such as those used in financial services, will apply later, giving financial institutions time to prepare and ensure compliance [7].

The Central Bank of Ireland is responsible for regulating high-risk AI systems used by Irish financial institutions [7]. The Central Bank is actively developing its supervisory expectations for AI in financial services, focusing on responsible AI, risk management, and consumer protection [3]. It emphasizes the need for financial institutions to understand the technology they are using, avoid exploiting customer behaviours, and ensure clarity of accountability for AI-driven decisions [3].

In addition to the AI Act, Ireland has a National AI Strategy that emphasizes a human-centric approach to AI development and use [14]. This strategy promotes ethical AI principles, public trust, and responsible innovation. It also highlights the importance of collaboration between government, industry, research institutions, and civil society to ensure that AI is used for the benefit of society. To foster innovation and responsible AI development, Ireland has established an AI regulatory sandbox, providing a controlled environment for businesses to test and validate their AI systems before wider deployment [2]. This sandbox can be a valuable tool for promoting ethical AI practices and ensuring that AI systems are fair and non-discriminatory.

3.2.3 AI in Irish Enterprise

The Irish government is actively promoting the adoption of AI in Irish enterprises, recognizing its potential to enhance competitiveness, productivity, and innovation [2]. Initiatives such as the Enterprise Digital Advisory Forum, established by the Department of Enterprise, Trade and Employment (DETE), aim to drive industry-wide adoption of AI and provide guidance on responsible AI practices [2].

The Irish government is actively promoting the adoption of AI in Irish enterprises, recognizing its potential to enhance competitiveness, productivity, and and innovation [2]. Initiatives such as the Enterprise Digital Advisory Forum, established by the Department of Enterprise, Trade and Employment (DETE), aim to drive industry-wide adoption of AI and provide guidance on responsible AI practices [2]. The Forum brings together experts from various sectors to share best practices, develop standards, and create strategies for integrating AI technologies into business operations.

Additionally, Enterprise Ireland offers financial support and advisory services to help companies navigate the complexities of AI adoption, from initial planning to implementation and scaling. This support includes funding for research and development, access to specialized training programs, and opportunities to collaborate with leading AI researchers and developers.

3.2.4 AI Serving the Public

The Irish government is committed to leveraging AI to improve public services and address societal challenges [15]. This includes developing guidelines for ethical AI use in the public sector and launching pilot projects to explore AI applications in areas like policy research and service delivery [15]. These initiatives aim to ensure that AI is used to enhance efficiency, effectiveness, and fairness in public services while upholding ethical principles and protecting citizens' rights.

3.2.5 Research and Innovation

Ireland recognizes the importance of research and innovation in driving responsible AI development and addressing challenges related to fairness and non-discrimination. The National AI Research Nexus, a key initiative under the National AI Strategy, aims to unify Ireland's research efforts in AI, fostering collaboration between academia and industry [15]. This collaborative approach is crucial for advancing AI knowledge, developing ethical guidelines, and ensuring that AI technologies are used for the benefit of society.

> ***The National AI Research Nexus is a key pillar in Ireland's AI strategy, designed to centralize and coordinate AI research efforts across the country. It brings together leading researchers, academics, and industry professionals to address critical challenges in AI development, including ethical considerations, fairness, and non-discrimination.***

By fostering a collaborative environment, the Nexus aims to accelerate the discovery and application of AI technologies that can benefit society as a whole.

One of the primary objectives of the Nexus is to create a robust framework for ethical AI research. This includes developing comprehensive guidelines and standards that ensure AI systems are transparent, accountable, and aligned with societal values. The Nexus also supports multidisciplinary research projects that explore the social, economic, and cultural impacts of AI, providing valuable insights that can inform policy decisions and public discourse.

The National AI Research Nexus serves as a bridge between academia and industry, facilitating knowledge transfer and innovation. Through partnerships and joint ventures, the Nexus promotes the commercialization of cutting-edge AI research, enabling Irish businesses to leverage advanced technologies and maintain a competitive edge in the global market. This collaboration also helps to identify emerging trends and opportunities in AI, ensuring that Ireland remains at the forefront of AI innovation.

The Nexus is also committed to nurturing the next generation of AI talent. By offering scholarships, fellowships, and training programs, it aims to attract and retain top researchers and practitioners in the field. This investment in human capital is crucial for sustaining Ireland's leadership in AI and fostering a diverse and inclusive research community.

In summary, the National AI Research Nexus is a vital component of Ireland's AI ecosystem. It unifies research efforts, promotes ethical practices, and drives innovation, ensuring that AI technologies are developed and deployed for the greater good of society.

3.2.6 AI Education and Skills

To prepare the workforce for the growing use of AI, the Irish government is investing in AI education and skills development [15]. This includes expanding upskilling programs, apprenticeships, and AI-focused education initiatives to cultivate high-calibre AI talent and promote diversity and inclusion in the AI field [15]. These efforts are essential for ensuring that Ireland has a skilled workforce capable of developing and deploying AI systems responsibly and ethically.

3.2.7 Infrastructure for AI

The Irish government is committed to providing the necessary infrastructure to support ethical AI development and adoption [15]. This includes enhancing access to high-performance computing, strengthening cybersecurity measures, and promoting the use of renewable energy in data centers [15]. These initiatives are crucial for ensuring that AI systems are developed and operated securely, reliably, and sustainably.

3.2.8 AI Applications in Irish Financial Institutions

While specific examples of AI bias and discrimination in Irish financial institutions are limited in the research material, there are several examples of how AI is being used in the Irish financial sector:

- **Allied Irish Bank (AIB):** AIB has implemented the Tungsten Intelligent Automation Platform to automate over 200 customer-related processes, including document capture and processing, significantly improving customer response times and satisfaction [16].

The Tungsten Intelligent Automation Platform employed by Allied Irish Bank (AIB) is a comprehensive solution designed to streamline and enhance various customer-related processes. By leveraging advanced AI and machine learning algorithms, this platform automates over 200 distinct processes, ranging from document capture and processing to customer inquiry responses. The automation of these processes significantly reduces manual effort and minimises human error, leading to improved accuracy and efficiency.

One of the key advantages of the Tungsten Intelligent Automation Platform is its ability to process large volumes of data quickly and accurately. This capability allows AIB to handle customer requests and transactions at a much faster rate, resulting in reduced wait times and enhanced customer satisfaction. The platform also utilises natural language processing (NLP) to understand and respond to customer queries more effectively, providing a more personalised and seamless customer experience.

Tungsten Intelligent Automation Platform is designed to be highly scalable, allowing AIB to expand its automation capabilities as needed. This scalability ensures that the bank can continue to meet the evolving demands of its customers while maintaining high standards of service quality. Additionally, the platform includes robust security features to protect sensitive customer data and ensure compliance with regulatory requirements.

Overall, the Tungsten Intelligent Automation Platform represents a significant investment in technological innovation for AIB. By automating key processes and improving operational efficiency, the bank can better serve its customers and maintain a competitive edge in the financial sector.

- **KPMG Ireland:** KPMG is actively promoting the adoption of AI in Irish banks, highlighting its potential to drive sustainable growth, enhance customer experiences, and improve operational efficiency [17].

Specific initiatives and examples of KPMG's efforts include:

- AI Readiness Assessment: KPMG provides a comprehensive AI readiness assessment to Irish banks, helping them understand their current capabilities and identify areas for improvement. This assessment covers aspects such as data infrastructure, talent availability, regulatory compliance, and ethical standards.

- AI Strategy Development: KPMG collaborates with Irish banks to develop tailored AI strategies that align with their business objectives and regulatory requirements. This includes defining clear goals, selecting appropriate AI technologies, and establishing governance frameworks to oversee AI implementation.

- Pilot Projects: KPMG supports Irish banks in launching pilot projects to test and validate AI applications in a controlled environment. These projects often focus on specific use cases, such as fraud detection, customer service automation, and credit risk assessment. By demonstrating the tangible benefits of AI, KPMG helps banks build confidence in scaling these solutions across their operations.

- Training and Education: Recognising the importance of building AI literacy within the financial sector, KPMG offers training programmes and workshops for bank employees. These sessions cover fundamental AI concepts, ethical considerations, and practical applications, empowering staff to make informed decisions about AI adoption.

- Regulatory Compliance: KPMG assists Irish banks in navigating the complex regulatory landscape surrounding AI. This includes ensuring that AI systems adhere to data protection laws, anti-discrimination regulations, and industry standards. By providing expert guidance, KPMG helps banks mitigate legal risks and maintain trust with customers and regulators.

- Case Studies and Best Practices: KPMG shares case studies and best practices from successful AI implementations in other financial institutions worldwide. By showcasing real-world examples and lessons learned, KPMG helps Irish banks understand how AI can be effectively deployed to achieve specific business outcomes.

Through these initiatives, KPMG plays a crucial role in advancing the adoption of AI in the Irish financial sector, helping banks harness the power of AI to enhance their competitive edge and deliver better services to their customers.

These examples demonstrate the growing use of AI in Irish financial institutions to improve efficiency, customer service, and decision-making. However, it is crucial to ensure that these AI applications are developed and deployed responsibly, with careful consideration of fairness, non-discrimination, and ethical implications.

3.2.9 Potential examples of AI Discrimination

While specific examples of AI bias and discrimination in Irish financial institutions are not readily available, potential areas of concern include:

- **Credit scoring:** AI systems used for credit scoring could unfairly penalize applicants from certain demographics if the training data reflects historical biases in lending practices. For example, if past lending decisions have disproportionately disadvantaged certain minority groups, an AI system trained on this data might perpetuate these biases, leading to unfair denials of credit or less favourable loan terms [6].

- **Loan approvals:** AI systems used for loan approvals could perpetuate existing disparities in access to credit if they are not carefully designed and monitored. For example, if an AI system relies on factors that are correlated with protected characteristics, such as postcode or employment history, it could inadvertently discriminate against certain groups, even if those characteristics are not explicitly included in the model [18].

- **Insurance pricing:** AI systems used for insurance pricing could lead to discriminatory outcomes if they rely on factors that are correlated with protected characteristics. For example, if an AI system uses data that shows a higher accident rate among younger drivers, it might charge them higher premiums, even if those drivers have good driving records. This could disproportionately affect young people from lower socio-economic backgrounds who may have limited access to safer vehicles or driving lessons [19].

These potential biases highlight the need for financial institutions to be vigilant in identifying and mitigating discrimination in their AI systems. This requires a comprehensive approach that includes careful data selection, algorithm design, ongoing monitoring, and human oversight to ensure fairness and compliance with anti-discrimination laws.

3.3 Challenges to AI Adoption in Ireland

While AI offers significant opportunities for the Irish financial sector, there are also challenges to its widespread adoption. These challenges include:

- **Conflicting views on AI applications:** There may be differing opinions within financial institutions about where and how AI should be applied, leading to uncertainty and delays in implementation [20].
- **Data quality issues:** The availability of high-quality data in sufficient quantity is crucial for the effective use of AI. However, many Irish financial institutions may face challenges in accessing or managing the data needed to train and operate AI systems effectively [20].
- **Lack of AI expertise:** There may be a shortage of skilled professionals with the necessary expertise to develop, deploy, and manage AI systems within financial institutions [20].
- **Overreliance on third-party AI providers:** Financial institutions need to be mindful of the risks associated with overreliance on third-party AI providers, including potential issues with data privacy, accountability, and commercial dependency [21].

Addressing these challenges is crucial for ensuring the responsible and ethical adoption of AI in the Irish financial sector. This requires investment in skills development, data management capabilities, and robust governance frameworks to guide AI implementation and mitigate potential risks.

3.4 Conclusion

AI has the potential to revolutionize financial services in Ireland, but it is crucial to ensure that these technologies are used fairly and responsibly. By understanding the issues of fairness, non-discrimination, and bias, and by taking proactive steps to mitigate risks, Irish financial institutions can harness the power of AI while upholding ethical principles and protecting consumers.

This guide has provided an overview of these key issues, along with practical steps and considerations for staff in Irish financial institutions. As the AI landscape continues to evolve, it is essential to stay informed about best practices, regulatory developments, and emerging challenges to ensure the responsible and ethical use of AI in financial services. This includes staying abreast of the phased implementation of the EU AI Act and the Central Bank of Ireland's evolving supervisory expectations for AI in finance.

It's crucial to recognize the connection between fairness in AI and the broader goal of financial inclusion. Biased AI systems can exacerbate existing inequalities and hinder access to financial services for marginalized groups.

> ***By prioritizing fairness and non-discrimination in their AI strategies, Irish financial institutions can contribute to a more inclusive and equitable financial system.***

Finally, it is important to emphasize that the risks associated with AI are constantly evolving. Financial institutions need to adopt a culture of ongoing learning and adaptation, staying informed about emerging challenges and adjusting their risk management strategies accordingly. This requires continuous monitoring, research, and collaboration to ensure the responsible and ethical use of AI in financial services for the benefit of both businesses and society.

3.5 References

1. Why avoiding bias is critical to AI success | Building successful AI that's grounded in trust and transparency | IBM, accessed on February 22, 2025, https://www.ibm.com/resources/guides/predict/trustworthy-ai/avoid-bias/
2. Ireland's national AI strategy refresh: the seven strands - Pinsent Masons, accessed on February 22, 2025, https://www.pinsentmasons.com/out-law/analysis/ireland-national-ai-strategy-refresh-the-seven-strands
3. Financial consumer protection and market conduct considerations of AI in finance - Remarks by Colm Kincaid, Director of Consumer Protection - Central Bank of Ireland, accessed on February 22, 2025, https://www.centralbank.ie/news/article/speech-colm-kincaid-financial-consumer-protection-and-market-conduct-considerations-of-AI-in-finance-22-may-2024
4. Fairness and Bias in AI Explained | SS&C Blue Prism, accessed on February 22, 2025, https://www.blueprism.com/resources/blog/bias-fairness-ai/
5. An AI fair lending policy agenda for the federal financial regulators - Brookings Institution, accessed on February 22, 2025, https://www.brookings.edu/articles/an-ai-fair-lending-policy-agenda-for-the-federal-financial-regulators/
6. AI Bias in Credit & Loan Processing: Is AI Biased When Assessing ..., accessed on February 22, 2025, https://www.itmagination.com/blog/credit-loan-processing-ai-biased-when-assessing-credit-worthiness
7. AI: Risk and Regulatory Considerations for Irish Regulated Firms - Maples Group, accessed on February 22, 2025, https://maples.com/knowledge/ai-risk-and-regulatory-considerations-for-irish-regulated-firms
8. AI discrimination and bias in financial services | EY - US, accessed on February 22, 2025, https://www.ey.com/en_us/insights/forensic-integrity-services/ai-discrimination-and-bias-in-financial-services
9. Building fairness into AI is crucial – and hard to get right -

Nextgov/FCW, accessed on February 22, 2025, https://www.nextgov.com/ideas/2024/03/building-fairness-ai-crucial-and-hard-get-right/395054/
10. Using AI for Financial Analysis: From Data Insights to Decision-Making - Ringy, accessed on February 22, 2025, https://www.ringy.com/articles/ai-for-financial-analysis
11. Responsible AI in Finance: A Guide for Employers on Ethical Implementation - Focus People, accessed on February 22, 2025, https://www.focuspeople.com/2023/11/01/responsible-ai-in-finance-a-guide-for-employers-on-ethical-implementation/
12. Explainable AI in finance: The key to harnessing its predictive power - N-iX, accessed on February 22, 2025, https://www.n-ix.com/explainable-ai-in-finance/
13. Exploring Explainable AI (XAI) in Financial Services: Why It Matters - Aspire Systems - blog, accessed on February 22, 2025, https://blog.aspiresys.com/artificial-intelligence/exploring-explainable-ai-xai-in-financial-services-why-it-matters/
14. National AI Strategy Refresh 2024 - Department of Enterprise, Trade and Employment, accessed on February 22, 2025, https://enterprise.gov.ie/en/publications/publication-files/national-ai-strategy-refresh-2024.pdf
15. Ireland Unveils Refreshed National AI Strategy to Lead in Ethical and Innovative AI Development, accessed on February 22, 2025, https://babl.ai/ireland-unveils-refreshed-national-ai-strategy-to-lead-in-ethical-and-innovative-ai-development/
16. Allied Irish Bank Transforms their Customer Response Time from Weeks to Minutes and Improving Customer Satisfaction | Tungsten Automation, accessed on February 22, 2025, https://www.tungstenautomation.com/learn/case-studies/2023/allied-irish-bank
17. Intelligent banking transformation - AI-driven change - KPMG Ireland, accessed on February 22, 2025, https://kpmg.com/ie/en/home/insights/2025/02/intelligent-fs-banking.html
18. British and American banks put under spotlight for discriminatory mortgage lending practices, accessed on February 22, 2025,

https://www.nortonrosefulbright.com/en/knowledge/publications/c4b529bb/british-and-american-banks-put-under-spotlight-for-discriminatory-mortgage-lending-practices
19. How the Irish insurance sector's reliance on AI is impacting customers - Pinsent Masons, accessed on February 22, 2025, https://www.pinsentmasons.com/out-law/analysis/irish-insurance-sector-reliance-ai-impacting-customers
20. AI and Risk Management in Ireland | Deloitte Ireland, accessed on February 22, 2025, https://www.deloitte.com/ie/en/services/risk-advisory/research/_ai-and-risk-management-in-ireland.html
21. The new AI Act has Big Implications for the Financial Services Sector - Institute of Directors Ireland, accessed on February 22, 2025, https://www.iodireland.ie/images/uploads/downloads/8300_IOD_FactSheet_June_Big_Data%2C_Big_Change_The_new_AI_Act_has_Big_Implications_for_the_Financial_Services_Sector.pdf

4 Transparency & Explainability

Artificial intelligence (AI) is rapidly transforming the financial services industry, offering the potential to improve efficiency, reduce costs, and enhance customer experiences[1]. However, the increasing complexity of AI models raises concerns about their transparency and explainability, particularly in a sector where trust and accountability are paramount. This primer provides a short guide to the issues of transparency and explainability in the responsible use of AI in financial services, with a specific focus on the Irish context.

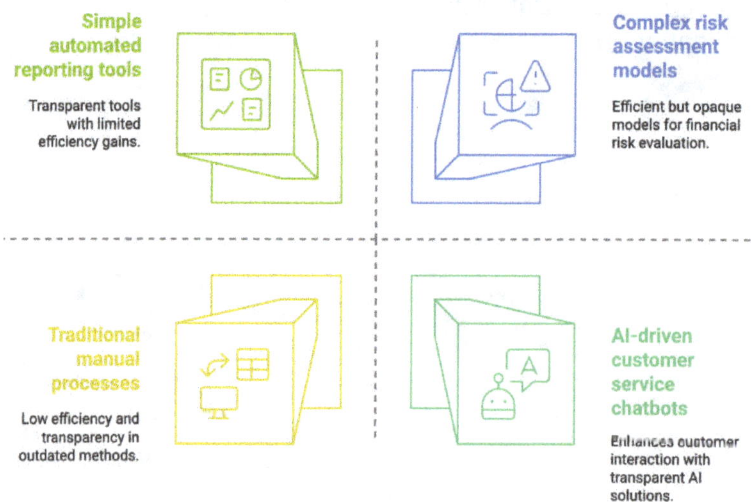

4.1 Transparency in AI for Financial Services

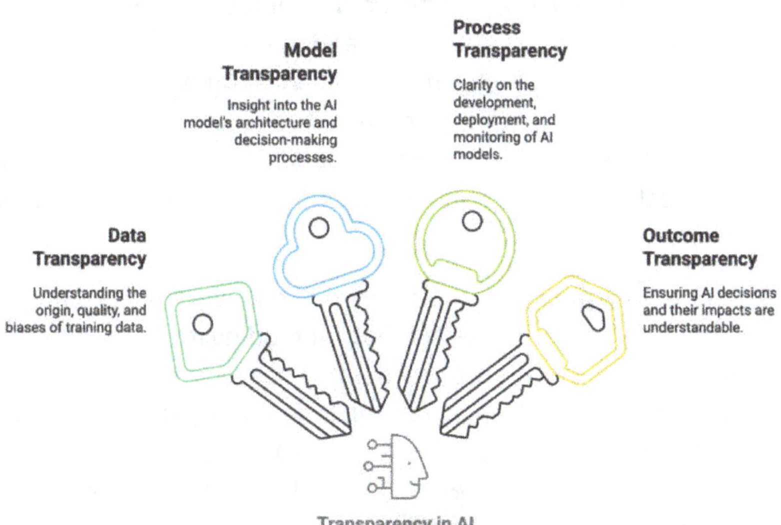

Transparency in AI refers to the ability to understand how an AI system works and makes decisions. This includes understanding the data used to train the model, the model's architecture and decision-making processes, and the overall process of developing, deploying, and monitoring the AI system. Robust AI governance needs to be built on three core pillars: transparency, accountability, and collaboration[2]. In the context of financial services, transparency is crucial for building trust with customers, ensuring fairness and avoiding bias in AI decisions, facilitating regulatory compliance, and improving risk management.

4.1.1 Dimensions of Transparency

Transparency in AI can be broken down into several key dimensions:

- **Data Transparency:** This involves understanding the origin, quality, and potential biases of the data used to train AI models. It is crucial to ensure that the data is representative, accurate, and free from biases that could lead to unfair or discriminatory outcomes. For example, in credit scoring, data transparency would involve understanding where the credit history data comes from, how it was collected, and whether it contains any historical biases that could disadvantage certain demographic groups.
- **Model Transparency:** This refers to the ability to understand the inner workings of the AI model, including its architecture and decision-making processes. This can be challenging with complex AI models, such as deep learning algorithms, which can be difficult to interpret even for experts. For instance, model transparency in a fraud detection system might involve understanding the specific factors and patterns the AI model considers when flagging a transaction as potentially fraudulent.
- **Process Transparency:** This encompasses clarity on how AI models are developed, deployed, and monitored within financial institutions. It includes documentation of the development process, model validation procedures, and ongoing monitoring mechanisms to ensure the AI system is functioning as intended. For example, process transparency might involve documenting the steps taken to validate a new AI-powered investment advice tool, including the testing procedures and performance metrics used.
- **Outcome Transparency:** This ensures that the results and impacts of AI decisions are clear and understandable to customers and stakeholders. It involves providing clear explanations for AI-driven decisions, such as loan approvals or

credit scoring, and enabling individuals to understand how those decisions affect them. For instance, if a customer is denied a loan application, outcome transparency would involve providing a clear explanation of the factors that contributed to the decision, such as their credit score, debt-to-income ratio, or employment history.

4.1.2 Benefits of Transparency

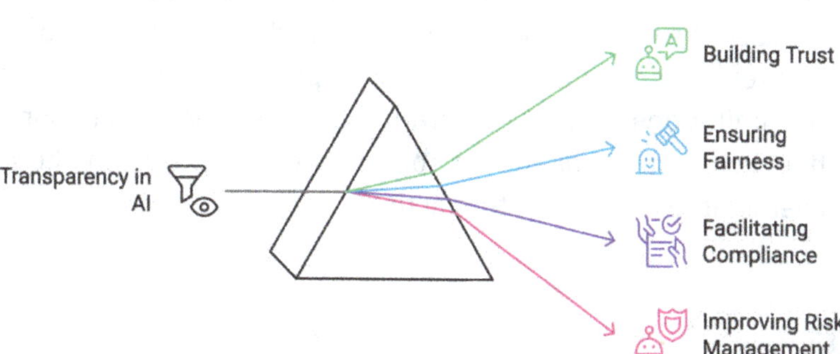

Transparency in AI offers several potential benefits for financial services:

- **Building Trust:** By providing clear explanations for AI decisions, financial institutions can build trust with customers and demonstrate that their AI systems are fair, unbiased, and reliable. For example, if a customer receives investment advice from an AI-powered tool, transparency about how the advice was generated can increase their confidence in the recommendation.
- **Ensuring Fairness:** Transparency helps to identify and mitigate potential biases in AI models, ensuring that AI-driven decisions are fair and equitable for all customers. For instance, by analysing the data used to train a loan approval model, financial

institutions can identify and address any potential biases that might unfairly disadvantage certain groups of applicants.

- **Facilitating Compliance:** Transparency is essential for complying with regulations and guidelines on AI in financial services, such as the EU AI Act[3]. By documenting their AI development processes and providing clear explanations for AI decisions, financial institutions can demonstrate compliance with regulatory requirements.
- **Improving Risk Management:** By understanding how AI models work and make decisions, financial institutions can better manage the risks associated with AI, such as model errors or unintended consequences. For example, transparency about the limitations of an AI-powered fraud detection system can help institutions implement appropriate safeguards and human oversight to mitigate potential risks.

4.2 Explainability in AI for Financial Services

Explainability in AI goes beyond transparency by providing clear and understandable explanations for why an AI system makes a specific decision. It enables users to understand the reasoning behind AI-driven outcomes and to trust that those outcomes are justified and reliable. In financial services, explainability is crucial for enabling customers to understand the reasons behind AI decisions that affect them, supporting regulatory compliance and auditability, improving model debugging and troubleshooting, and enhancing human oversight of AI systems.

However, it's important to acknowledge the inherent tension between accuracy and explainability in AI models[4]. Often, the most accurate models, such as deep neural networks, are the least explainable due to their complexity. Conversely, simpler models like decision trees may be more interpretable but might not capture the intricate relationships within data as effectively, leading to lower accuracy. This trade-off presents a challenge for financial institutions in balancing predictive performance with interpretability.

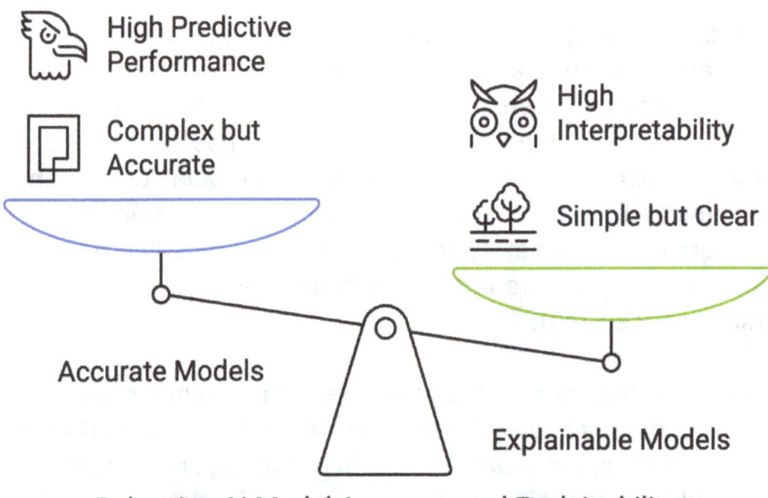

Balancing AI Model Accuracy and Explainability

There can be a conflict between explainability and intellectual property protection[5]. Financial institutions developing proprietary AI models may be hesitant to disclose the details of their algorithms due to concerns about revealing trade secrets or losing their competitive advantage. This tension can create challenges in balancing transparency with the need to protect intellectual property.

Despite these challenges, it's crucial to emphasize the importance of validating AI results, even with explainable models[5]. A "trust but verify" approach is essential for ensuring responsible AI use and mitigating potential risks. This involves critically evaluating AI outputs, implementing human oversight mechanisms, and continuously monitoring AI systems for accuracy and fairness.

4.2.1 Methods for Achieving Explainability

Several methods can be used to achieve explainability in AI:

- **Model-Agnostic Explainability:** These techniques can be applied to any AI model, regardless of its complexity. Examples include LIME (Local Interpretable Model-Agnostic Explanations) and SHAP (Shapley Additive exPlanations). LIME explains individual predictions by approximating the model locally with a simpler, interpretable model. SHAP assigns importance values to features based on their contribution to the prediction. For instance, in a credit scoring model, SHAP could be used to explain how different factors, such as income, credit history, and employment status, contributed to the final credit score.

- **Model-Specific Explainability:** These techniques are tailored to specific types of AI models. For example, decision trees can be visualized to show the decision-making process, while rule-based models provide explicit rules that can be easily understood. In an AI system used for fraud detection, a decision tree could be used to illustrate the specific rules and thresholds that trigger a fraud alert.

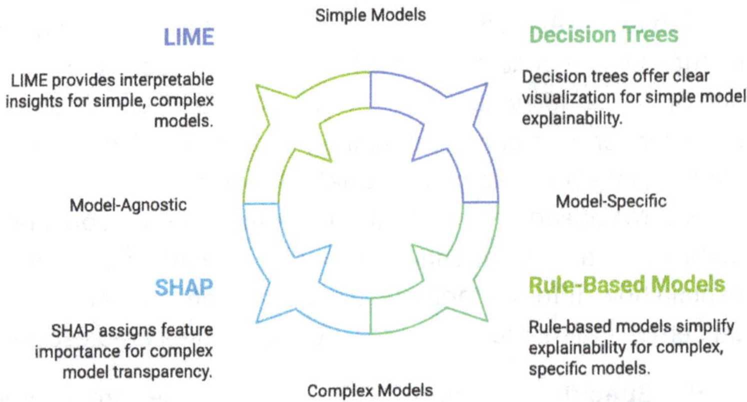

4.2.2 Benefits of Explainability

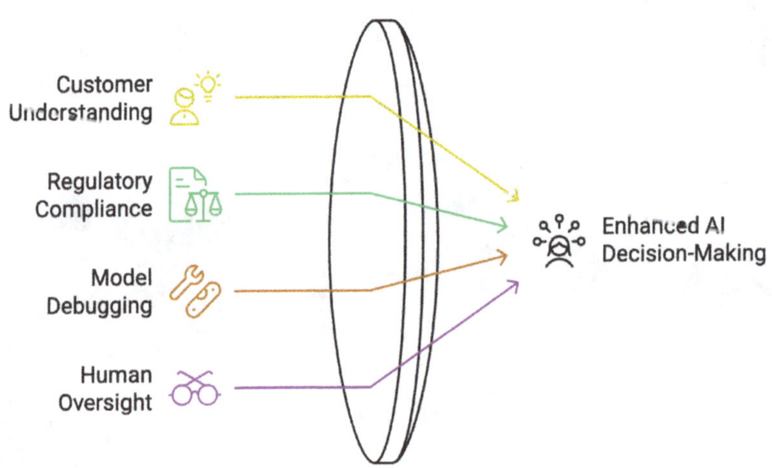

Explainability in AI offers several potential benefits for financial services:

- **Customer Understanding:** Explainability enables customers to understand the reasons behind AI decisions that affect them, such as loan applications or credit scoring. This can improve customer satisfaction and trust in the financial institution. For example, if an AI system recommends a particular investment portfolio, explainability would allow the customer to understand why that portfolio was chosen based on their risk tolerance, financial goals, and market conditions.
- **Regulatory Compliance:** Explainability supports regulatory compliance by providing evidence that AI systems are making decisions in a fair and unbiased manner. By explaining the reasoning behind AI-driven outcomes, financial institutions can demonstrate compliance with regulations like the EU AI Act.
- **Model Debugging:** Explainability helps to identify and correct errors in AI models by providing insights into the model's decision-making process. For instance, if an AI system for loan approvals is consistently denying loans to a specific demographic group, explainability techniques can help identify potential biases or errors in the model.
- **Human Oversight:** Explainability enhances human oversight of AI systems by enabling humans to understand and validate AI-driven decisions. This is particularly important in high-stakes decisions, such as credit scoring or investment advice, where human review can help ensure fairness and accuracy.

4.2.3 Irish Context and Practical Examples

In Ireland, the Central Bank of Ireland (CBI) is actively involved in shaping the regulatory landscape for AI in financial services. The CBI emphasizes the importance of responsible AI, with a focus on consumer protection, fairness, and transparency in AI deployment[6]. This includes ensuring that AI systems are used in a way that prioritizes the interests of customers and avoids any unfair or discriminatory outcomes.

The EU AI Act, which is expected to be fully implemented in 2025, will further strengthen the regulatory framework for AI in Ireland and across the EU[3]. The AI Act adopts a risk-based approach, classifying AI systems into different categories with varying levels of regulatory scrutiny.

The AI Act prohibits AI systems that pose an unacceptable risk, such as social scoring systems and manipulative AI applications. High-risk AI systems, including those used in credit scoring and financial risk management, are subject to strict requirements for risk management, data quality, and human oversight. Limited-risk AI systems, like chatbots, primarily focus on transparency obligations, ensuring users are aware they are interacting with an AI[7].

The AI Act also outlines specific fines for different categories of infringements. For instance, violations related to prohibited practices or non-compliance with data requirements can result in fines of up to €35 million or 7% of the total worldwide annual turnover of the preceding financial year, whichever is higher. Non-compliance with other requirements can lead to fines of up to €15 million or 3% of turnover[3].

The implementation of the AI Act follows a staggered approach. Prohibited AI systems will need to be phased out within six months of the legislation coming into force. Obligations for general-purpose AI governance will apply after 12 months. All rules, including those for high-risk systems, will apply after 24 months, and obligations for high-risk systems defined in Annex II will apply after 36 months[3].

Ireland has also developed a National AI Strategy, which aligns with the EU AI Act by promoting responsible AI practices and cultivating AI talent[8]. This strategy focuses on building public trust in AI, improving policy outcomes, and fostering a thriving AI ecosystem in Ireland.

Furthermore, Ireland has designated nine national authorities to oversee the protection of fundamental rights in the context of AI[9]. These authorities, including the Data Protection Commission and the Central Bank of Ireland, play a crucial role in ensuring that AI systems are developed and deployed in a manner that respects fundamental rights and avoids discriminatory outcomes.

Collaboration between financial institutions and regulatory bodies is essential in shaping AI's future in the banking industry[2]. As AI evolves, regulatory frameworks must adapt to the complexities of this technology. Financial institutions need to work closely with regulators to create policies that promote innovation while ensuring AI is used safely and responsibly.

4.2.3.1 *Practical Use Cases of AI in Irish Financial Institutions*

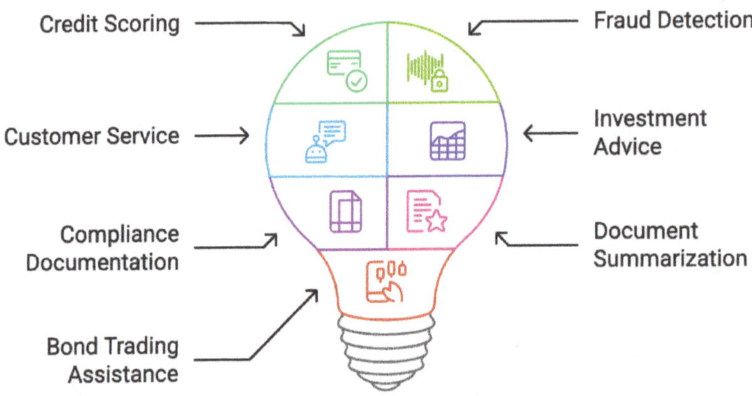

AI is being used in various ways by Irish financial institutions, including:

- **Credit Scoring:** AI models are used to assess creditworthiness and determine loan eligibility, automating the credit scoring process and potentially reducing bias.
- **Fraud Detection:** AI systems can analyse transaction data in real-time to identify and prevent fraudulent activities, improving security and protecting customers.
- **Customer Service:** AI-powered chatbots and virtual assistants are used to provide personalized customer support, answering queries and resolving issues efficiently.
- **Investment Advice:** AI algorithms can analyse market data and provide investment recommendations, potentially improving investment outcomes for customers.

- **Compliance and Offering Documentation:** In the Irish funds industry, AI can be used to prepare first drafts of compliance documents and offering documentation, such as AML policies and prospectuses[10].
- **Document Summarisation:** AI can summarize complex regulatory, financial, and operational documents, allowing professionals to quickly extract key information[10].
- **Bond Trading Assistance:** AI-powered tools like BondGPT can assist bond traders by providing real-time liquidity information, analytical models, and explainable AI features[10].

4.2.3.2 Challenges to AI Adoption in Ireland

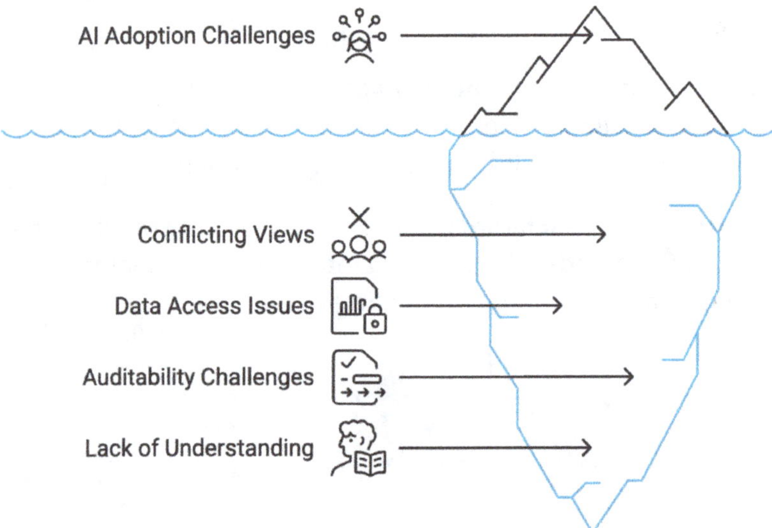

Despite the potential benefits of AI, there are challenges to its widespread adoption in the Irish financial sector:

- **Conflicting views on where AI needs to be applied:** There may be disagreements within institutions about the most appropriate use cases for AI.
- **High quality and quantity of data is crucial for the decisions made by AI:** Access to sufficient and reliable data can be a barrier to AI implementation.
- AI which evolves over time contains many processing layers that make auditability and traceability challenging: The complexity of some AI models can make it difficult to understand their decision-making processes.
- **Understanding AI and its implications on the specific case:** A lack of understanding of AI and its risks can hinder adoption[1].

4.3 Applying Transparency and Explainability in the Irish Context

Irish financial institutions can implement transparency and explainability measures in their AI systems by:

- **Providing clear explanations for AI-driven decisions:** This can be achieved through personalized explanations, interactive tools, or visualizations that help customers understand how AI models are making decisions that affect them.
- **Documenting the AI development and deployment process:** This includes maintaining records of data sources, model architectures, validation procedures, and monitoring mechanisms.
- **Using explainable AI techniques:** This involves selecting AI models that are inherently explainable or using model-agnostic explainability techniques to provide insights into the decision-making process of complex models.
- **Training staff on AI transparency and explainability:** This ensures that staff members understand the importance of these concepts and can contribute to ensuring responsible AI practices within the institution.

4.4 Open Banking and AI

Open banking initiatives can contribute to a more transparent and customer-centric financial ecosystem, which aligns with the principles of responsible AI[11]. By enabling customers to share their financial data with third-party providers, open banking promotes greater transparency and control over their financial information. This can foster greater trust between financial institutions and customers, as well as encourage innovation in financial services.

4.5 Practical Considerations for Staff in Irish Financial Institutions

Different staff members have distinct roles and responsibilities in relation to AI transparency and explainability:

Staff Role	Responsibilities related to AI Transparency & Explainability
Data Scientists	Developing and validating AI models, ensuring data quality, and implementing explainability techniques.
Compliance Officers	Ensuring that AI systems comply with relevant regulations and guidelines, such as the EU AI Act and CBI guidance.
Business Analysts	Translating business requirements into AI solutions, ensuring that AI systems meet the needs of the business while adhering to responsible AI principles.
Customer Service Representatives	Communicating AI-driven decisions to customers, providing clear explanations and addressing any concerns.

4.5.1 Practical Guidance for Staff

Staff can contribute to ensuring transparency and explainability in AI systems by:

- **Understanding the AI system's limitations:** Recognizing that AI models are not perfect and may produce errors or unintended consequences.
- **Documenting their work:** Maintaining clear records of data sources, model development, and validation procedures.
- **Communicating effectively:** Providing clear and concise explanations to customers and stakeholders about how AI systems work and make decisions.
- **Raising concerns:** Reporting any potential issues or biases in AI systems to appropriate personnel.

4.5.2 Training and Education

Training and education are crucial for staff to understand AI transparency and explainability. This includes:

- Technical training on AI concepts and explainability techniques.
- Ethical training on responsible AI practices and potential risks.
- Regular updates on regulatory developments and industry best practices.

4.6 Implementation Framework and Roadmap

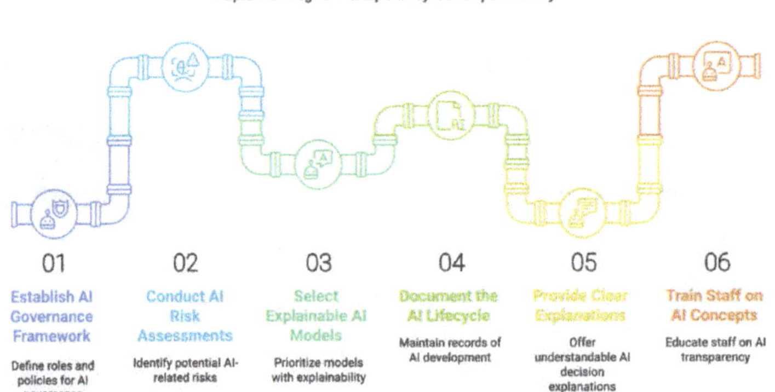

Irish financial institutions can implement transparency and explainability in their AI systems by following a structured framework:

1. **Establish an AI Governance Framework:** Define roles and responsibilities, establish clear policies and procedures, and ensure alignment with relevant regulations.
2. **Conduct AI Risk Assessments:** Identify potential risks associated with AI, including bias, fairness, and explainability concerns.
3. **Select Explainable AI Models:** Prioritize AI models that are inherently explainable or use model-agnostic explainability techniques.
4. **Document the AI Lifecycle:** Maintain clear records of data sources, model development, validation procedures, and monitoring mechanisms.
5. **Provide Clear Explanations:** Develop mechanisms to provide clear and understandable explanations for AI-driven decisions

to customers and stakeholders.

6. **Train Staff on AI Transparency and Explainability:** Ensure that staff members understand the importance of these concepts and can contribute to responsible AI practices.
7. **Monitor and Evaluate AI Systems:** Continuously monitor AI systems for performance, bias, and explainability issues, and make adjustments as needed.

4.6.1 Risk Management Lifecycle for AI

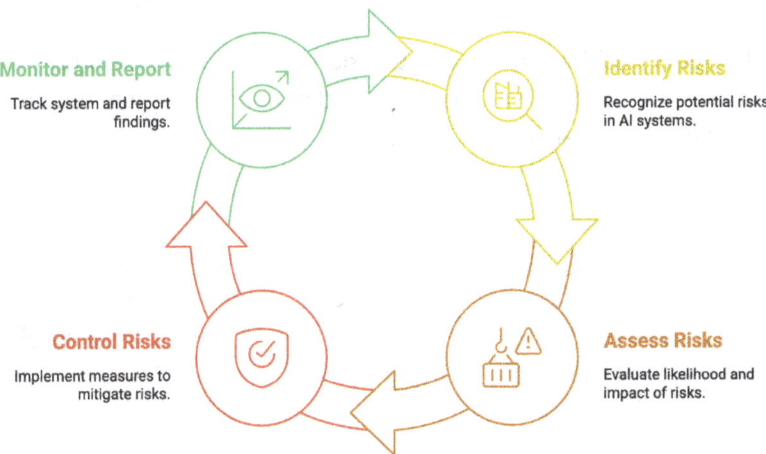

To effectively manage the risks associated with AI, a robust risk management framework should be implemented. This framework should include the following four key stages: [1]

- **Identify:** Identify all potential risks associated with the AI system, including operational, ethical, data privacy, and regulatory compliance risks.
- **Assess:** Evaluate the likelihood and potential impact of each identified risk.
- **Control:** Implement appropriate controls to mitigate the identified risks. This may involve data quality checks, model validation procedures, human oversight mechanisms, and ongoing monitoring.
- **Monitor and report:** Continuously monitor the AI system for any emerging risks or control failures. Regularly report on the effectiveness of the risk management framework to senior

management and relevant stakeholders.

4.6.2 Third-Party AI Providers

When working with third-party AI providers, Irish financial institutions should consider the following: [1]

- **Due diligence:** Conduct thorough due diligence on the provider to assess their expertise, security practices, and compliance with relevant regulations.
- **Testing and monitoring:** Ensure that the AI model provided by the third party undergoes rigorous testing and monitoring, similar to internally developed models.
- **Continuity planning:** Have a robust continuity plan in place to ensure business operations can continue in case the third-party AI solution ceases operation or malfunctions.

4.7 Case Studies

While specific case studies of Irish-based companies successfully implementing transparency and explainability in their AI systems were not found in the provided research material, the research did highlight several examples of AI applications in Irish financial institutions. These examples can provide valuable insights into how transparency and explainability can be applied in practice.

BondGPT, an AI application developed by Broadridge, is used by asset managers and dealers to inform their corporate bond trading. This tool incorporates "Explainable AI" by implementing a "Show your work" function that displays every step taken to generate a response, such as database searches or calculations[10].

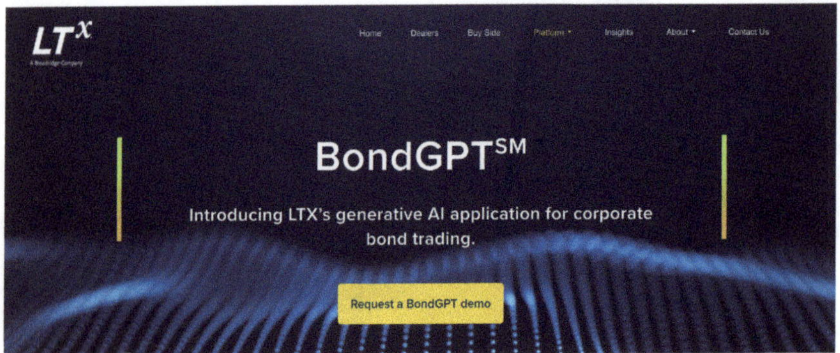

4.8 Synthesis and Recommendations

Transparency and explainability are crucial for the responsible use of AI in financial services. By implementing these concepts, Irish financial institutions can build trust with customers, ensure fairness, comply with regulations like the EU AI Act, and manage the risks associated with AI. This involves understanding the different dimensions of transparency, applying appropriate explainability techniques, and establishing a robust AI governance framework.

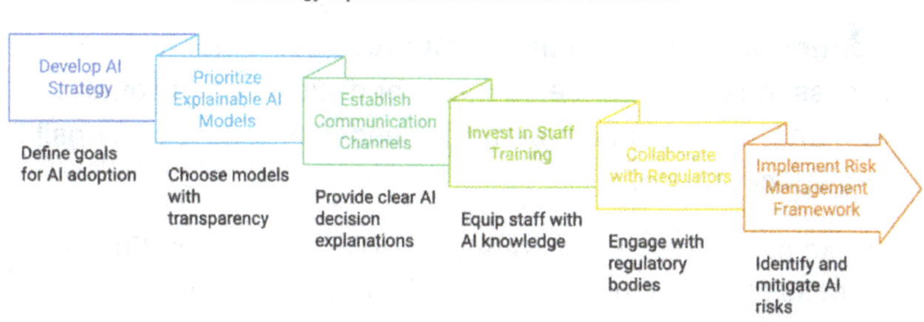

Irish financial institutions should prioritize the following actions:

- **Develop a clear AI strategy:** Define the institution's goals for AI adoption, considering ethical principles, risk management, and regulatory compliance.
- **Prioritize explainable AI models:** Choose AI models that are inherently explainable or utilize model-agnostic explainability techniques to provide insights into the decision-making process.
- **Establish clear communication channels:** Provide clear and understandable explanations for AI-driven decisions to customers and stakeholders, using personalized explanations, interactive tools, or visualizations.
- **Invest in staff training:** Equip staff with the necessary knowledge and skills to understand and contribute to

responsible AI practices.

- **Collaborate with regulators:** Engage in open dialogue with regulatory bodies to ensure alignment with evolving regulatory frameworks and contribute to shaping the future of AI in financial services.
- **Implement a robust risk management framework:** Follow a structured approach to identify, assess, and mitigate AI-related risks, including those associated with data quality, model bias, and third-party providers.
- **Continuously monitor and evaluate AI systems:** Regularly assess the performance, fairness, and explainability of AI systems, making adjustments as needed to ensure responsible and ethical AI use.

By embracing these recommendations, Irish financial institutions can harness the full potential of AI while upholding ethical and responsible practices, ultimately contributing to a more trustworthy and customer-centric financial ecosystem.

4.9 References

1. AI and Risk Management in Ireland | Deloitte Ireland, accessed on February 25, 2025, https://www.deloitte.com/ie/en/services/risk-advisory/research/_ai-and-risk-management-in-ireland.html
2. Transparency, Accountability and Collaboration: Harnessing the power of artificial intelligence in banking, accessed on February 25, 2025, https://www.globalbankingandfinance.com/transparency-accountability-and-collaboration-harnessing-the-powe-of-artificial-intelligence-inbanking
3. The EU AI Act: What you need to know - PwC Ireland, accessed on February 25, 2025, https://www.pwc.ie/services/audit-assurance/insights/eu-ai-act.html
4. Assessing the Transparency and Explainability of AI Algorithms in Planning and Scheduling tools: A Review of the Literature - ResearchGate, accessed on February 25, 2025, https://www.researchgate.net/publication/372468692_Assessing_the_Transparency_and_Explainability_of_AI_Algorithms_in_Planning_and_Scheduling_tools_A_Review_of_the_Literature
5. Transparency, Explainability, and Interpretability of AI - Cimplifi, accessed on February 25, 2025, https://www.cimplifi.com/resources/transparency-explainability-and-interpretability-of-ai/
6. (PDF) Central Bank Perspectives on AI: A Comparative Analysis of Key Issues, accessed on February 25, 2025, https://www.researchgate.net/publication/388817991_Central_Bank_Perspectives_on_AI_A_Comparative_Analysis_of_Key_Issues
7. AI: Considerations for Irish Fund Management Companies | Commercial Law Firm, accessed on February 25, 2025, https://www.dilloneustace.com/insights/ai-considerations-for-irish-fund-management-companies/
8. Central Bank of Ireland and Insight Research Ireland Centre at University of Limerick Join Forces to Boost AI Research, accessed on February 25, 2025, https://www.researchireland.ie/news/central-bank-of-ireland-and-insight-research-ireland-to-boost-ai-research/
9. Ireland Designates Nine Authorities to Safeguard Fundamental Rights Under the EU AI Act, accessed on February 25, 2025,

https://www.williamfry.com/knowledge/ireland-designates-nine-authorities-to-safeguard-fundamental-rights-under-the-eu-ai-act/
10. Unlocking Potential AI Use Cases in the Funds Industry, accessed on February 25, 2025, https://www.irishfunds.ie/news-knowledge/newsletter/unlocking-potential-ai-use-cases-in-the-funds-industry/
11. Unlocking Financial Innovation: Strategic Approaches to Open Banking Implementation, accessed on February 25, 2025, https://bpfi.ie/publications/unlocking-financial-innovation-strategic-approaches-to-open-banking-implementation/

5 Privacy & Data Protection

The Irish financial services sector is undergoing a profound transformation driven by the integration of Artificial Intelligence (AI) across various operational domains. This technological evolution promises significant enhancements in efficiency, more effective risk management strategies, and the ability to offer increasingly personalized customer experiences. However, as AI technology continues to advance, it brings to the forefront critical challenges related to privacy and data protection.

At the heart of virtually all AI systems lies their reliance on extensive datasets, often containing sensitive personal and financial information. These datasets are indispensable for the training, validation, and ongoing operation of AI models, and the precision and effectiveness of any AI model are directly correlated with the quality and volume of the data used.

Consequently, the dependency of AI on data underscores the vital importance of privacy and data protection for its responsible deployment within the financial sector.

Maintaining customer trust and ensuring ongoing compliance with evolving regulatory frameworks are paramount. Robust privacy safeguards and stringent data handling protocols are essential to mitigate risks such as data breaches, misuse of sensitive information, and significant regulatory penalties. Financial institutions must prioritize proactive measures to anticipate and mitigate potential issues before they arise.

5.1 The Imperative of Privacy & Data Protection

The Irish financial services sector is experiencing a significant transformation with the increasing integration of Artificial Intelligence (AI) across various operational domains [1]. This adoption is fuelled by the potential for substantial enhancements in efficiency, more effective risk management strategies, and the ability to offer increasingly personalized customer experiences [1]. Examples of AI applications being actively explored and implemented within Ireland include sophisticated systems for fraud detection, advanced credit scoring methodologies, customer service chatbots designed for seamless interaction, and sophisticated tools for market analysis [2].

This rapid evolution in AI technology and its application within finance underscores a critical need for financial institutions to adopt a proactive and thoroughly informed approach to both privacy and data protection [1]. Maintaining customer trust and ensuring ongoing compliance with evolving regulatory frameworks are paramount in this dynamic environment.

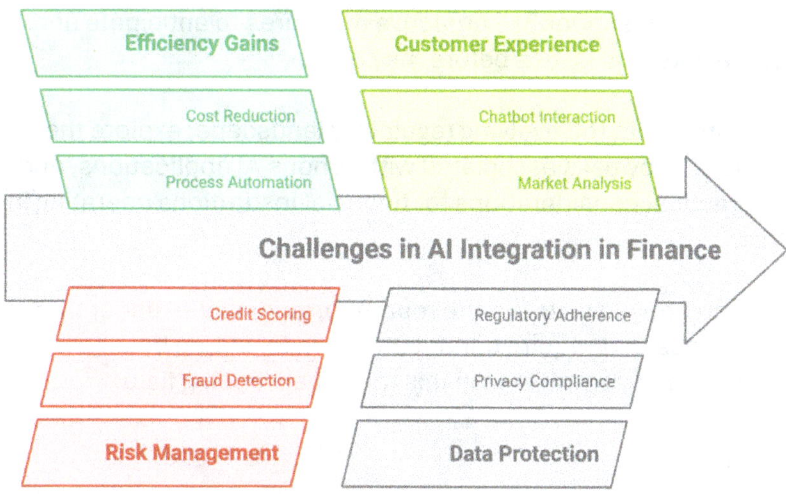

> ***The foundation of virtually all AI systems lies in their reliance on extensive datasets, which frequently contain sensitive personal and financial information. These datasets are crucial for the training, validation, and ongoing operation of AI models*** [6]***.***

The ultimate precision and overall effectiveness of any AI model are directly correlated with the quality and the sheer volume of the data upon which it is built [6]. Consequently, the inherent dependency of AI on data establishes privacy and data protection as fundamental principles for its responsible deployment within the financial sector [8].

Without the implementation of robust privacy safeguards and stringent data handling protocols, the risk of potentially damaging data breaches, the misuse of sensitive information, and significant regulatory penalties increases substantially. Therefore, financial institutions must prioritize proactive measures to anticipate and mitigate potential issues before they arise.

This chapter into the evolving regulatory landscape, explore the specific privacy risks associated with various AI applications, and offer practical considerations for financial institutions operating in Ireland.

We'll also provide a structured roadmap, guiding the reader through the key areas that require careful attention to ensure both innovation and compliance in this rapidly advancing field.

5.2 The Evolving Regulatory Landscape for AI and Data Protection

5.2.1 General Data Protection Regulation (GDPR)

Ensuring Compliance and Trust with GDPR in AI-Driven Finance

Lawfulness & Fairness

Ensures data processing is legal and equitable.

Transparency

Requires clear and open data processing practices.

Purpose Limitation

Restricts data collection to specific, legitimate purposes.

Data Minimization

Advocates for the minimal necessary data use.

Accountability

Mandates responsibility and compliance demonstration.

The cornerstone of data protection within the European Union, and by direct extension within Ireland, is the General Data Protection Regulation (GDPR) [1]. This regulation establishes a comprehensive set of principles that govern the processing of personal data. Several of these principles hold particular relevance for the implementation and use of AI in financial services.

These include the necessity for lawfulness, fairness, and transparency in all data processing activities, the principle of purpose limitation which dictates that data should only be collected for specified, explicit, and legitimate purposes, and the principle of data minimization, emphasizing that only data adequate, relevant, and limited to what is necessary in relation to the purposes for which they are processed should be used [13].

GDPR mandates the accuracy of personal data and its storage for no longer than is necessary for the purposes for which it is processed. The principles of integrity and confidentiality require that personal data is processed in a manner that ensures appropriate security, and finally, the principle of accountability obliges data controllers to be responsible for and able to demonstrate compliance with the GDPR.

Obtaining explicit consent for processing personal data that will be used in AI systems is of paramount importance under GDPR. This necessitates the implementation of consent mechanisms that are prominent, easily understandable, and provide granular options for users to specify their preferences regarding different types of data processing [11].

GDPR also enshrines a range of rights for data subjects, and any implementation of AI within financial institutions must be carefully designed to respect these rights. These include the right of individuals to access their personal data, to request rectification of inaccurate data, to demand erasure of data under certain circumstances, to restrict the processing of their data, to receive their data in a portable format, and to object to automated decision-making, particularly when such decisions produce legal effects or similarly significantly affect them [10].

While the GDPR itself is technologically neutral in its drafting, its core principles present specific challenges that require meticulous consideration during the design and deployment phases of AI systems within the financial services sector. The inherent complexity of AI algorithms and the increasing prevalence of automated decision-making necessitate a profound understanding of GDPR principles to ensure ongoing compliance. For instance, fulfilling the transparency principle by providing a clear explanation of the logic behind an AI-driven credit decision to a data subject can be a technically demanding task.

5.2.2 EU Artificial Intelligence Act (AI Act)

Complementing the GDPR is the EU Artificial Intelligence Act (AI Act), a more recent and groundbreaking regulation specifically aimed at addressing both the potential risks and the considerable opportunities presented by AI [16].

> ***The AI Act adopts a risk-based framework, categorizing AI systems into four distinct levels of risk: unacceptable, high, limited, and minimal [17].***

This categorization directly impacts the obligations placed on both the providers and the deployers of these systems.

Notably, within the financial sector, AI systems that are employed for the purpose of evaluating the creditworthiness of individuals and for risk assessment and pricing related to life and health insurance are classified as high-risk [17]. This classification triggers a set of stringent obligations for financial institutions, including:

- enhanced requirements for data governance
- the maintenance of comprehensive technical documentation
- ensuring transparency in the system's operation
- implementing robust human oversight mechanisms
- adhering to high standards of cybersecurity [16].

The AI Act also explicitly prohibits certain AI practices deemed to pose an unacceptable level of risk to fundamental rights [22]. It is important to note that the AI Act is being implemented in a phased manner, with various obligations coming into effect over the next few years. Irish financial institutions must be keenly aware of these timelines to ensure they are prepared to meet the new regulatory requirements [19].

The EU AI Act introduces sector-specific regulations that directly affect financial services, necessitating that Irish institutions undertake a proactive assessment of their current and planned AI deployments to ensure full compliance with the newly established obligations [21].

> ***The high-risk designation for AI used in credit scoring and insurance pricing directly impacts core business functions for many financial institutions.***

These institutions must thoroughly understand the specific requirements associated with these high-risk systems, such as the need for detailed documentation outlining the system's functionality and decision-making processes, as well as the implementation of effective human oversight to avoid potentially significant penalties for non-compliance [21].

Compliance and Risk Management in AI for Financial Services

5.2.3 Irish Regulatory Authorities

Within Ireland, several regulatory authorities play crucial roles in overseeing the intersection of AI and data protection in the financial sector.

The Data Protection Commission (DPC) serves as the national independent authority responsible for upholding the fundamental rights of individuals concerning the protection of their personal data under the GDPR [10]. The DPC has increasingly focused its attention on the implications of AI for data privacy, undertaking inquiries and engaging with technology companies on their use of personal data in AI models [34].

Under the EU AI Act, it is highly likely that the Central Bank of Ireland (CBI) will be designated as the market surveillance authority for high-risk AI systems that are utilized by regulated financial institutions within Ireland [17].

The CBI has already articulated its focus on achieving a balance between the opportunities and potential risks associated with the growing use of AI in the financial sector [37].

Ireland has also designated other authorities to oversee the protection of fundamental rights in the context of AI, including the Financial Services and Pensions Ombudsman (FSPO), which is expected to monitor the use of AI within financial services, with a particular focus on consumer protection [24].

Given this multi-faceted regulatory landscape, it is imperative that Irish financial institutions actively engage with both the DPC and the CBI, as well as other relevant authorities, to effectively navigate the complexities of AI and data protection regulations.

The DPC's deep expertise in GDPR and the CBI's extended role in financial supervision to include AI mean that maintaining open and consistent communication with both is essential to ensure that AI practices align with all pertinent legal and regulatory requirements.

The potential for regulatory authorities to conduct technical testing of AI models [24] further underscores the critical need for financial institutions to establish and maintain robust compliance measures. To provide a clear overview of the key regulatory players in the Irish context, their primary areas of focus regarding AI in financial services, and their core responsibilities, the following table is provided:

Table 1: Key Irish Regulatory Bodies for AI in Financial Services

Regulatory Body	Primary Focus	Key Responsibilities
Data Protection Commission (DPC)	Data Protection (GDPR, ePrivacy)	Enforcing GDPR, investigating data breaches, issuing guidance on data protection and AI
Central Bank of Ireland (CBI)	Market Surveillance for High-Risk AI in Financial Sector (EU AI Act)	Supervising financial institutions' compliance with the AI Act, conducting market surveillance, potentially carrying out technical testing
Financial Services and Pensions Ombudsman (FSPO)	Consumer Protection in Financial Services (including AI-driven decisions)	Investigating complaints from consumers regarding financial services, including those involving AI

This table serves as a valuable resource for staff within Irish financial institutions, enabling them to quickly understand the regulatory landscape and identify the appropriate bodies to engage with for specific issues related to AI and data protection.

5.3 AI Applications and Associated Privacy Risks

Balancing AI Fraud Detection and Privacy

Pattern Recognition
AI identifies patterns in transaction data

Anomaly Detection
AI detects anomalies indicating potential fraud

Privacy Risks
Identifying privacy risks and data security concerns

Data Security Measures
Implementing measures to secure sensitive data

Fairness and Bias Mitigation
Ensuring algorithms are unbiased and fair

5.3.1 Fraud Detection and Prevention

AI algorithms are increasingly employed by Irish financial institutions for the detection and prevention of fraud [2]. These systems analyse vast datasets of transaction records to identify patterns and anomalies that may indicate fraudulent activities. For example, companies like Feedzai offer platforms that utilize AI to analyse transaction patterns and spot fraudulent anomalies, while FICO Platform deploys AI to detect real-time fraud, particularly in credit card transactions and payments [4]. However, this application of AI presents several privacy risks.

There is the potential for false positives, where legitimate transactions might be incorrectly flagged as fraudulent, causing inconvenience to customers. The effectiveness of these systems relies on the processing of large volumes of personal data, including detailed transaction histories and account information. This aggregation of sensitive financial information also creates a significant risk of data breaches, making financial institutions attractive targets for cybercriminals seeking to exploit these valuable datasets [8].

While AI undeniably enhances fraud detection capabilities, financial institutions operating in Ireland must ensure the implementation of robust data security measures and diligently work to ensure that the underlying algorithms are not inherently biased, which could lead to the unfair scrutiny of specific customer groups. The ability of AI to significantly improve fraud detection relies on access to and the analysis of personal data.

Institutions must carefully balance the critical need for enhanced security with the fundamental principles of data minimization and fairness to avoid unintended and potentially negative consequences for their customers.

5.3.2 Credit Scoring and Risk Assessment

Credit scoring and risk assessment represent another significant area where AI is being actively utilized by financial institutions in Ireland [3]. AI algorithms analyse a wide array of data points, including traditional credit history as well as alternative data sources such as rent payments and utility bills, to evaluate an individual's creditworthiness. This application, however, is not without its privacy risks.

> ***A key concern is the potential for algorithmic bias, which can lead to discriminatory outcomes, such as the unfair denial of loan applications to certain demographic groups [9].***

There is also the issue of a lack of transparency in how these AI-driven credit scores are calculated, making it difficult for individuals to understand the rationale behind the decisions [2].

The use of AI in credit scoring falls under the purview of Article 22 of the GDPR, which addresses automated individual decision-making, including profiling, that has legal or similarly significant effects on individuals [11].

The EU AI Act further underscores the importance of this area by classifying AI systems used for evaluating creditworthiness as high-risk [20]. Consequently, the utilization of AI in credit scoring necessitates meticulous attention to principles of fairness, ensuring transparency in the processes, and maintaining full compliance with the regulatory frameworks governing automated decision-making. Irish financial institutions must be particularly cognizant of the high-risk classification assigned under the EU AI Act and the associated stringent requirements.

The potential for AI to inadvertently perpetuate or even amplify existing biases in credit scoring can have severe and far-reaching financial consequences for individuals. Therefore, financial institutions need to implement robust mechanisms for the detection and effective mitigation of such biases, as well as ensure a reasonable degree of explainability regarding the outcomes and provide individuals with the opportunity to request a human review of the AI-driven decisions.

5.3.3 Customer Service Chatbots and Virtual Assistants

AI-powered chatbots and virtual assistants are increasingly being deployed by Irish financial institutions to enhance customer service, handle a wide range of customer inquiries, provide personalized financial advice, and automate routine tasks [3]. Examples of such implementations include Bank of America's virtual assistant, Erica, and NatWest's Cora+ [38].

While these AI tools offer significant improvements in customer service efficiency and accessibility, they also introduce certain privacy risks. A primary concern is the collection of personal data during customer interactions, which can include sensitive information.

There is also the potential for this data to be stored indefinitely within the AI systems and their associated logs [11]. It is therefore crucial for financial institutions to obtain clear and explicit consent from customers regarding how their data will be used, particularly if it is used to improve the accuracy and overall performance of the chatbots [11].

> ***The EU AI Act imposes transparency requirements, mandating that users should be clearly informed when they are interacting with an AI system, unless it is obvious from the context [18].***

While AI-driven chatbots undoubtedly enhance the efficiency of customer service operations, Irish financial institutions must ensure that they have established robust processes for obtaining proper and informed consent for all data processing activities, implement well-defined data retention policies that align with GDPR principles, and maintain transparency with their customers by clearly indicating when they are interacting with an AI rather than a human agent.

Clear communication and a firm commitment to the principles of data minimization are essential for maintaining customer trust and ensuring compliance with both the GDPR and the EU AI Act.

5.3.4 Algorithmic Trading and Investment Strategies

Algorithmic trading and investment strategies represent another area where AI is increasingly being leveraged within the financial sector in Ireland [1]. AI algorithms are used to analyse vast quantities of market data, identify subtle trends and patterns that might be missed by human analysts, and ultimately automate trading decisions based on these insights.

Examples of key players in this space include Numerai, an AI-run hedge fund, and BlackRock, which utilizes AI extensively within its Aladdin investment management platform for sophisticated market risk analysis [4]. In contrast to the more direct impact on individual customer privacy seen in other AI applications, the privacy risks associated with algorithmic trading and investment are less pronounced. However, potential concerns can still arise, particularly in areas such as the risk of market manipulation through sophisticated AI algorithms and the potential for the misuse of non-public information, although these issues typically fall under broader regulatory compliance rather than strict data privacy regulations.

Despite the primary focus on market dynamics, financial institutions that employ AI in their trading operations must still ensure that the data used for both training and the ongoing operation of these algorithms is ethically sourced and handled in a manner that is fully compliant with all relevant regulations.

Even though the direct impact on the privacy of individual customers may be less evident in this domain, the extensive datasets utilized in algorithmic trading could still contain aggregated or anonymized personal data derived from various sources. This necessitates that institutions maintain careful consideration of data governance practices to ensure that all data is handled responsibly and in accordance with legal requirements.

5.3.5 Other AI Applications and the Importance of Privacy by Design

Beyond these core applications, AI is also being increasingly used in other areas within Irish financial services. These include the processing of Anti-Money Laundering (AML) documentation and the enhancement of Know Your Customer (KYC) procedures [4]. Additionally, AI is being deployed to provide more tailored and personalized financial guidance to customers based on the analysis of their individual financial data [5].

> ***These applications inherently involve the processing of sensitive personal and financial data, underscoring the critical need for financial institutions to implement robust security measures to protect this information.***

It is essential to ensure that the AI algorithms used in these contexts operate with fairness and do not lead to discriminatory recommendations or outcomes. Across all the various applications of AI within Irish financial services, a consistent and unwavering focus on the principles of data privacy by design and by default is absolutely essential for financial institutions.

This proactive approach means integrating privacy considerations right from the initial stages of any AI project, rather than treating them as an afterthought. By embedding privacy into the very fabric of their AI initiatives, institutions can most effectively mitigate potential risks and ensure ongoing compliance with the complex and evolving regulatory landscape.

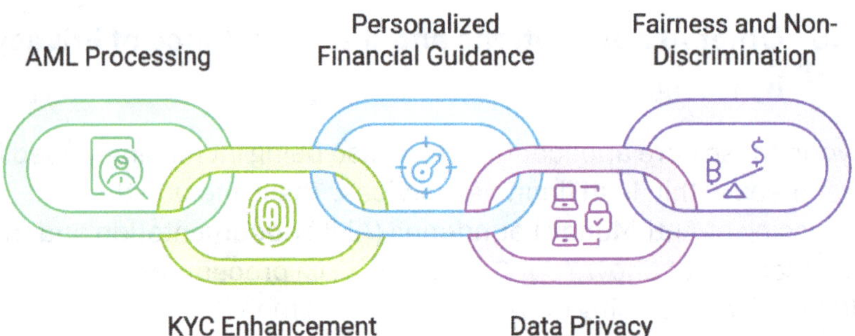

5.4 Key Privacy and Data Protection Considerations for Responsible AI

5.4.1 Effective Consent Management

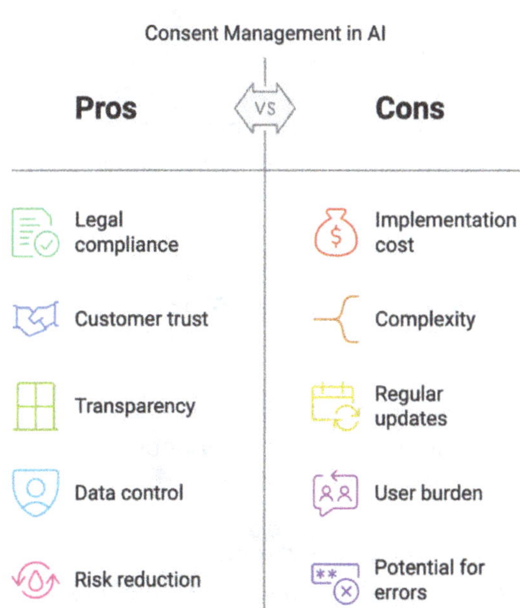

Effective consent management is a cornerstone of responsible AI deployment, particularly in customer-facing applications within Irish financial services.

Financial institutions must implement clear, user-friendly, and easily accessible mechanisms for obtaining and diligently managing consent for the collection and subsequent processing of personal data that will be utilized by their AI systems [11].

It is crucial to ensure that granular consent options are provided to users, allowing them to specify their preferences for different purposes of data processing, especially in scenarios where AI is employed for multiple distinct functions [11].

Institutions should establish a practice of regularly reviewing and updating their consent management processes to ensure they remain aligned with evolving data protection regulations and the ever-changing expectations of their customers.

> ***Robust consent management is not only a legal imperative under the GDPR but is also paramount for building and maintaining customer trust in the institution's handling of their personal information when utilizing AI technologies.***

By providing individuals with genuine control over their data and ensuring they understand how it is being used by AI systems, financial institutions can foster a more transparent and trustworthy relationship with their clientele, while simultaneously reducing the potential risk of non-compliance and associated penalties under the GDPR.

5.4.2 Adherence to Data Minimization and Purpose Limitation

Adherence to the principles of data minimization and purpose limitation is another critical consideration for Irish financial institutions as they integrate AI into their operations [11].

This involves a commitment to collecting and processing only the personal data that is strictly necessary to achieve the specific and legitimate purpose of the particular AI application.

Financial institutions should actively avoid the indefinite storage of personal data within their AI systems and must establish and consistently adhere to clear and well-defined data retention policies that align with GDPR requirements.

It is essential to ensure that any personal data initially collected for a specific purpose is not subsequently reused for other purposes that are incompatible with the original intent, without obtaining explicit and informed consent from the individuals concerned.

By diligently adhering to the principles of data minimization and purpose limitation, financial institutions can significantly reduce the

potential attack surface for data breaches and demonstrate their ongoing commitment to safeguarding the privacy of their customers in accordance with the stipulations of the GDPR.
Limiting both the amount of personal data that is processed and the duration for which it is stored minimizes the potential harm that could occur in the event of a security incident and reinforces the institution's dedication to responsible data handling practices.

5.4.3 Transparency and Explainability

Transparency and explainability are increasingly important aspects of responsible AI in financial services. Irish institutions should strive to provide data subjects with meaningful and easily understandable information about the underlying logic involved in AI-driven automated decision-making processes, particularly when these decisions have a significant impact on individuals [2].

> ***Where feasible and appropriate, financial institutions should aim for explainable AI (XAI), which enables individuals to gain insights into how AI systems arrive at specific decisions, fostering greater understanding and trust [8].***

Furthermore, it is essential to maintain transparency by clearly disclosing to customers when they are interacting with an AI system, such as a customer service chatbot, rather than a human representative [18]. Enhancing transparency and the level of explainability in AI systems is crucial for building customer trust and also facilitates more effective oversight by regulatory authorities.

The inherent "black box" nature of some sophisticated AI algorithms can often create a barrier to both trust and regulatory compliance. Therefore, concerted efforts to make the decision-making processes of AI more transparent and readily understandable are vital for ensuring accountability and promoting fairness in the application of these technologies within the financial sector.

5.4.4 Mitigation of Algorithmic Bias

Financial institutions in Ireland must be acutely aware that AI models have the potential to inherit and even amplify biases that may be present within the datasets used for their training [1]. To address this critical issue, institutions need to implement rigorous and comprehensive testing and validation processes specifically designed to identify and effectively mitigate bias in their AI algorithms [9].

The ultimate goal is to ensure that the AI systems deployed do not inadvertently lead to discriminatory outcomes for any particular groups of individuals. Taking proactive measures to identify and mitigate algorithmic bias is not only an ethical imperative but is also essential for safeguarding the institution's reputation and preventing potentially significant regulatory penalties.

> ***Biased AI systems can lead to unfair or discriminatory decisions, which can severely erode customer trust and potentially result in violations of anti-discrimination laws.***

Therefore, Irish financial institutions must place a high priority on ensuring fairness in all aspects of their AI deployments.

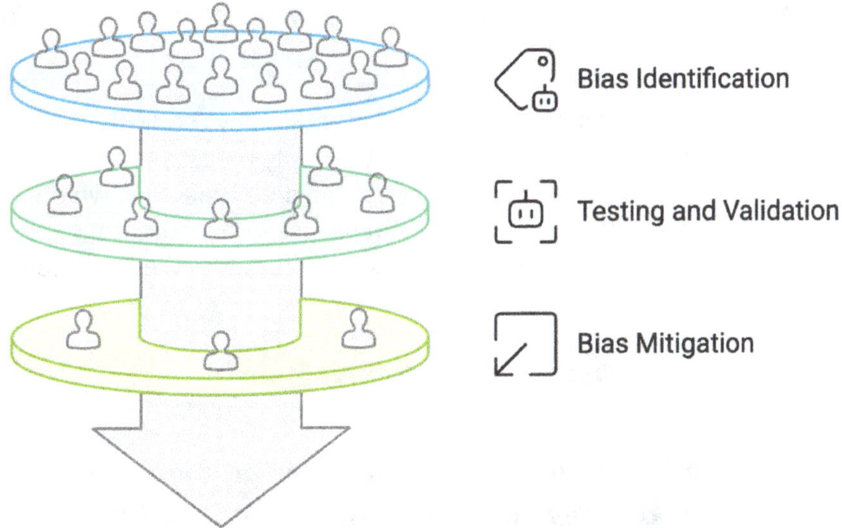

5.4.5 Robust Cybersecurity Measures

Implementing robust cybersecurity measures is absolutely paramount for Irish financial institutions that utilize AI systems, particularly to protect the sensitive personal and financial data that these systems process [1].

These measures must be designed to prevent unauthorized access, manipulation, and theft of this valuable data. This includes the strategic utilization of encryption technologies to secure data both when it is stored (at rest) and when it is being transmitted (in transit), as well as the implementation of stringent access controls to ensure that only authorized personnel can interact with the data and the AI systems.

Financial institutions must also commit to regularly assessing and proactively updating their security measures to effectively address the ever-evolving landscape of cyber threats. Given the highly regulated nature of the financial sector, coupled with the immense value of the data they hold, strong data security is not just an operational necessity but a non-negotiable requirement for maintaining the integrity and confidentiality of customer information processed by AI systems.

Financial institutions are consistently targeted by cyberattacks, making the implementation of robust security measures absolutely crucial to prevent potentially catastrophic data breaches, which could lead to substantial financial losses, severe regulatory sanctions, and irreparable damage to their reputation and customer trust.

5.4.6 Human Oversight and Intervention

> ***Establishing clear and well-defined protocols for human oversight of AI systems is another critical consideration for responsible AI implementation in Irish financial services [9].***
>
> ***This is particularly important for AI systems that make decisions that could have a significant impact on individuals, such as loan approvals or insurance claim processing.***

Implementing "kill switches" or "exit chutes" provides a necessary safety mechanism, allowing for the immediate disabling of AI systems if any discrepancies or unintended and potentially harmful behaviours are detected [3]. Furthermore, financial institutions should provide clear and accessible mechanisms for individuals to appeal or request a manual review of decisions that have been made by AI systems [11].

The inclusion of human oversight in AI processes serves as a crucial safety net, ensuring accountability for the outcomes of these systems and providing the necessary ability to identify and correct any errors or inherent biases that may arise.

While AI offers the potential to automate numerous processes and enhance efficiency, human judgment and intervention remain essential, particularly when dealing with complex or unusual cases, and are vital for ultimately ensuring fairness and accuracy in critical decision-making processes that affect individuals' financial well-being.

5.5 Practical Implications and Recommendations

5.5.1 Develop Robust AI Governance Frameworks

Irish financial institutions should prioritize the development of robust AI governance frameworks to ensure the responsible adoption and use of artificial intelligence. This involves establishing clear and comprehensive policies and procedures that govern the entire lifecycle of AI systems, from their initial development and deployment to their ongoing monitoring and eventual decommissioning.

> ***These frameworks should explicitly incorporate the principles of privacy by design, ensuring that data protection is considered at every stage of the AI system's development*** [3]**.**

Clearly defined roles and responsibilities for AI governance should be established across all relevant departments within the institution [16]. Furthermore, a comprehensive inventory of all AI systems currently in use, as well as those planned for future implementation, should be meticulously maintained [16].

A well-defined AI governance framework is absolutely essential for ensuring the responsible integration of AI technologies and for maintaining full compliance with the complex and evolving regulatory landscape.

Without such a framework, financial institutions face a significant risk of deploying AI systems that are not aligned with their core values, do not meet their legal and ethical obligations, or fail to meet the expectations of their customers.

AI Governance Framework Development
Identify Need for AI Governance
Recognizing the necessity for structured AI oversight
Establish Policies and Procedures
Creating comprehensive guidelines for AI lifecycle management
Define Roles and Responsibilities
Assigning clear roles for AI governance across departments
Maintain AI Systems Inventory
Keeping an updated record of current and planned AI systems
Ensure Compliance with Regulations
Aligning AI practices with legal and ethical standards

5.5.2 Conduct Thorough Data Protection Impact Assessments (DPIAs)

Conducting thorough Data Protection Impact Assessments (DPIAs) is a critical step for Irish financial institutions embarking on AI initiatives.

> ***DPIAs are mandatory under the GDPR for any processing activities, including the deployment of AI, that are likely to result in a high risk to the rights and freedoms of individuals, particularly when the AI systems will be processing sensitive personal data or making automated decisions that have significant effects on individuals' lives [11].***

These assessments should be structured to provide a clear outline of the data flow within the AI system, identify any potential risks to data privacy, and detail the specific measures that will be implemented to mitigate these risks [11]. When institutions are uncertain about the necessity or the scope of a DPIA, or when dealing with particularly complex AI deployments, seeking guidance from the Irish Data Protection Commission (DPC) or consulting with legal experts in data protection is highly recommended [11].

DPIAs serve as an invaluable tool for proactively identifying and addressing potential privacy risks associated with the deployment of AI technologies. By systematically assessing the potential impact of AI on personal data, financial institutions can ensure that they implement appropriate safeguards and minimize the likelihood of data breaches or instances of non-compliance with regulatory requirements.

5.5.3 Implement Staff Training and Awareness Programs

Irish financial institutions must establish clear and comprehensive policies and procedures that specifically guide their staff on the responsible and ethical use of AI tools within the workplace [16]. This includes developing detailed guidelines that outline expected behaviors and practices when interacting with or utilizing AI systems.

It iis essential to implement robust training and awareness programs to educate employees on the fundamental principles of AI, the relevant data privacy regulations (including GDPR and the EU AI Act), and the institution's own internal policies regarding AI usage [2].

Defining clear and acceptable use policies for AI in the workplace helps to ensure that employees understand the boundaries of appropriate AI usage and the potential risks associated with its misuse [46]. Educating and empowering staff to use AI responsibly is absolutely crucial for fostering a strong culture of data privacy and ethical AI practices throughout the entire organization.

> ***Human error remains a significant contributing factor to data breaches and compliance failures.***

Therefore, well-informed and properly trained staff are significantly better equipped to recognize and understand the potential risks associated with the use of AI and to consistently adhere to the institution's established policies and procedures.

5.5.4 Ensure Ongoing Regulatory Compliance

To ensure ongoing compliance with the evolving regulatory landscape for both AI and data protection, Irish financial institutions need to adopt a proactive and systematic approach.

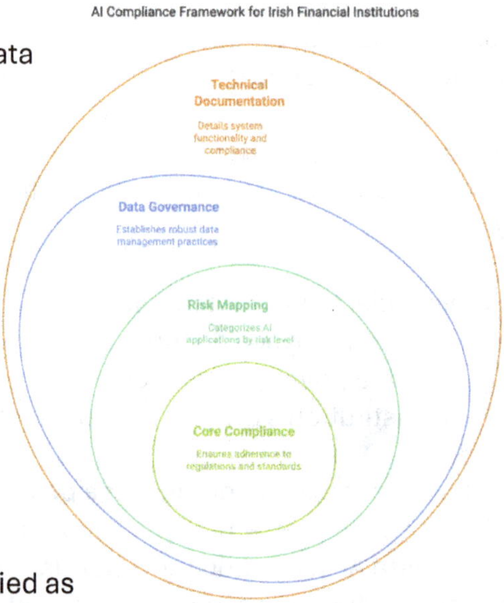

AI Compliance Framework for Irish Financial Institutions

Technical Documentation
Details system functionality and compliance

Data Governance
Establishes robust data management practices

Risk Mapping
Categorizes AI applications by risk level

Core Compliance
Ensures adherence to regulations and standards

This includes meticulously mapping their various AI applications to the specific risk categories as defined within the EU AI Act [16].

For those AI systems classified as high-risk, institutions must diligently implement all the specific requirements stipulated by the Act, such as establishing robust data governance frameworks, maintaining comprehensive technical documentation detailing the system's functionality and compliance measures, and ensuring effective human oversight of the system's operation [16].

It is also essential to establish well-defined processes for the continuous monitoring and regular auditing of all AI systems to verify their ongoing compliance with both the GDPR and the EU AI Act [11]. The regulatory environment for AI and data protection is not static; it continues to evolve with technological advancements and societal considerations.

Therefore, Irish financial institutions must remain agile and committed to continuous learning and adaptation, establishing internal processes to actively track regulatory changes and proactively update their AI governance frameworks, policies, and procedures to ensure sustained compliance and maintain a competitive edge in the rapidly transforming financial services landscape.

5.5.5 Implement Best Practices for Third-Party Vendor Management

Given the increasing trend of financial institutions in Ireland relying on third-party vendors for the provision of AI solutions, establishing best practices for the selection and ongoing management of these vendors is of paramount importance.

This includes conducting thorough due diligence on any potential AI vendors to rigorously assess their data protection practices, their overall security posture, and their level of compliance with all relevant data protection regulations, such as the GDPR and any applicable provisions of the EU AI Act [11].

It is also essential to ensure that legally sound and comprehensive data processing agreements are in place with all AI vendors. These agreements should clearly define the responsibilities of both the institution and the vendor regarding data processing, security, and any potential liabilities in the event of a data breach or other security incident [11].

> ***Financial institutions must have a clear understanding of where the vendor's data is hosted and ensure that these hosting arrangements comply with all applicable data transfer requirements, particularly if data is being transferred outside of the European Economic Area (EEA)*** [11]***.***

Robust vendor management practices are absolutely critical for effectively mitigating potential privacy and security risks associated with the use of third-party AI services. By implementing a rigorous vendor selection process and establishing clear contractual obligations, institutions can help to ensure that their AI vendors adhere to the same high standards of data privacy and security that the institutions themselves are committed to upholding.

5.6 Case Studies of Privacy and Data Protection in AI

5.6.1 An Post Money

An Post Money, the financial services division of the Irish postal service, provides a compelling case study in the application of AI within the Irish financial landscape. Their ongoing digital transformation initiatives, including a significant partnership with Cognizant, underscore the increasing adoption of technology to enhance customer experiences and operational efficiency [51]. Notably, An Post Money utilizes facial recognition technology within its mobile application as part of the identity verification process for anti-money laundering purposes .

This application of biometric data highlights the critical importance of clearly outlining privacy considerations. An Post provides comprehensive privacy statements detailing how they manage personal data across their various services, including An Post Money [52]. These statements explain the types of personal data collected, the purposes for which it is processed, and the measures taken to ensure its security and confidentiality [5].

An Post has implemented various security measures to protect customer data and actively prevent fraudulent activities, providing information and tips to customers on how to stay safe online and avoid scams [55]. An Post Money's approach exemplifies the practical application of AI for crucial functions like customer onboarding and identity verification, while simultaneously demonstrating a clear emphasis on data privacy and security through the implementation of transparent privacy policies and robust technological safeguards. As a significant player in the Irish financial services sector, An Post Money offers a tangible example of how AI is being integrated into operations while actively addressing the associated privacy concerns through measures such as publicly available and detailed privacy statements and the implementation of stringent security protocols.

5.6.2 "BIG Bank" (Anonymized Case Study)

While specific publicly available case studies detailing the AI deployments of other Irish financial institutions are somewhat limited within the provided snippets, the research material does indicate a general trend towards the adoption of AI for various purposes. For instance, Irish banks are increasingly leveraging AI for the enhancement of their fraud detection capabilities . Additionally, there is evidence suggesting that some Irish financial institutions are utilizing AI platforms to deliver more personalized interactions with their customers.

Although these examples provide a general overview of AI adoption, they do not address the specific privacy and data protection measures implemented by these institutions.

However, a valuable anonymized case study from the Irish Banking Culture Board [61] focuses on the use of AI in credit decision-making within a "BIG Bank." This case study, while not naming the institution, offers significant insights into the critical importance of board-level oversight, the necessity of conducting thorough due diligence before implementing AI systems, and the crucial need for financial institutions to effectively address customer complaints that may arise in relation to AI-driven decisions [61]. This anonymized example underscores the privacy and ethical challenges that Irish financial institutions are likely facing as they explore and implement AI technologies.

Even in the absence of explicit, named Irish case studies across all areas of AI application in finance, the general trends identified in the research, coupled with the anonymized case study, strongly suggest that Irish financial institutions are actively exploring and implementing AI solutions across a range of their operations.

In doing so, they are likely encountering similar privacy and ethical considerations and challenges as their counterparts in other regions globally. The relative lack of readily available public case studies specifically detailing these implementations and the associated privacy measures highlights a potential need for greater transparency within the sector regarding AI deployments and the steps being taken to ensure robust privacy and data protection for customers. The provided anonymized case study serves as a crucial reminder of the importance of governance and oversight in the context of AI adoption in financial services.

5.6.3 Finclude

While not a traditional financial institution, Finclude, a company that aims to help individuals open bank accounts across the EU, provides an interesting case study related to AI and data protection in the Irish context [62]. They partnered with IBM and, in the process of seeking authorization from the Central Bank of Ireland, demonstrated a strong commitment to privacy and security [62].

This highlights that even companies working with financial data in Ireland face stringent scrutiny from regulatory bodies regarding their data handling practices, including those related to AI [62].
From these examples and the broader analysis, several key lessons and actionable insights emerge for Irish financial institutions.

> ***Transparency with customers regarding the use of AI is paramount for building and maintaining trust. Robust due diligence processes and the establishment of ongoing monitoring mechanisms for AI systems are essential to ensure their continued accuracy, fairness, and compliance.***

Finally, it is critical for institutions to establish clear lines of accountability and ensure that appropriate human oversight is in place for all AI-driven decisions, particularly those that could significantly impact their customers.

5.7 The Future of AI and Data Protection

The landscape of AI and data protection in Irish financial services is poised for continued evolution, driven by several emerging trends. One significant trend is the increasing utilization of Generative AI technologies within the financial sector, which presents novel and complex privacy challenges that institutions must address [16]. The potential for AI-powered cyber threats is a growing concern, necessitating the implementation of even more sophisticated and robust cybersecurity measures to safeguard sensitive financial data .

Ongoing developments and increasing adoption of "open banking" initiatives will also have significant data privacy implications due to the enhanced sharing of financial data across various platforms and providers [17].

> ***These emerging trends indicate that the future will likely see a proliferation of increasingly sophisticated AI applications within Irish financial services, demanding an even greater level of vigilance and proactive measures concerning both privacy and data protection.***

Technologies such as Generative AI and the open banking framework introduce new layers of complexity in how data is handled, shared, and secured, requiring financial institutions to continuously adapt and strengthen their privacy and security frameworks to meet these evolving challenges.

The regulatory environment surrounding AI and data protection is also expected to continue to evolve at both the European Union and national levels. Ongoing development of AI regulations and guidelines will likely shape how financial institutions in Ireland can deploy and utilize these technologies [16].

Therefore, it is of paramount importance for Irish financial institutions to remain consistently informed about the latest regulatory developments and to actively adopt best practices in the realm of responsible AI.

The potential for increased scrutiny and more stringent enforcement actions by regulatory authorities further underscores the need for proactive compliance measures [59].
In this dynamic and evolving landscape, continuous learning and a commitment to adaptation will be crucial for Irish financial institutions to effectively navigate the complexities of AI and data protection.

The regulatory environment for AI is still in its formative stages, and financial institutions must cultivate agility and a proactive mindset to ensure that their policies and operational practices are regularly updated to maintain ongoing compliance and to sustain a competitive advantage within the rapidly transforming financial services sector.

5.8 Conclusion: Fostering Trust and Responsibility in the Age of AI

In conclusion, the integration of Artificial Intelligence into Irish Financial Services presents significant opportunities for innovation and efficiency, but it also brings with it the critical imperative of prioritizing privacy and data protection. This chapter has highlighted the key regulatory considerations, primarily the GDPR and the EU AI Act, and their practical implications for financial institutions operating in Ireland.

> ***The analysis underscores the necessity of establishing robust governance frameworks that embed privacy by design, conducting thorough risk assessments, and fostering a culture of responsible AI use among staff.***

The case study of An Post Money provides a concrete example of how AI can be implemented while addressing privacy concerns through transparent policies and technological safeguards. While specific examples from other Irish institutions are less readily available, the broader trends and the anonymized case study on AI in credit decision-making indicate that the sector is actively engaging with AI and facing similar challenges in ensuring privacy and ethical practices.

The case of Finclude further emphasizes the regulatory scrutiny applied to companies handling financial data in Ireland, particularly concerning data protection in the context of AI.

Looking ahead, the increasing sophistication of AI, particularly with the emergence of Generative AI, and the evolving regulatory landscape will demand continuous vigilance and adaptation from Irish financial institutions. Staying informed about regulatory developments, adopting best practices in responsible AI, and maintaining open communication with regulatory authorities will be crucial for navigating the future.

Ultimately, by integrating privacy and data protection into all aspects of their AI adoption strategies, Irish financial institutions can foster trust with their customers and ensure the responsible and sustainable growth of AI within the sector, realizing its potential benefits while upholding fundamental rights and maintaining the integrity of the financial system.

5.9 References

1. (PDF) Data privacy, security, and ethical considerations in AI ..., accessed on March 20, 2025, https://www.researchgate.net/publication/379078709_Data_privacy_security_and_ethical_considerations_in_AI-powered_finance

2. Transforming Ireland's Financial Industry through AI & Data Literacy - University College Dublin, accessed on March 20, 2025, https://www.ucd.ie/professionalacademy/resources/finance-industry-ai-transformation/

3. AI and Risk Management in Ireland | Deloitte Ireland, accessed on March 20, 2025, https://www.deloitte.com/ie/en/services/risk-advisory/research/_ai-and-risk-management-in-ireland.html

4. The Role of AI in Finance: Real-World Examples and Opportunities | Agicap, accessed on March 20, 2025, https://agicap.com/en/article/ai-finance/

5. 8 Applications of Finance AI in Financial Management - Tipalti, accessed on March 20, 2025, https://tipalti.com/en-eu/financial-operations-hub/finance-ai/

6. Managing Artificial Intelligence-Specific Cybersecurity Risks in the Financial Services Sector - Treasury Department, accessed on March 20, 2025, https://home.treasury.gov/system/files/136/Managing-Artificial-Intelligence-Specific-Cybersecurity-Risks-In-The-Financial-Services-Sector.pdf

7. ARTIFICIAL INTELLIGENCE IN FINANCIAL SERVICES - Treasury Department, accessed on March 20, 2025, https://home.treasury.gov/system/files/136/Artificial-

Intelligence-in-Financial-Services.pdf

8. (PDF) Data Privacy Challenges in AI-Driven Financial Services, accessed on March 20, 2025, https://www.researchgate.net/publication/389466331_Data_Privacy_Challenges_in_AI-Driven_Financial_Services

9. ijrpr.com, accessed on March 20, 2025, https://ijrpr.com/uploads/V5ISSUE10/IJRPR34234.pdf

10. Data Protection Commission: Homepage, accessed on March 20, 2025, https://www.dataprotection.ie/

11. Navigating AI and GDPR in Ireland: 6 Pitfalls to Avoid - ProfileTree, accessed on March 20, 2025, https://profiletree.com/navigating-ai-and-gdpr-in-ireland/

12. A Global Spotlight on Ireland's role in Data Protection - FTI Strategic Communications, accessed on March 20, 2025, https://fticommunications.com/a-global-spotlight-on-irelands-role-in-data-protection/

13. Practical Solutions for Harmonized Compliance with GDPR and AI, accessed on March 20, 2025, https://gdprlocal.com/practical-solutions-for-harmonized-compliance-with-gdpr-and-ai/

14. Irish businesses must act now to navigate the impact of AI and the EU AI Act, accessed on March 20, 2025, https://www.pinsentmasons.com/out-law/analysis/irish-businesses-must-act-navigate-impact-eu-ai-act

15. The impact of the General Data Protection Regulation (GDPR) on artificial intelligence - European Parliament, accessed on March 20, 2025, https://www.europarl.europa.eu/RegData/etudes/STUD/2020/641530/EPRS_STU(2020)641530_EN.pdf

16. Responsible AI in Financial Services | EY - Global, accessed

on March 20, 2025, https://www.ey.com/en_gl/responsible-ai-financial-services

17. The new AI Act has Big Implications for the Financial Services Sector - Institute of Directors Ireland, accessed on March 20, 2025, https://www.iodireland.ie/images/uploads/downloads/8300_IOD_FactSheet_June_Big_Data%2C_Big_Change_The_new_AI_Act_has_Big_Implications_for_the_Financial_Services_Sector.pdf
18. Big Data, Big Change: The new AI Act has Big Implications for the Financial Services Sector, accessed on March 20, 2025, https://www.mccannfitzgerald.com/knowledge/financial-services-regulation/new-artificial-intelligence-act-has-big-implications-for-the-financial-services-sector
19. Artificial Intelligence and Insurance - Insurance Ireland, accessed on March 20, 2025, https://insuranceireland.eu/news-and-publications/blog/artificial-intelligence-and-insurance/
20. AI: Risk and Regulatory Considerations for Irish Regulated Firms | Maples Group, accessed on March 20, 2025, https://maples.com/wp-content/uploads/2024/09/AI-Risk-and-Regulatory-Considerations-for-Irish-Regulated-Firms.pdf
21. The EU AI Act: The impact on financial services institutions - Consultancy.eu, accessed on March 20, 2025, https://www.consultancy.eu/news/11237/the-eu-ai-act-the-impact-on-financial-services-institutions
22. EU Artificial Intelligence (AI) Act - Department of Enterprise, Trade and Employment, accessed on March 20, 2025,

https://enterprise.gov.ie/en/what-we-do/innovation-research-development/artificial-intelligence/eu-ai-act/

23. EU law is changing the landscape for AI in financial services - Pinsent Masons, accessed on March 20, 2025, https://www.pinsentmasons.com/out-law/analysis/eu-law-changing-landscape-ai-financial-services
24. Ireland Designates Nine Authorities to Safeguard Fundamental Rights Under the EU AI Act, accessed on March 20, 2025, https://www.williamfry.com/knowledge/ireland-designates-nine-authorities-to-safeguard-fundamental-rights-under-the-eu-ai-act/
25. EU AI Act adopted by the Parliament: What's the impact for financial institutions? - Deloitte, accessed on March 20, 2025, https://www.deloitte.com/lu/en/Industries/investment-management/perspectives/european-artificial-intelligence-act-adopted-parliament.html
26. Understanding the Impact of the EU AI Act: A Primer for Financial Institutions - Protiviti, accessed on March 20, 2025, https://www.protiviti.com/us-en/insights-paper/understanding-impact-eu-ai-act
27. EU AI Act: Key Points for Financial Services Businesses | Insights & Resources | Goodwin, accessed on March 20, 2025, https://www.goodwinlaw.com/en/insights/publications/2024/08/alerts-practices-pif-key-points-for-financial-services-businesses
28. AI Watch: Global regulatory tracker - European Union | White & Case LLP, accessed on March 20, 2025,

https://www.whitecase.com/insight-our-thinking/ai-watch-global-regulatory-tracker-european-union

29. The implications of using AI in fraud prevention and detection - KPMG International, accessed on March 20, 2025, https://kpmg.com/nl/en/home/insights/2025/01/the-implications-of-using-ai-in-fraud-prevention-and-detection.html
30. How organisations can embrace responsible AI | EY - Ireland, accessed on March 20, 2025, https://www.ey.com/en_ie/insights/assurance/how-organisations-can-embrace-responsible-ai
31. EU: Artificial Intelligence Regulation Should Ban Social Scoring | Human Rights Watch, accessed on March 20, 2025, https://www.hrw.org/news/2023/10/09/eu-artificial-intelligence-regulation-should-ban-social-scoring
32. AI, Machine Learning & Big Data Laws 2024 | Ireland - Global Legal Insights, accessed on March 20, 2025, https://www.globallegalinsights.com/practice-areas/ai-machine-learning-and-big-data-laws-and-regulations/ireland/
33. Rapid Rise and GDPR Scrutiny of New AI Systems - Deloitte, accessed on March 20, 2025, https://www.deloitte.com/se/sv/services/legal/perspectives/rapid-rise-and-gdpr-scrutiny-of-new-ai-systems.html
34. EDPB Opinion on AI Models and Data Protection Compliance - Byrne Wallace Shields LLP, accessed on March 20, 2025, https://byrnewallaceshields.com/news-and-recent-work/publications/edpb-opinion-on-ai-

models-and-data-protection-compliance.html

35. Irish Data Regulators Put Google AI Model Under Review | PYMNTS.com, accessed on March 20, 2025, https://www.pymnts.com/news/regulation/2024/google-artificial-intelligence-model-faces-european-union-data-privacy-investigation/

36. The EDPB Opinion on training AI models using personal data and recent Garante fine – lawful deployment of LLMs, accessed on March 20, 2025, https://www.dataprotectionreport.com/2025/01/the-edpb-opinion-on-training-ai-models-using-personal-data-and-recent-garante-fine-lawful-deployment-of-llms/

37. Regulatory & Supervisory Outlook Report | Central Bank of Ireland, accessed on March 20, 2025, https://www.centralbank.ie/publication/regulatory---supervisory-outlook-report

38. AI Applications in Banking: Real-World Examples - Blocshop, accessed on March 20, 2025, https://blocshop.ie/blog/ai-applications-in-banking-real-world-examples

39. Revolutionising Finance: How AI is Shaping the Future of the Financial Sector | HLB Ireland, accessed on March 20, 2025, https://www.hlb.ie/revolutionising-finance-how-ai-is-shaping-the-future-of-the-financial-sector/

40. How artificial intelligence is reshaping the financial services industry | EY - Greece, accessed on March 20, 2025, https://www.ey.com/en_gr/insights/financial-services/how-artificial-intelligence-is-reshaping-the-financial-services-industry

41. Guiding AI development: The path to responsible and effective banking solutions, accessed on March 20,

2025, https://ibsintelligence.com/blogs/guiding-ai-development-the-path-to-responsible-and-effective-banking-solutions/

42. Cybersecurity Challenges in an AI-Driven Financial Services World - FTF - FinTech Frontiers, accessed on March 20, 2025, https://fintechfrontiers.live/cybersecurity-challenges-in-an-ai-driven-financial-services-world/

43. CJEU Rules that GDPR Prohibition on Automated Decision-Making Applies to Credit Scoring - Hunton Andrews Kurth LLP, accessed on March 20, 2025, https://www.hunton.com/privacy-and-information-security-law/cjeu-rules-that-gdpr-prohibition-on-automated-decision-making-applies-to-credit-scoring

44. Ruling to concern service-providers using AI - Law Society of Ireland Gazette, accessed on March 20, 2025, https://www.lawsociety.ie/gazette/top-stories/2024/january/ruling-to-concern-service-providers-using-ai/

45. Financial consumer protection and market conduct considerations of AI in finance - Remarks by Colm Kincaid, Director of Consumer Protection - Central Bank of Ireland, accessed on March 20, 2025, https://www.centralbank.ie/news/article/speech-colm-kincaid-financial-consumer-protection-and-market-conduct-considerations-of-AI-in-finance-22-may-2024

46. Artificial Intelligence Risk Management: A Practical Step-by-Step Guide - GDPR Local, accessed on March 20, 2025, https://gdprlocal.com/artificial-intelligence-risk-management-a-practical-step-by-step-guide/

47. Treasury's Post-2024 RFI Report on AI in Financial Services – Uses, Opportunities, and Risks | 01 | 2025 | Publications,

accessed on March 20, 2025, https://www.debevoise.com/insights/publications/2025/01/treasurys-post-2024-rfi-report-on-ai-in-financial

48. Nearly 8 in 10 Financial Services Firms View AI as Critical to Industry's Success, Finds New Report from Smarsh, accessed on March 20, 2025, https://www.smarsh.com/press-release/nearly-8-in-10-financial-services-firms-view-ai-as-critical-to-industrys-success-finds-new-report-from-smarsh

49. How Responsible AI can improve business and preserve value - PwC, accessed on March 20, 2025, https://www.pwc.com/gx/en/services/ai/responsible-ai.html

50. Responsible AI — Technology Services - PwC Ireland, accessed on March 20, 2025, https://www.pwc.ie/services/consulting/technology/artificial-intelligence/responsible-ai.html

51. An Post Money Builds New Digital Bank - Cognizant, accessed on March 20, 2025, https://www.cognizant.com/us/en/case-studies/an-post-new-digital-bank

52. Group Data Privacy Statement - An Post, accessed on March 20, 2025, https://www.anpost.com/Privacy/Group-Data-Privacy-Statement

53. Data Protection Mails Notice - An Post, accessed on March 20, 2025, https://www.anpost.com/Privacy/Data-Protection-Privacy-Notice

54. Privacy - An Post, accessed on March 20, 2025, https://www.anpost.com/Privacy

55. An Post Money App Terms of Use, accessed on March 20, 2025, https://www.anpost.com/Terms-of-Use/App-Terms-of-Use

56. Security - An Post, accessed on March 20, 2025,

https://www.anpost.com/Security

57. Reflections on US Treasury Department Report on AI in Financial Services | New York City Bar Association, accessed on March 20, 2025, https://www.nycbar.org/reports/reflections-on-us-treasury-department-report-on-ai-in-financial-services/
58. AI users trust on medical advice GenAI | Deloitte Ireland, accessed on March 20, 2025, https://www.deloitte.com/ie/en/about/press-room/trust-gen-ai-medical-advice.html
59. How AI is reshaping the P&C (re)insurance market - DOCOsoft, accessed on March 20, 2025, https://docosoft.com/how-ai-is-reshaping-the-pc-reinsurance-market/
60. AI and Privacy in the New Age of Open Banking - American Bar Association, accessed on March 20, 2025, https://www.americanbar.org/groups/business_law/resources/business-law-today/2024-february/ai-and-privacy-in-the-new-age-of-open-banking/
61. Case Study Two: AI Decision Making - Irish Banking Culture Board, accessed on March 20, 2025, https://www.irishbankingcultureboard.ie/wp-content/uploads/2024/10/Case-Study-2-30.10.24.pdf
62. Finclude - IBM, accessed on March 20, 2025, https://www.ibm.com/case-studies/finclude

6 Accountability & Responsibility

The financial services sector in Ireland is increasingly embracing artificial intelligence (AI) to enhance efficiency, improve customer experiences, and gain competitive advantages. This growing reliance on AI necessitates a robust understanding and implementation of accountability and responsibility frameworks to ensure ethical, fair, and trustworthy deployment.

This chapter analyses academic literature, industry insights, and Irish regulatory guidelines, particularly those from the Central Bank of Ireland, to explore how these crucial concepts are defined, assigned, and addressed within the context of AI in financial services.

The analysis reveals a strong consensus on the paramount importance of accountability and responsibility in mitigating the inherent risks of AI, such as bias, lack of transparency, and potential harm to consumers and the financial system. While academic and industry sources look into the theoretical and practical aspects of these concepts, **Irish regulators are actively establishing expectations and legal obligations, primarily through the Central Bank of Ireland and the impending EU Artificial Intelligence Act (AI Act).**

Key challenges remain in navigating the complexities of AI decision-making and ensuring clear lines of responsibility across the AI lifecycle. We finish by offering actionable recommendations for Irish financial institutions to foster a culture of responsible AI adoption underpinned by strong accountability and responsibility mechanisms.

6.1 Introduction

6.1.1 Background on AI Adoption

The financial services industry in both the UK and Ireland has witnessed a significant surge in the adoption of artificial intelligence in recent years.[1] This transformation is driven by advancements in technology, the availability of large datasets, and the increasing need for efficiency and innovation.[1] Generative AI and large language models, in particular, are gaining traction, expanding the scope of AI applications beyond traditional areas.[1]

Financial institutions are leveraging AI across a wide spectrum of their operations, primarily focusing on enhancing internal processes and improving regulatory compliance.[1] However, there is a growing interest in exploring AI's potential to generate new revenue streams and personalize customer offerings.[2]

> ***This widespread integration signifies a fundamental shift in how financial services operate, making the establishment of clear accountability and responsibility frameworks more critical than ever before.***

In Ireland, this trend is equally evident, with financial institutions increasingly adopting AI-driven solutions for various purposes, including automation, customer service enhancement, and improved decision-making.[5]

The Central Bank of Ireland has acknowledged AI as a technology with significant transformative potential for both regulated entities and itself as a regulator.[7] This recognition underscores the importance of understanding and managing the implications of AI in the Irish financial landscape.

6.1.2 Importance of Accountability and Responsibility

Accountability and responsibility are paramount for ensuring the ethical, fair, and trustworthy deployment of AI within the financial services sector.[4] As AI systems become more sophisticated and integrated into critical financial processes, the potential for risks such as bias, discrimination, lack of transparency, and even financial instability increases significantly if these frameworks are absent.[1] Algorithmic bias, for instance, can lead to discriminatory outcomes in lending and credit scoring, potentially excluding certain demographic groups from essential financial services.[8]

The "black box" nature of some AI models can make it difficult to understand how decisions are made, hindering effective oversight and accountability.[10] Without clear lines of responsibility, it becomes challenging to address errors, misconduct, or regulatory violations arising from the use of AI.[12] Therefore, establishing robust accountability and responsibility mechanisms is crucial for maintaining public trust in AI-driven financial services and safeguarding the integrity of the financial system.

Balancing AI Accountability and Risk Management in Financial Services

6.1.3 Scope and Objectives

This chapter aims to provide a comprehensive analysis of accountability and responsibility in the context of responsible AI use within the financial services sector, with a specific focus on Ireland. It will examine the definitions of these concepts as presented in academic literature and industry reports. Furthermore, it will examine the guidelines and regulations issued by Irish regulatory bodies, primarily the Central Bank of Ireland, concerning AI in finance.

The chapter will also explore how accountability and responsibility are addressed in practical AI applications within the financial sector and compare the perspectives of academic/industry sources with the regulatory stance in Ireland.

Ultimately, this analysis will inform actionable recommendations for financial institutions in Ireland to ensure responsible AI adoption with clear accountability and responsibility frameworks.

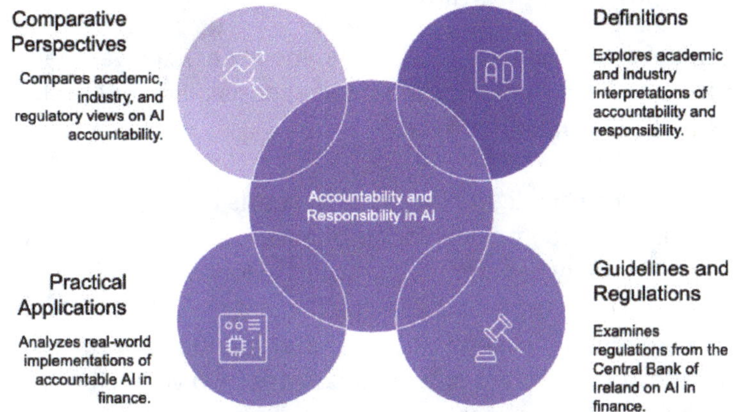
Ensuring Responsible AI in Ireland's Financial Sector
Comparative Perspectives
Compares academic, industry, and regulatory views on AI accountability.
Definitions
Explores academic and industry interpretations of accountability and responsibility.
Accountability and Responsibility in AI
Practical Applications
Analyzes real-world implementations of accountable AI in finance.
Guidelines and Regulations
Examines regulations from the Central Bank of Ireland on AI in finance.

6.2 Defining Accountability and Responsibility

6.2.1 Defining Accountability

Accountability in the realm of AI within financial services generally refers to the obligation to justify and take responsibility for AI-related decisions, actions, and outcomes.[10]

Academic literature highlights that as AI systems become increasingly integrated into financial processes, establishing clear lines of accountability becomes paramount.[9] However, a key challenge arises from the fact that AI itself is not a legal entity and cannot be held directly accountable.[10] Therefore, the focus shifts to identifying the human actors and organizations involved in the AI lifecycle who can be held responsible for its consequences.[10]

> ***This includes individuals who develop, test, deploy, and oversee AI tools within financial institutions.[10]***

The concept of accountability in this context involves not only being answerable for what the AI does but also having mechanisms in place to ensure that appropriate action can be taken in case of errors, biases, or unintended negative impacts.[10]

6.2.2 Defining Responsibility

Responsibility in the context of AI in financial services encompasses a broader set of duties and ethical considerations related to the development and deployment of these technologies.[2]

> ***It involves a proactive obligation to ensure that AI systems are designed, developed, and used ethically and without causing harm.***[4]

This includes adhering to principles of responsible AI, such as fairness, transparency, safety, and the ethical use of data.[4] Responsibility in this context goes beyond mere legal liability after an event occurs; it entails a continuous commitment to ethical practices and risk mitigation throughout the entire AI lifecycle.[4]

Financial institutions have a responsibility to ensure that their AI systems are not only compliant with regulations but also align with societal values and do not lead to discriminatory or unfair outcomes for consumers.

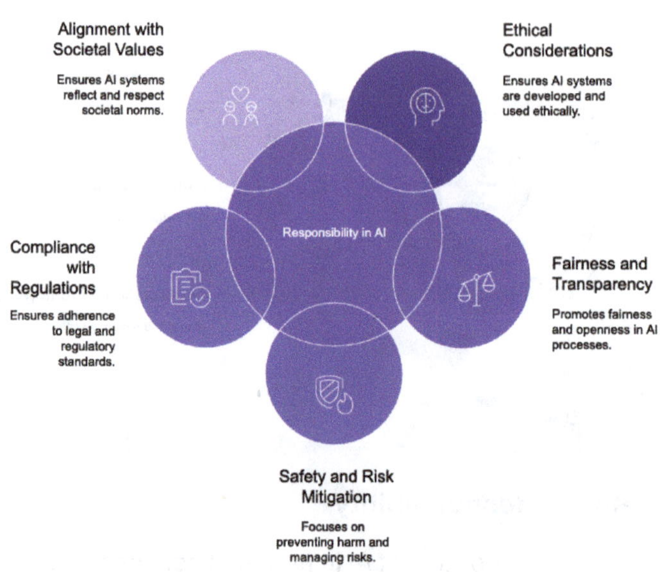
Alignment with Societal Values
Ensures AI systems reflect and respect societal norms.
Ethical Considerations
Ensures AI systems are developed and used ethically.
Responsibility in AI
Compliance with Regulations
Ensures adherence to legal and regulatory standards.
Fairness and Transparency
Promotes fairness and openness in AI processes.
Safety and Risk Mitigation
Focuses on preventing harm and managing risks.

6.3 Accountability and Responsibility in Literature and Industry Reports

6.3.1 Academic Perspectives on Accountability

Academic literature on AI in financial services underscores the intricate nature of establishing accountability.[9] A significant challenge identified is the "black box" problem, where the decision-making processes of complex AI algorithms are opaque and difficult to understand.[10] This lack of transparency complicates efforts to trace the causes of errors or biases and assign accountability effectively.[10]

To address this, academics propose multi-faceted approaches that focus on the human element involved in AI development and deployment, as well as the regulation of the data used to train these systems.[10]

The development of interpretable AI models, which provide insights into their decision-making processes, is also suggested as a potential solution.[11] The importance of establishing robust governance structures and ethical guidelines for the use of AI in financial decision-making is consistently emphasized in academic research.[9] These frameworks should clearly define roles, responsibilities, and processes for overseeing AI systems and ensuring accountability for their outcomes.[11]

6.3.2 Industry Perspectives on Accountability and Responsibility

Industry reports reflect a growing awareness among financial institutions regarding the critical need for responsible AI practices, driven by both regulatory pressures and the imperative to maintain customer trust.[2]

These reports explore the assignment of responsibility within organizations, the implementation of AI governance models, and the adoption of best practices to ensure ethical and accountable AI deployment.[2]

> ***Managing AI-related risks, such as bias, data privacy breaches, and security vulnerabilities, is a central theme in industry discussions.***[15]

Compliance with emerging regulations, particularly the EU AI Act, is also a significant driver for adopting responsible AI frameworks that emphasize accountability and transparency.[15] Industry watchdogs have called for clear regulatory guardrails and accountability mechanisms to ensure the safe and responsible use of AI in financial services, highlighting the potential for harm to consumers and the financial system if these are lacking.[13]

Overall, industry perspectives recognize that building and maintaining stakeholder trust requires a proactive commitment to responsible AI, with accountability and responsibility serving as fundamental pillars.

6.4 The Irish Regulatory Landscape for AI in Financial Services

6.4.1 Central Bank of Ireland's Stance

The Central Bank of Ireland (CBI) has increasingly focused on the implications of AI for the financial services sector, emphasizing the importance of regulatory transparency, oversight, and compliance when firms utilize AI technologies.[27]

In its supervisory communications, the CBI has highlighted the need for financial institutions to possess a clear understanding of the AI technology they employ and the specific business challenges it is intended to address.[8]

> ***A key expectation from the CBI is that firms ensure clarity of accountability for all decisions made concerning the use of AI.***[8]

This includes establishing who within the organization is responsible for overseeing the AI systems, managing their risks, and ensuring they are not used in a manner that could exploit customer behaviours or lead to detrimental outcomes.[8] The CBI's supervisory approach is risk-based, focusing on how firms identify and prepare for new sources of operational risk arising from AI adoption.[8]

The CBI is expected to play a significant role in the enforcement of the EU AI Act in Ireland, likely being designated as a Market Surveillance Authority for the financial services sector.[25] This indicates a proactive stance towards regulating AI in finance, with a clear emphasis on accountability and the protection of consumers and the financial system.

CBI's AI Regulatory Framework in Finance

Regulatory Transparency

Ensuring clear guidelines for AI use

Accountability

Defining responsibility for AI decisions

Risk Management

Identifying and preparing for AI risks

EU AI Act Enforcement

Implementing EU AI regulations in Ireland

6.4.2 Other Relevant Irish Regulatory Bodies

Beyond the Central Bank of Ireland, other Irish regulatory bodies also have a role in overseeing the ethical and responsible use of AI in the financial services sector, particularly concerning consumer protection and fundamental rights.[38]

The Irish Human Rights and Equality Commission (IHREC) is expected to examine AI applications where human rights concerns may arise, especially in areas prone to discrimination, such as financial services.[38] IHREC's role will likely involve ensuring that AI-driven decisions are free from bias and do not unfairly impact individuals based on protected characteristics.[38]

The Financial Services and Pensions Ombudsman (FSPO) is another key body expected to monitor the use of AI within financial services, with a specific focus on consumer protection.[38] The FSPO will likely scrutinize AI-driven decisions in areas like credit scoring, loan approvals, and insurance underwriting to prevent unfair treatment or discriminatory outcomes for consumers.[38]

The designation of these and other authorities under the EU AI Act signifies a federated approach to AI regulation in Ireland, leveraging the expertise of existing sectoral regulators to ensure comprehensive oversight.[37]

6.4.3 Implications of the EU AI Act

The EU Artificial Intelligence Act (AI Act) will have significant implications for Irish financial institutions regarding accountability and responsibility for their AI systems.[7] The Act establishes a risk-based framework, categorizing AI systems into different risk levels: unacceptable, high, limited, and minimal.[7]

The use of AI for evaluating creditworthiness or establishing credit scores is classified as high-risk [16], subjecting financial institutions deploying such systems to stringent obligations related to accountability and responsibility.[15]

These obligations include implementing risk management systems, ensuring data governance and quality, maintaining technical documentation and record-keeping, providing transparency about the system's functioning, ensuring human oversight, and maintaining accuracy and cybersecurity.[15]

> ***The AI Act came into force in August 2024, with its requirements being progressively implemented from February 2025 to August 2027 and beyond.***[15]

Non-compliance can result in significant penalties, including substantial fines.[15] Therefore, Irish financial institutions must proactively prepare to meet these new legal requirements to ensure responsible AI deployment with clear accountability and responsibility frameworks.

6.5 Analysis of Accountability in AI Applications

6.5.1 Conceptualizing Accountability in AI Use Cases

Accountability is conceptualized and addressed differently across various AI applications within financial services.[2] In credit scoring, for example, the focus on accountability revolves around ensuring fairness and preventing discriminatory outcomes.[11]

> ***The challenge lies in understanding how AI models arrive at creditworthiness assessments and ensuring these assessments are not biased against certain demographic groups.[11]***

Similarly, in loan approvals, accountability involves determining who is responsible if an AI system makes an erroneous decision, potentially denying a qualified applicant a loan.[18] For insurance pricing, ethical considerations and the avoidance of bias in pricing models are key aspects of accountability.[19]

In fraud detection, while AI enhances accuracy, accountability is crucial to address instances where legitimate transactions might be wrongly flagged as fraudulent, requiring mechanisms for redress.[2] Across these diverse applications, the inherent complexity and often opaque nature of AI decision-making processes pose significant challenges in attributing accountability effectively.[10]

6.5.2 Mechanisms for Ensuring Accountability

Several technical and organizational mechanisms can be employed to enhance accountability in AI applications within financial services.[4] Auditability is a crucial aspect, requiring the ability to track and review the data, algorithms, and decisions made by AI systems.[11]

> ***Explainability, which involves making AI decision-making processes more transparent and understandable, is also vital for accountability.***[4]

Implementing human oversight mechanisms, where human experts review and can override AI-driven decisions, provides an essential layer of accountability.[4] Furthermore, establishing robust AI governance frameworks and internal controls within financial institutions is critical for defining responsibilities, setting standards, and ensuring ongoing monitoring of AI systems to promote accountability.[11]

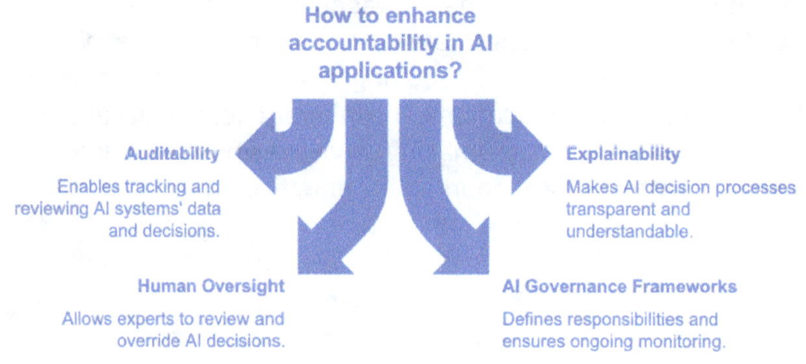

6.6 Analysis of Responsibility in AI Applications

6.6.1 Defining and Assigning Responsibility

Responsibility for AI applications in financial services is a multifaceted concept that requires careful definition and assignment across various stakeholders.[2] While AI developers play a role in ensuring the safety and reliability of their algorithms, financial institutions deploying AI ultimately bear the responsibility for how these systems are used and the outcomes they produce.[10]

This responsibility extends to individual employees who are tasked with overseeing AI systems and ensuring their appropriate use.[15]

> ***The "human-in-the-loop" approach emphasizes the assignment of responsibility to designated managers who are accountable for the proper development, implementation, and use of AI models.[10]***

Financial institutions need to establish clear organizational structures and policies that explicitly define the roles and responsibilities of different actors involved in the AI lifecycle to ensure effective responsibility.[15]

6.6.2 Ethical Considerations and Responsibility

Ethical considerations form a crucial foundation for responsibility in AI applications within financial services.[7] Financial institutions have a responsibility to ensure that their AI systems are developed and deployed in a manner that avoids bias and discrimination against any individuals or groups.[7]

Protecting the privacy and security of sensitive data used by AI systems is another critical ethical responsibility.[1] Furthermore, promoting fairness and transparency in how AI systems operate is essential for building trust with consumers and ensuring responsible use.[4] Financial institutions must proactively address these ethical considerations and ensure that their AI systems align with these principles to prevent harm to consumers and maintain the integrity of the financial system.[1]

6.7 Recommendations from Irish Regulatory Guidelines

6.7.1 Central Bank of Ireland's Requirements

The Central Bank of Ireland (CBI) has outlined specific expectations regarding accountability and responsibility for AI in financial services.[7] The CBI expects firms to clearly understand the business challenge they are addressing with AI and to justify why their specific AI usage is an appropriate response.[7]

A strong emphasis is placed on risk management, with firms expected to identify and prepare for any new sources of operational risk arising from AI adoption.[7]

> ***Crucially, the CBI requires clarity of accountability for all decisions made regarding the use of AI, ensuring that there are defined roles and responsibilities within the organization.***[7]

The CBI also stresses the importance of robust governance structures and regulatory compliance when using AI in financial services.[27]

6.7.2 EU AI Act Obligations for Irish Firms

The EU AI Act imposes several obligations on Irish financial institutions concerning accountability and responsibility for high-risk AI systems.[7]

These include the establishment of a risk management system to identify and mitigate risks associated with high-risk AI.[15] Firms must also ensure robust data governance and the quality of data used to train and operate AI systems.[15]

Maintaining comprehensive technical documentation detailing the system's functionalities and compliance measures is another key requirement.[15]

Transparency about how the AI system works and the decisions it makes is also mandated.[15]

> ***The Act requires the implementation of human oversight mechanisms to allow for intervention and correction of AI-driven decisions [15], along with***

> ***ensuring the accuracy and robustness of the AI systems and implementing adequate cybersecurity measures.***[15]

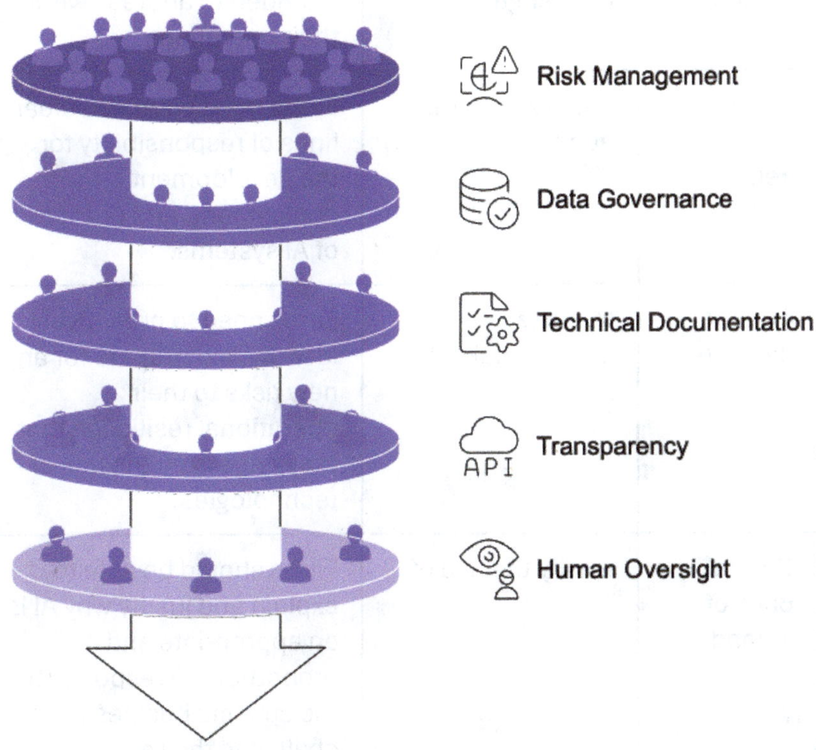

6.7.3 Table of Key Requirements and Recommendations

Regulatory Body	Specific Requirement / Recommendation	Description/Explanation
Central Bank of Ireland	Understand the business challenge	Firms should clearly define the problem that AI is intended to address within their operations.
Central Bank of Ireland	Ensure clarity of accountability	Firms must establish clear lines of responsibility for the development, deployment, and outcomes of AI systems.
Central Bank of Ireland	Manage operational risks	Firms need to proactively identify and prepare for any new risks to their operational resilience that may arise from the use of AI technologies.
Central Bank of Ireland	Justify the use of AI	Firms should be able to explain and justify why AI is an appropriate and proportionate response to the specific business challenge they are addressing.
EU AI Act	Implement risk management systems for high-risk AI	Establish, implement, document, and maintain a system throughout the lifecycle of high-risk AI systems to identify, assess,

		prevent, and mitigate risks.
EU AI Act	Ensure data governance and quality	Implement appropriate policies and procedures for the data used in the training, validation, and operation of high-risk AI systems to ensure its quality, relevance, and representativeness.
EU AI Act	Maintain technical documentation	Create and keep up-to-date comprehensive technical documentation for high-risk AI systems, providing all necessary information about the system and its development to demonstrate compliance.
EU AI Act	Provide transparency	Ensure appropriate levels of transparency regarding the capabilities and limitations of high-risk AI systems and provide clear and adequate information to users about how the system works and its potential impact.
EU AI Act	Ensure human oversight	Implement measures to ensure effective human oversight of high-risk AI systems, including the ability to intervene or override decisions made by

		the AI.
EU AI Act	Ensure accuracy	Develop and validate high-risk AI systems to achieve a high level of accuracy and robustness in their performance, particularly in areas where they could have significant impacts on individuals.
EU AI Act	Maintain cybersecurity	Implement appropriate measures to protect high-risk AI systems against cyber threats and ensure their resilience against attacks that could compromise their security, integrity, or availability.

6.8 Comparing Perspectives on Accountability and Responsibility

6.8.1 Convergence and Divergence

There is a notable convergence between the perspectives presented in academic literature, industry reports, and Irish regulatory guidelines regarding the fundamental importance of accountability and responsibility in the context of AI in financial services.[2]

All sources emphasize the necessity of human oversight in AI-driven processes to ensure accountability and prevent unintended consequences.[4]

> ***Transparency in AI systems is also consistently highlighted as a crucial element for building trust and enabling effective accountability.***[4]

All perspectives acknowledge the need to proactively manage risks associated with AI, particularly the risk of bias leading to unfair or discriminatory outcomes.[7]

Potential areas of divergence exist primarily in the level of technical detail and the specific focus of recommendations. Academic literature often looks at the intricacies of AI algorithms and proposes specific technical solutions for achieving explainability and mitigating bias.[10]

In contrast, regulatory guidelines, such as those from the Central Bank of Ireland and the EU AI Act, tend to provide broader principles and requirements, focusing on establishing governance frameworks and setting expectations for financial institutions.[8]

While academic research might explore the broader societal implications of AI in finance, regulations are typically more focused on ensuring financial stability, protecting consumers, and upholding fundamental rights within the specific context of financial services.[25]

6.8.2 Potential Gaps or Inconsistencies

One potential gap between academic/industry perspectives and current Irish regulatory guidelines might lie in the specific guidance on addressing the "black box" problem in highly complex AI models.

While regulations emphasize the need for transparency, they may not yet provide detailed technical instructions on how financial institutions should achieve explainability in cutting-edge AI systems. Academic literature, on the other hand, actively explores various techniques and methodologies for making complex AI more interpretable.[4]

Another potential area for consideration is the rapidly evolving nature of AI. Academic research may identify new risks and challenges associated with emerging AI technologies faster than regulatory frameworks can be updated to address them.

For instance, the ethical implications of increasingly autonomous AI systems might require further regulatory scrutiny beyond the current scope of the EU AI Act.[4] Continuous dialogue and collaboration between academia, industry, and regulatory bodies will be crucial to identify and address such potential gaps and ensure that the regulatory landscape remains relevant and effective in the face of ongoing AI innovation.

How to address gaps in AI regulation?

Enhance Transparency Guidelines

Develop detailed technical instructions for explainability in AI systems.

Update Regulatory Frameworks

Adapt regulations to keep pace with rapidly evolving AI technologies.

Foster Collaboration

Encourage continuous dialogue between academia, industry, and regulators.

6.9 Conclusion and Recommendations

6.9.1 Summary of Key Findings

The analysis reveals a strong consensus across academic literature, industry reports, and Irish regulatory guidelines on the critical importance of accountability and responsibility in the responsible use of AI within financial services.

> ***Accountability entails being answerable for AI-related decisions and outcomes, with a focus on the human actors and organizations involved in the AI lifecycle.***
>
> ***Responsibility encompasses a broader ethical duty to ensure AI systems are developed and deployed fairly, transparently, safely, and without causing harm.***

While academic and industry sources explore the theoretical and practical aspects of these concepts, the Central Bank of Ireland is actively setting supervisory expectations, and the impending EU AI Act will impose concrete legal obligations on Irish financial institutions, particularly for high-risk AI applications like credit scoring.

Key mechanisms for ensuring accountability include auditability, explainability, and human oversight, all underpinned by robust AI governance frameworks.

6.9.2 Comprehensive Recommendations for Financial Institutions

To effectively address accountability and responsibility in their AI strategies and operations, Irish financial institutions should consider the following recommendations:

- **Develop and implement robust AI governance frameworks:** Establish clear policies, procedures, and organizational structures that define roles, responsibilities, and accountability for all stages of the AI lifecycle, from development to deployment and monitoring.[11]
- **Establish processes for regular audits and assessments of AI systems:** Conduct periodic reviews to evaluate AI systems for potential biases, fairness issues, accuracy, and compliance with ethical guidelines and regulatory requirements.[11]
- **Invest in explainable AI technologies and techniques:** Explore and implement methods to enhance the transparency and interpretability of AI decision-making processes, particularly for high-risk applications, to facilitate understanding and accountability.[4]
- **Ensure adequate human oversight and the ability to intervene:** Implement mechanisms that allow human experts to review, validate, and, if necessary, override AI-driven decisions, especially in critical areas that could significantly impact consumers.[4]
- **Provide comprehensive training to staff:** Educate employees across relevant departments on AI ethics, potential risks, and applicable regulatory requirements, including the EU AI Act, to foster a culture of responsible AI adoption.[7]
- **Maintain thorough documentation:** Keep detailed records of AI systems, including their design, development, data sources,

decision-making processes, testing procedures, and any modifications made over time, to ensure auditability and accountability.[15]

- **Implement mechanisms for addressing and redressing harm:** Establish clear processes for individuals to raise concerns or complaints about AI-driven decisions and ensure that there are effective mechanisms in place to investigate and redress any harm caused by AI systems.[16]
- **Stay informed and adapt to evolving regulations:** Continuously monitor developments in AI regulation, particularly the implementation of the EU AI Act, and proactively adapt their AI strategies and operations to ensure ongoing compliance.[7]

By implementing these recommendations, financial institutions in Ireland can navigate the complexities of AI adoption responsibly, ensuring that accountability and responsibility are embedded at the core of their AI strategies and operations, ultimately fostering trust and innovation within the sector.

6.10 References

1. The Financial Stability Implications of Artificial Intelligence, accessed on April 4, 2025, https://www.fsb.org/uploads/P14112024.pdf

2. Artificial Intelligence in Financial Services - Publications - The World Economic Forum, accessed on April 4, 2025, https://reports.weforum.org/docs/WEF_Artificial_Intelligence_in_Financial_Services_2025.pdf

3. Artificial Intelligence in Financial Services | Treasury, accessed on April 4, 2025, https://home.treasury.gov/system/files/136/Artificial-Intelligence-in-Financial-Services.pdf

4. www.turing.ac.uk, accessed on April 4, 2025, https://www.turing.ac.uk/sites/default/files/2021-06/ati_ai_in_financial_services_lores.pdf

5. Harnessing AI to drive financial services enterprise transformation in Ireland, accessed on April 4, 2025, https://www.irishtimes.com/sponsored/2025/03/25/harnessing-ai-to-drive-financial-services-enterprise-transformation-in-ireland/

6. Transforming Ireland's Financial Industry through AI & Data Literacy - University College Dublin, accessed on April 4, 2025, https://www.ucd.ie/professionalacademy/resources/finance-industry-ai-transformation/

7. AI: Considerations for Irish Fund Management Companies | Commercial Law Firm, accessed on April 4, 2025, https://www.dilloneustace.com/insights/ai-considerations-for-irish-fund-management-companies/

8. Financial consumer protection and market conduct considerations of AI in finance - Remarks by Colm Kincaid, Director of Consumer Protection - Central Bank of Ireland, accessed on April 4, 2025, https://www.centralbank.ie/news/article/speech-colm-kincaid-financial-consumer-protection-and-market-conduct-considerations-of-AI-in-finance-22-may-2024

9. Artificial Intelligence for Financial Accountability and Governance in the Public Sector: Strategic Opportunities and Challenges - MDPI, accessed on April 4, 2025, https://www.mdpi.com/2076-3387/15/2/58

10. The Future of AI Accountability in the Financial Markets - Duke Law ..., accessed on April 4, 2025, https://scholarship.law.duke.edu/cgi/viewcontent.cgi?article=7081&context=faculty_scholarship

11. Ethical Implications of AI in Financial Services: Bias, Transparency, and Accountability, accessed on April 4, 2025, https://www.researchgate.net/publication/384713108_Ethical_Implications_of_AI_in_Financial_Services_Bias_Transparency_and_Accountability

12. Legal accountability and ethical considerations of AI in financial services, accessed on April 4, 2025, https://gsconlinepress.com/journals/gscarr/content/legal-accountability-and-ethical-considerations-ai-financial-services

13. Report – Artificial intelligence in finance: how to trust a black box?, accessed on April 4, 2025, https://www.finance-watch.org/policy-portal/digital-finance/report-artificial-intelligence-in-finance/

14. Responsible AI in finance: 3 key actions to take now - PwC, accessed on April 4, 2025, https://www.pwc.com/us/en/tech-effect/ai-analytics/responsible-ai-in-finance.html

15. Responsible AI in Financial Services | EY - Global, accessed on April 4, 2025, https://www.ey.com/en_gl/responsible-ai-financial-services

16. Navigating AI Regulations in the UK and Ireland: An Easy Guide, accessed on April 4, 2025, https://profiletree.com/ai-regulations-in-the-uk-and-ireland/

17. Transparency, Accountability and Collaboration: Harnessing the power of artificial intelligence in banking, accessed on April 4, 2025, https://www.globalbankingandfinance.com/transparency-accountability-and-collaboration-harnessing-the-powe-of-artificial-intelligence-inbanking

18. AI and Business Ethics: Balancing Efficiency with Responsibility - 4 Leaf Performance, accessed on April 4, 2025, https://www.4leafperformance.com/ai-and-business-ethics-balancing-efficiency-with-responsibility/

19. Embracing artificial intelligence responsibly in the insurance industry - RSM US, accessed on April 4, 2025, https://rsmus.com/insights/industries/insurance/embracing-artificial-intelligence-responsibly-in-the-insurance-i.html

20. Safeguarding Society: Financial Crash Lessons Shaping AI's Future - Grant Thornton Ireland, accessed on April 4, 2025, https://www.grantthornton.ie/insights/factsheets/safeguarding-society-financial-crash-lessons-shaping-ais-future/

21. AI Ethics and Responsible Deployment: A Roadmap for Businesses - ProfileTree, accessed on April 4, 2025, https://profiletree.com/ai-ethics-and-responsible-deployment/

22. Guiding AI development: The path to responsible and effective banking solutions, accessed on April 4, 2025, https://ibsintelligence.com/blogs/guiding-ai-development-the-path-to-responsible-and-effective-banking-solutions/

23. AI Compliance in Banking: Ireland's New Legal Challenges (Ireland) - AI Law, accessed on April 4, 2025, https://www.reviewofailaw.com/Tool/Evidenza/Single/view_html?id_evidenza=2993

24. Balancing Act: Managing AI Governance Risks in Financial Services | Alvarez & Marsal, accessed on April 4, 2025, https://www.alvarezandmarsal.com/insights/balancing-act-managing-ai-governance-risks-financial-services

25. www.centralbank.ie, accessed on April 4, 2025, https://www.centralbank.ie/docs/default-source/publications/regulatory-and-supervisory-outlook-reports/regulatory-supervisory-outlook-report 2025.pdf?sfvrsn=e185651a_9

26. Financial Services Union response to CP158 - Central Bank of Ireland, accessed on April 4, 2025, https://www.centralbank.ie/docs/default-source/publications/consultation-papers/cp158/financial-services-union-response-to-cp158.pdf?sfvrsn=f3426a1a_2

27. Initial guidance on the use of AI in the provision of investment services - Walkers Global, accessed on April

4, 2025, https://www.walkersglobal.com/Insights/2024/06/Initial-guidance-on-the-use-of-AI-in-the-provision-of-investment-services

28. EU law is changing the landscape for AI in financial services - Pinsent Masons, accessed on April 4, 2025, https://www.pinsentmasons.com/out-law/analysis/eu-law-changing-landscape-ai-financial-services

29. The new AI Act has Big Implications for the Financial Services Sector - Institute of Directors Ireland, accessed on April 4, 2025, https://www.iodireland.ie/images/uploads/downloads/8300_IOD_FactSheet_June_Big_Data%2C_Big_Change_The_new_AI_Act_has_Big_Implications_for_the_Financial_Services_Sector.pdf

30. Responsible AI in Insurance — Insight - PwC Ireland, accessed on April 4, 2025, https://www.pwc.ie/industries/insurance/insights/responsible-ai-for-insurers.html

31. The current and future impacts of AI in the insurance sector - Kennedys Law, accessed on April 4, 2025, https://kennedyslaw.com/en/thought-leadership/article/2024/the-current-and-future-impacts-of-ai-in-the-insurance-sector/

32. AI: Risk and Regulatory Considerations for Irish Regulated Firms - Maples Group, accessed on April 4, 2025, https://maples.com/knowledge/ai-risk-and-regulatory-considerations-for-irish-regulated-firms

33. ADAPT researcher to lead AI Accountability Lab at Trinity College Dublin, accessed on April 4, 2025, https://www.researchireland.ie/news/adapt-researcher-to-

lead-ai-accountability-lab/

34. Case Study Two: AI Decision Making - Irish Banking Culture Board, accessed on April 4, 2025, https://www.irishbankingcultureboard.ie/wp-content/uploads/2024/10/Case-Study-2-30.10.24.pdf
35. AI and Risk Management in Ireland | Deloitte Ireland, accessed on April 4, 2025, https://www.deloitte.com/ie/en/services/risk-advisory/research/_ai-and-risk-management-in-ireland.html
36. www.walkersglobal.com, accessed on April 4, 2025, https://www.walkersglobal.com/Insights/2024/06/Initial-guidance-on-the-use-of-AI-in-the-provision-of-investment-services#:~:text=ESMA%20and%20the%20Central%20Bank,risk%20management%20when%20using%20AI
37. Ministers Burke and Smyth welcome government approval of roadmap for implementing the EU Artificial Intelligence Act - Department of Enterprise, Trade and Employment, accessed on April 4, 2025, https://enterprise.gov.ie/en/news-and-events/department-news/2025/march/20250305.html
38. Ireland Designates Nine Authorities to Safeguard Fundamental Rights Under the EU AI Act, accessed on April 4, 2025, https://www.williamfry.com/knowledge/ireland-designates-nine-authorities-to-safeguard-fundamental-rights-under-the-eu-ai-act/
39. Ireland's Federated Approach to AI Regulation - Byrne Wallace Shields LLP, accessed on April 4, 2025, https://byrnewallaceshields.com/news-and-recent-work/publications/irelands-federated-approach-to-ai-

regulation.html

40. Irish Firms Embrace Responsible AI: Adoption of Guidelines Doubles in 12 Months | IFSC, accessed on April 4, 2025, https://www.ifsc.ie/news/irish-firms-embrace-responsible-ai-adoption-of-guidelines-doubles-in-12-months
41. EU Artificial Intelligence (AI) Act - Department of Enterprise, Trade and Employment, accessed on April 4, 2025, https://enterprise.gov.ie/en/what-we-do/innovation-research-development/artificial-intelligence/eu-ai-act/
42. Irish businesses must act now to navigate the impact of AI and the EU AI Act, accessed on April 4, 2025, https://www.pinsentmasons.com/out-law/analysis/irish-businesses-must-act-navigate-impact-eu-ai-act
43. Artificial Intelligence and Insurance - Insurance Ireland, accessed on April 4, 2025, https://insuranceireland.eu/news-and-publications/blog/artificial-intelligence-and-insurance/
44. The EU AI Act: proactivity is crucial for financial institutions to meet key deadlines - fscom, accessed on April 4, 2025, https://fscom.co/ie/blog/the-eu-ai-act-proactivity-is-crucial-for-financial-institutions-to-meet-key-deadlines/
45. Fintech 2025 - Ireland | Global Practice Guides, accessed on April 4, 2025, https://practiceguides.chambers.com/practice-guides/fintech-2025/ireland/trends-and-developments
46. Businesses urged to review AI policies as Ireland prepares to implement EU AI Act, accessed on April 4, 2025, https://www.pinsentmasons.com/out-law/analysis/businesses-urged-review-ai-policies-ireland-implement-eu-ai-act

47. Fintech Laws & Regulations 2024 | Ireland - Global Legal Insights, accessed on April 4, 2025, https://www.globallegalinsights.com/practice-areas/fintech-laws-and-regulations/ireland/

48. Ireland's national AI strategy refresh: the seven strands - Pinsent Masons, accessed on April 4, 2025, https://www.pinsentmasons.com/out-law/analysis/ireland-national-ai-strategy-refresh-the-seven-strands

49. EU AI Act Roadmap: What does the AI act mean for your organization? | EY - Netherlands, accessed on April 4, 2025, https://www.ey.com/en_nl/insights/ai/eu-ai-act-roadmap-what-does-the-ai-act-mean-for-your-organization

50. Ministers Richmond and Calleary launch Ireland's AI Standards and Assurance Roadmap | NSAI, accessed on April 4, 2025, https://www.nsai.ie/about/news/ministers-richmond-and-calleary-launch-irelands-ai-standards-and-assurance-roadmap/

51. AI Standards & Assurance Roadmap, accessed on April 4, 2025, https://www.nsai.ie/images/uploads/general/NSAI_AI_report_digital.pdf

52. How embedded finance and AI impact the lending sector | EY - Belgium, accessed on April 4, 2025, https://www.ey.com/en_be/insights/financial-services/how-embedded-finance-and-ai-impact-the-lending-sector

53. AI in credit scoring: A comprehensive review of models and predictive analytics - Semantic Scholar, accessed on April 4, 2025, https://pdfs.semanticscholar.org/5d0e/c362c11511ffccdc2d0b54d8bf7144c7845b.pdf

54. Spotlight on AI - KPMG Ireland, accessed on April 4, 2025, https://kpmg.com/ie/en/home/insights/2024/11/spotlight-on-ai-fs-insurance-art-int.html

55. www.globalgovernmentforum.com, accessed on April 4, 2025, https://www.globalgovernmentforum.com/the-taixman-how-ai-is-transforming-irelands-revenue-collection/#:~:text=An%20adaptable%20assistant,fraud%20detection%20and%20customer%20service.

56. Artificial Intelligence (AI) in Banking | SAS Ireland, accessed on April 4, 2025, https://www.sas.com/en_ie/solutions/ai/banking.html

57. The tAIxman: how AI is transforming Ireland's revenue collection - Global Government Forum, accessed on April 4, 2025, https://www.globalgovernmentforum.com/the-taixman-how-ai-is-transforming-irelands-revenue-collection/

58. Industry Insights: Finding Operational and Investment Alpha - How AI is Reshaping the ... - Irish Funds, accessed on April 4, 2025, https://www.irishfunds.ie/news-knowledge/newsletter/member-thought-leadership-finding-operational-and-investment-alpha-how-ai-is-reshaping-the-investment-industry/

59. AI Accountability Lab - School of Computer Science and Statistics | Trinity College Dublin, accessed on April 4, 2025, https://www.tcd.ie/scss/news/2024/ai-accountability-lab/

60. AI Board Governance Roadmap | Deloitte US, accessed on April 4, 2025, https://www2.deloitte.com/us/en/pages/center-for-board-effectiveness/articles/board-of-directors-governance-framework-artificial-intelligence.html

7 Governance

Artificial Intelligence (AI) presents transformative opportunities for Irish financial institutions, promising enhanced efficiency, improved customer experiences, and sophisticated risk management. However, realising these benefits responsibly necessitates robust AI governance.

This chapter provides a comprehensive overview of AI governance within the Irish financial services sector, tailored for professionals undertaking studies in the responsible and ethical use of AI.

It defines AI governance and its core principles – accountability, transparency, fairness, security, and privacy – highlighting their critical importance in a high-stakes, heavily regulated industry built on trust.

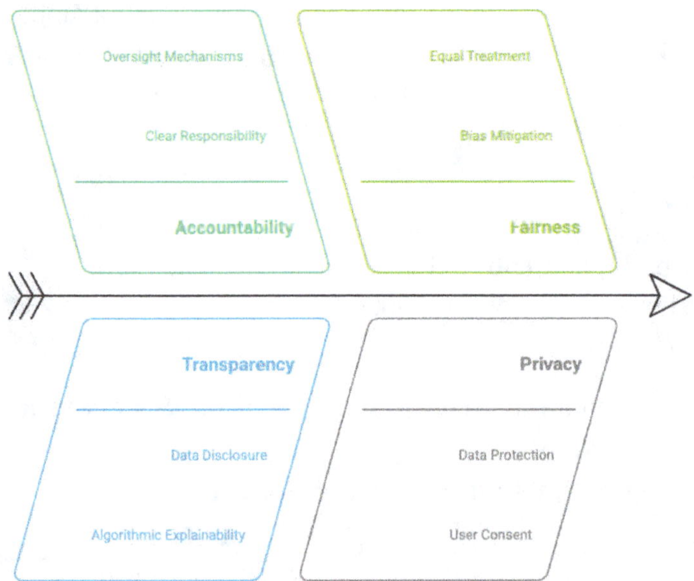

The regulatory landscape is rapidly evolving, dominated by the landmark EU AI Act, which imposes significant obligations, particularly on 'high-risk' systems prevalent in finance, such as credit scoring.

Concurrently, the Central Bank of Ireland is developing its supervisory expectations, emphasising firm responsibility, consumer protection, operational resilience, and clear accountability. Existing frameworks like GDPR remain fundamental, with the Data Protection Commission playing a key enforcement role.

Financial institutions in Ireland are exploring AI across various applications, from operational automation and fraud detection to customer service chatbots and algorithmic trading. Yet, these applications introduce significant risks, including algorithmic bias leading to discrimination, lack of transparency hindering trust and compliance, potential data privacy violations, model inaccuracies, and amplified cybersecurity threats. Systemic risks related to third-party dependencies and market correlations are also emerging concerns.

Established governance frameworks like ISO/IEC 42001 and the NIST AI RMF offer structured approaches to manage these risks, aligning well with regulatory demands.

> ***Ethical challenges persist, particularly concerning consumer protection, ensuring fairness, preventing exclusion, and establishing clear lines of accountability for AI-driven decisions.***

Implementing effective AI governance faces practical hurdles, including resource constraints, skills gaps in AI and data literacy, the complexity of integrating governance into existing processes, and navigating the interpretation of new regulations.

Addressing these requires a strategic approach, viewing governance not merely as a compliance burden but as an enabler of trustworthy innovation and a potential source of competitive advantage.

Proactive engagement, investment in skills and frameworks, fostering a culture of responsibility, and continuous adaptation are crucial for Irish financial institutions to navigate the future of AI successfully.

7.1 Defining AI Governance

AI governance encompasses the framework of policies, regulations, principles, and best practices designed to ensure that artificial intelligence is developed, deployed, and managed in a responsible and ethical manner.[1] It extends beyond purely technical safeguards to include essential mechanisms for oversight, accountability, and transparency, ensuring AI systems align with both organisational objectives and broader societal values.[1]

> ***Fundamentally, AI governance provides organisations with a structured methodology for navigating the complex ethical considerations inherent in AI implementation.***[2]

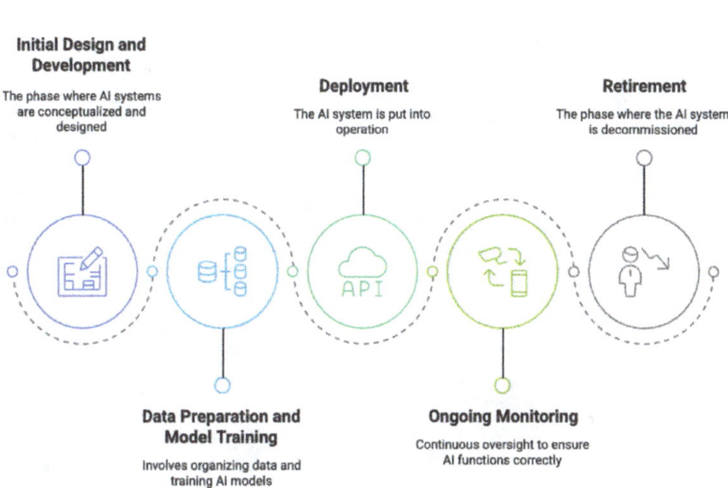

The scope of AI governance is comprehensive, covering the entire lifecycle of an AI system. This begins with the initial design and development phases, extends through data preparation and model training, and continues into deployment, ongoing monitoring, and eventual retirement.[1]

Its primary objectives are multi-faceted:

- to mitigate the inherent risks associated with AI technologies, such as algorithmic bias, data privacy violations, and opaque decision-making [2]
- to ensure compliance with a growing body of legal and regulatory requirements [2]
- to build and maintain trust among users, customers, and regulators [2]
- to guarantee that AI is used for beneficial purposes that reflect ethical standards.[1]

7.2 Core Principles of AI Governance

The practice of AI governance is guided by several foundational principles. While the specific terminology and grouping may vary slightly across different frameworks and sources, a core set of principles consistently emerges as essential for responsible AI deployment.[1] These principles provide the ethical and operational compass for navigating the complexities of AI.

- **Transparency & Explainability:** This principle dictates that AI systems and their decision-making processes should be understandable to relevant stakeholders.[1] Achieving this involves clear documentation of system design and data usage, the application of techniques that make model logic interpretable (Explainable AI or XAI), and open disclosures about how AI is employed.[1]
- Explainability is not merely a technical desideratum; it is fundamental for building user trust [2] and is increasingly a regulatory expectation, particularly when AI makes decisions with significant consequences, such as loan application assessments.[10]
- **Accountability & Ownership:** Organisations must establish clear lines of responsibility for the outcomes and actions of their AI systems.[1] This involves designating specific individuals or teams responsible for each system [10], implementing mechanisms to track AI decision-making, and having defined processes for addressing errors, biases, or unintended negative consequences.[2] The Central Bank of Ireland, for instance, explicitly requires clarity on accountability for AI use within regulated firms.[12]
- **Fairness & Non-Discrimination:** AI systems must be designed, trained, and deployed in ways that prevent unfair bias and ensure equitable treatment for all individuals and groups.[1] This

requires proactive measures such as using diverse and representative training data, conducting regular bias audits, employing fairness metrics during development and monitoring, and potentially implementing bias mitigation techniques.[1] Addressing bias is a critical ethical challenge and a major focus for financial regulators concerned about discriminatory outcomes in lending, insurance, and other areas.[12]

- **Privacy & Data Governance:** Given AI's reliance on data, protecting personal and sensitive information is paramount.[1] This principle encompasses robust data security measures (like encryption and access controls), data handling practices that comply with regulations such as GDPR (including requirements for lawful basis, data minimisation, and respecting data subject rights), and techniques like anonymisation or pseudonymisation where appropriate.[1] Foundational to this is ensuring high-quality data – data that is accurate, complete, and consistent – as poor data quality undermines AI performance and reliability.[1]
- **Security & Robustness/Reliability:** AI systems must be protected against unauthorised access, manipulation, and other security threats.[2] Simultaneously, they need to be robust, meaning they function reliably and consistently under various conditions and stresses, avoiding unexpected failures or erratic behaviour.[2] This includes ensuring the integrity of the data they process and maintaining resilience against disruptions.[2]
- **Human Oversight/Agency:** Particularly for high-risk AI applications, effective governance requires meaningful human oversight.[6] This ensures that humans can monitor AI operations, intervene when necessary, understand system decisions, and potentially override automated outputs, providing a crucial fallback mechanism.[6]

- **Ethical Considerations:** Beyond specific technical or procedural requirements, AI governance involves aligning the development and deployment of AI with broader ethical principles, human rights, and societal values.[1] This involves considering the potential impact of AI on individuals and society and striving for outcomes that are beneficial and just.[3]

These core principles are summarised in Table 1, highlighting their relevance within the Irish financial context.
Table 1: Core Principles of AI Governance and Relevance in Irish Finance

Principle	Definition	Relevance in Irish Finance	Key Sources
Transparency & Explainability	AI systems and decision-making processes should be understandable to stakeholders.	Builds customer trust; Enables bias detection; Required by EU AI Act for high-risk systems; Facilitates regulatory scrutiny (CBI, DPC); Supports accountability.	1
Accountability & Ownership	Clear responsibility assigned for AI outcomes; processes exist	Essential for risk management; Required by CBI;	1

	to address errors/harm.	Underpins ethical use; Enables redress for negative outcomes; Key component of EU AI Act compliance.	
Fairness & Non-Discrimination	AI designed and trained to prevent biases and ensure equitable treatment/outcomes.	Prevents consumer harm/exclusion; Mitigates reputational risk; Legal requirement (anti-discrimination laws, GDPR, AI Act); Key CBI/DPC focus; Ethical imperative.	6
Privacy & Data Governance	Protecting personal/sensitive data used by AI; ensuring compliance with data protection laws (e.g., GDPR). Ensuring data quality.	Mandatory under GDPR (DPC oversight); Critical for customer trust; Manages security risks; Fundamental for reliable AI performance;	1

		Addresses CBI concerns.	
Security & Robustness	Protecting AI systems from threats; ensuring reliable, consistent performance under various conditions.	Protects sensitive financial data; Ensures operational resilience (DORA compliance); Prevents system failures/disruption; Mitigates cyber risks; Underpins trustworthy AI.	2
Human Oversight/Agency	Appropriate human involvement in AI operation, monitoring, and decision-making, especially for high-risk systems.	Provides fallback/intervention capability; Required by EU AI Act for high-risk systems; Addresses limitations of automation; Enhances accountability; Mitigates risk of errors.	6
Ethical Considerations	Aligning AI development and deployment	Builds long-term trust; Guides	3

	with ethical principles, human rights, and societal values.	decision-making beyond compliance; Addresses societal concerns; Reflects organisational values; Supports responsible innovation mandate from CBI.	

It is crucial to recognise that these principles are not independent but deeply interconnected. For instance, achieving genuine fairness often necessitates transparency and explainability to allow for the detection and correction of biases.[8]

> ***Without understanding how an AI system arrives at a decision, it is impossible to verify its fairness.***

Similarly, accountability hinges on transparency – knowing how a system operated – and clear ownership structures.[1] The protection of privacy is fundamentally dependent on robust security measures; data cannot be private if it is not secure.[1]

This interdependence underscores the need for a holistic approach to AI governance, where all principles are considered and addressed concurrently within a unified framework, rather than being treated as separate, sequential checklist items.

7.3 Specific Importance for Financial Institutions

While AI governance is important across many sectors, it holds particular significance for financial institutions operating in Ireland due to a confluence of factors:

- **High Stakes and Regulatory Intensity:** The financial services sector operates within a stringent regulatory environment.[10] Decisions made by financial institutions, increasingly influenced or automated by AI, involve sensitive customer data and have critical impacts on individuals' financial well-being (e.g., access to credit, investment outcomes).[10] Consequently, failures or errors in AI systems can lead to severe financial losses, significant reputational damage, regulatory penalties, and broader societal harm.[10]

- **Complex Risk Landscape:** AI introduces novel and complex risks alongside its potential benefits. These include model risk (the potential for models to be flawed or misused), algorithmic bias, cybersecurity vulnerabilities specific to AI, operational disruptions, significant dependencies on third-party AI providers, and even potential impacts on market stability through correlated behaviour.[10]

- Robust AI governance frameworks are therefore indispensable tools for systematically identifying, assessing, monitoring, and mitigating these multifaceted risks.[2] Emerging concerns about financial stability implications are also driving regulatory attention.[30]

- **The Imperative of Trust:** Trust is the bedrock of the financial services industry.[2] The opacity and perceived autonomy of AI systems can potentially erode this trust if not managed carefully. AI governance, by promoting transparency in how decisions are made, ensuring fairness in outcomes, establishing clear accountability, and safeguarding data, is essential for building and sustaining the confidence of customers, regulators, and the wider public in the use of AI by financial institutions.[1]

- **Navigating Compliance:** Financial institutions in Ireland must navigate a complex web of regulations pertaining to AI. This includes the overarching EU AI Act with its specific requirements for high-risk systems [26], the foundational requirements of the GDPR regarding personal data processing [18], the operational resilience mandates of DORA [38], and the evolving guidance and expectations set forth by the Central Bank of Ireland.[12] Strong AI governance structures are not optional but a prerequisite for demonstrating compliance and avoiding substantial penalties for breaches.[21]

- **Enabling Responsible Innovation:** Effective governance should not be viewed solely as a constraint. By providing clear rules of the road, ethical guardrails, and a framework for managing risks, AI governance can actually foster confidence and encourage responsible innovation within financial institutions.[2] The Central Bank of Ireland itself seeks to support innovation, provided it occurs within a safe and trustworthy framework.[42]

- **Realising Benefits Sustainably:** AI offers considerable potential benefits, including significant operational efficiencies, cost reductions, enhanced fraud detection, improved customer experiences through personalisation, and potentially new revenue streams.[28] AI governance ensures that these benefits are pursued and realised in a manner that is responsible, ethical, and sustainable over the long term, mitigating potential downsides.[25]

Beyond these core imperatives, establishing robust AI governance can evolve into a source of competitive differentiation. In a market where trust and reputation are paramount, institutions that can demonstrably prove their commitment to ethical, transparent, and fair AI practices may gain an edge in attracting and retaining customers, securing investment, and recruiting top talent.[11] Proactive and well-implemented governance signals a level of responsibility and trustworthiness that resonates positively with stakeholders, potentially translating into tangible business value rather than being merely a cost of compliance.

7.4 Regulatory and Supervisory Landscape in Ireland

The regulatory environment governing the use of AI by financial institutions in Ireland is complex and rapidly evolving, shaped primarily by EU-level legislation and national supervisory oversight. Key components include the EU AI Act, specific guidance from the Central Bank of Ireland, and the enduring requirements of data protection law.

7.4.1 The EU AI Act and its Implications for Irish Finance

The EU AI Act, which entered into force in August 2024 with phased implementation over the following years [21], represents the most comprehensive legal framework for AI globally to date.[22] It establishes harmonised rules across the EU, adopting a risk-based approach to regulate AI systems.[21]

> ***Significantly, the Act has extraterritorial scope, impacting any organisation that provides or uses AI systems within the EU market, regardless of where the organisation is headquartered.[21]***

The Act categorises AI systems based on the level of risk they pose:

- **Unacceptable Risk:** Systems posing a clear threat to safety, livelihoods, and rights are banned outright. Examples include social scoring by public authorities, real-time remote biometric identification in public spaces (with narrow exceptions for law enforcement), and AI designed to manipulate human behaviour to circumvent free will.[23] These prohibitions take effect early in the implementation timeline (e.g., February 2025).[40]
- **High Risk:** This category captures AI systems used in critical sectors or applications where they could significantly impact fundamental rights or safety. These systems are subject to the most stringent requirements under the Act.[22]

- **Limited Risk:** Systems like chatbots or deepfakes are subject to specific transparency obligations, ensuring users are aware they are interacting with an AI or viewing AI-generated content.[23]
- **Minimal or No Risk:** The vast majority of AI systems (e.g., AI-enabled video games, spam filters) fall into this category, facing no additional obligations under the Act, although voluntary codes of conduct are encouraged.[23]
- **General-Purpose AI (GPAI):** The Act includes specific rules for GPAI models (like large language models), with additional obligations for those deemed to pose systemic risks.[33]

> ***For Irish financial institutions, the 'high-risk' category is particularly pertinent. The Act explicitly lists certain financial applications as potentially falling under this classification, most notably:***

- AI systems intended to be used to evaluate the creditworthiness of natural persons or establish their credit score, as these determine access to financial resources.[21]
- AI systems used for risk assessment and pricing in relation to natural persons in the case of life and health insurance.[38]

Other common financial use cases, such as AI for fraud detection, anti-money laundering (AML), algorithmic trading, investment advice (robo-advisory), and customer due diligence, may also be classified as high-risk depending on their specific characteristics and potential impact.[21]

This prevalence of high-risk applications means that a substantial portion of AI deployment within the Irish financial sector will be subject to the Act's strictest compliance regime.

While the Act aims for proportionality through its risk tiers [21], the practical effect for many core financial functions is the application of the highest level of regulatory scrutiny.

> ***Financial institutions utilising AI for these common purposes must therefore prepare for significant governance overhead and cannot assume a 'light touch' approach applies.***

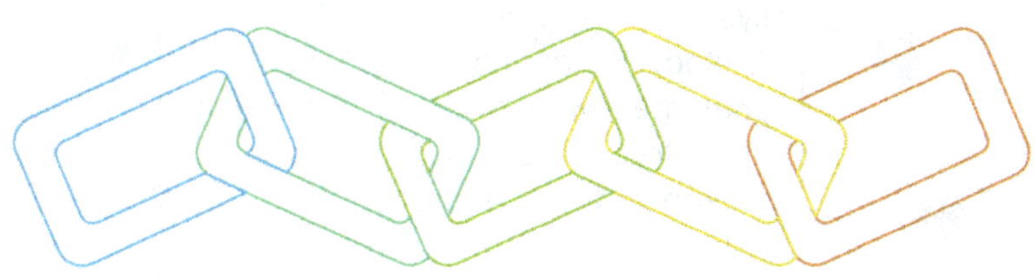

Both providers (developers) and deployers (users, i.e., financial institutions) of high-risk AI systems face extensive obligations throughout the system's lifecycle.[21] These are summarised in Table 2.

Table 2: EU AI Act - Key Requirements for High-Risk Financial Systems

Requirement Area	Specific Obligation	Relevant Financial Use Cases	Key Sources
Risk Management System	Establish, implement, document, and maintain a continuous risk management system throughout the AI lifecycle. Identify, estimate, evaluate, and adopt measures for known/foreseeable risks.	Credit Scoring, Insurance Pricing, AML, Fraud Detection	21
Data & Data Governance	Use high-quality training, validation, and testing datasets. Ensure data is relevant, representative, error-free, complete, and governed appropriately (bias detection/mitigation).	Credit Scoring, Insurance Pricing, Fraud Detection	22
Technical Documentation	Draw up and maintain comprehensive technical	All High-Risk Systems	21

	documentation demonstrating compliance *before* placing the system on the market or putting it into service. Keep documentation updated.		
Record-Keeping (Logs)	Ensure high-risk systems technically allow for automatic recording of events ('logs') relevant for traceability and monitoring throughout the lifecycle.	All High-Risk Systems	21
Transparency & User Info	Design systems for transparency. Provide deployers with clear, adequate information about the system's capabilities, limitations, intended purpose, and necessary user actions for compliance.	Credit Scoring, Robo-Advisory, Insurance Pricing	21
Human Oversight	Design systems to be effectively overseen by humans. Implement appropriate human oversight measures (defined by provider/deployer) to	Credit Scoring, Automated Trading, Insurance Underwriting	21

	prevent or minimise risks. Ensure humans can intervene or disregard output.		
Accuracy, Robustness,	Ensure systems achieve appropriate levels of accuracy, robustness (resilience against errors/inconsistencies), and cybersecurity throughout their lifecycle.	All High-Risk Systems	38
Conformity Assessment	Undergo a conformity assessment procedure (potentially involving notified bodies for some systems) *before* being placed on the market or put into service. Affix CE marking.	All High-Risk Systems	26
EU Database Registration	Register the high-risk AI system in a public EU database managed by the Commission.	All High-Risk Systems	41
Post-Market Monitoring	Establish and implement a post-market monitoring system to collect, document, and analyse data on the system's performance throughout its	All High-Risk Systems	38

	lifetime. Report serious incidents.		

A critical aspect for financial institutions is the **shared responsibility model.**[21] When an institution uses a high-risk AI system provided by a third party, both the vendor (provider) and the institution (deployer) have distinct but overlapping compliance duties. The institution, as the deployer, is responsible for using the system according to its instructions, ensuring human oversight, monitoring its operation, and maintaining logs.[21]

Crucially, if the institution substantially modifies a third-party system, it may be reclassified as a provider, inheriting a much broader set of obligations.[26] This shared responsibility significantly elevates the importance of third-party risk management. Financial institutions cannot simply procure an AI tool; they must conduct thorough due diligence on the provider's compliance with the AI Act (e.g., regarding data quality, bias testing, documentation) and ensure this aligns with their own obligations.

This requirement dovetails with the stringent third-party risk management mandates under the Digital Operational Resilience Act (DORA) [38], necessitating an integrated approach to vendor assessment and ongoing monitoring specific to AI Act compliance. Failure by a vendor can translate directly into a compliance breach for the deploying institution.

Supervision of the AI Act for financial institutions in Ireland is expected to fall under the remit of the existing financial supervisory authorities, widely anticipated to be the Central Bank of Ireland.[33] These authorities will be granted market surveillance powers under the Act.[36]

For institutions participating in the Single Supervisory Mechanism (SSM), national supervisors will report relevant findings to the European Central Bank (ECB).[38]

> ***Non-compliance with the Act carries the threat of substantial fines, potentially reaching up to €35 million or 7% of global annual turnover for the most serious infringements.***[21]

The AI Act is designed to complement, not replace, existing sector-specific financial regulations like DORA, MiFID II, and the Capital Requirements Directive (CRD).[13]

In recognition of the existing robust governance and risk management requirements in finance, the Act includes provisions suggesting that compliance with certain existing financial rules may satisfy corresponding requirements under the AI Act, particularly concerning internal governance, risk management processes, and documentation.[38]

> ***However, the AI Act remains the primary legislation governing AI-specific risks and obligations.***[38]

7.4.2 Central Bank of Ireland: Guidance and Expectations

The Central Bank of Ireland (CBI) plays a pivotal role in overseeing the adoption and governance of AI within the financial institutions it regulates. While acknowledging AI's significant transformative potential for the sector and its own operations [12], the CBI is concurrently focused on the associated risks and the need for responsible implementation.

The CBI is actively developing its specific supervisory expectations regarding AI use by regulated firms, with dedicated work planned for 2024/2025.[12] In the interim, its approach is characterised as risk-based and proportionate, placing primary responsibility on the firms themselves – specifically their boards and senior management – to ensure AI is adopted and managed responsibly.[33]

Several key areas of supervisory focus have emerged from CBI communications:

- **Appropriateness and Understanding:** A recurring theme is the expectation that firms must not only understand the AI technology they deploy but also be able to clearly articulate the specific business challenge being addressed and justify *why* AI is an appropriate solution.[12]
- The CBI explicitly notes that just because AI *can* perform a task does not automatically mean it *should* be used for that purpose, implying a need for careful judgement considering potential downsides.[33] This emphasis signals an expectation that goes beyond mere technical validation, requiring firms to demonstrate thoughtful consideration of ethical implications, consumer impact, and potential alternatives *before* deploying AI.
- **Consumer Protection:** Safeguarding consumer interests is paramount.[12] Supervisors will scrutinise whether AI is being used in ways that could exploit consumer behaviours or

vulnerabilities, leading to detriment.[12] Concerns include the potential for data or algorithmic bias to result in unfair or discriminatory treatment [12], and the risk that AI could inadvertently or deliberately lead to the exclusion of certain individuals or groups from accessing financial services.[12]

- **Operational Resilience:** Firms are expected to proactively identify, assess, and manage any new or amplified operational risks arising from the use of AI systems.[12] This includes risks during transition phases or when integrating AI with legacy systems.[40] This focus aligns closely with the requirements of DORA.[42]
- **Governance and Accountability:** The CBI demands clarity regarding accountability for decisions related to the use of AI within firms.[12] Robust internal governance frameworks, overseen by the board and senior management, are expected to be in place to manage AI deployment responsibly.[33]
- **Risk Management:** Firms must ensure their existing risk management frameworks are reviewed and updated to adequately capture and manage AI-specific risks on an ongoing basis.[33] This includes grappling with the 'downside risks' highlighted by the CBI, such as the lack of transparency in some AI models (particularly generative AI), the potential for misinformation or market manipulation, and the financial stability risk posed by models trained on common datasets producing highly correlated outputs.[33]

While the CBI's current stance relies heavily on firm responsibility and high-level principles, this places a significant onus on institutions to proactively interpret these principles and demonstrate robust internal governance.

It suggests a supervisory approach that, initially at least, may focus more on the overall governance culture and risk management capabilities rather than prescriptive rule-checking, although compliance with the detailed AI Act requirements remains mandatory.

The CBI is not operating in isolation; it actively collaborates with research bodies like the Insight Research Ireland Centre at the University of Limerick to deepen understanding of AI applications and risks [53] and aligns its approach with broader EU frameworks, including the AI Act and guidance from bodies like the European Securities and Markets Authority (ESMA).[12] It also supports innovation through initiatives like its Innovation Sandbox Programme, aiming to facilitate technological advancement within a safe and regulated environment.[43]

7.4.3 Irish Data Protection Law (GDPR) and AI Systems

Alongside the new AI-specific regulations, the General Data Protection Regulation (GDPR), as implemented in Ireland via the Data Protection Act 2018, remains a cornerstone of the legal framework governing AI systems that process personal data.[18] This applies both to the data used to train AI models and any personal data input into or generated by the system during operation.[56]

Key GDPR considerations for AI in Irish financial institutions include:

- **Core Principles:** All processing must adhere to GDPR's core principles: lawfulness, fairness, and transparency; purpose limitation; data minimisation; accuracy; storage limitation; integrity and confidentiality; and accountability.[19] Applying these principles to complex AI systems presents unique challenges. For example, the principle of data minimisation (processing only necessary data) [19] can be in tension with the tendency for many AI models, particularly large language models, to be trained on vast, diverse datasets, often scraped from public sources.[20] This necessitates careful justification and documentation, especially regarding the lawful basis for processing such extensive training data.
- **Lawful Basis:** A valid legal basis under Article 6 of GDPR (e.g., consent, performance of a contract, legal obligation, legitimate interests) is required for any processing of personal data by AI systems.[18] Relying on 'legitimate interests' requires a documented balancing test, weighing the institution's interest against the rights and freedoms of individuals, considering their reasonable expectations.[19] Recent guidance from the European Data Protection Board (EDPB) clarifies that legitimate interest *can* be a basis for AI development and deployment, but requires strict necessity and robust safeguards like transparency and opt-out mechanisms.[19]

- **Data Subject Rights:** Financial institutions must ensure their AI systems and associated processes allow individuals to effectively exercise their GDPR rights, including rights of access, rectification, erasure ('right to be forgotten'), restriction of processing, data portability, and the right to object.[18] Fulfilling these rights can be technically challenging, for instance, definitively erasing an individual's data from a complex, already-trained model.[56]
- **Transparency:** Individuals must be clearly informed about how their personal data is being processed by AI systems, including the purposes of processing and any third parties involved.[18]
- **Data Protection Impact Assessments (DPIAs):** Given that AI processing, especially using new technologies or involving large-scale sensitive data, is often likely to result in a high risk to individuals' rights and freedoms, conducting a DPIA under Article 35 of GDPR is frequently mandatory.[19] The DPIA is a critical process for identifying and mitigating data protection risks before deployment.[39]
- **Automated Decision-Making:** GDPR Article 22 provides specific safeguards for individuals subject to decisions based solely on automated processing (including profiling) which produce legal or similarly significant effects. This is highly relevant for AI applications in areas like credit scoring or automated loan approval. Individuals generally have the right not to be subject to such decisions, the right to obtain human intervention, express their point of view, and contest the decision.[18]
- **Security:** Robust technical and organisational measures must be implemented to ensure the security and confidentiality of personal data processed by AI systems.[18]

- **Anonymisation:** While processing anonymous data falls outside GDPR's scope, achieving true anonymisation in the context of AI models is difficult and subject to rigorous assessment on a case-by-case basis by data protection authorities (DPAs).[19] If personal data can still be inferred or extracted, the model is not anonymous, and GDPR applies.[19]
- **Unlawful Training Data:** A significant compliance risk arises from the EDPB's position that if an AI model was trained using personal data processed unlawfully (e.g., without a valid legal basis), the subsequent deployment of that model could also be deemed unlawful under GDPR, unless the model has been properly anonymised.[19] This creates a 'contagion' effect, meaning financial institutions deploying AI, particularly third-party or pre-trained models, must conduct due diligence on the provenance and lawfulness of the original training data, not just their own use of the model.[19]

The **Data Protection Commission (DPC) Ireland** serves as the national supervisory authority for GDPR and is the lead authority for many major technology companies with European headquarters in Ireland.[39] The DPC actively engages with AI-related data protection issues, issuing guidance [56], participating in EDPB discussions to achieve harmonised EU-wide interpretations [54], and conducting investigations into potential GDPR breaches involving AI, such as examining the adequacy of DPIAs for training large AI models.[39]

7.5 AI Applications in Irish Financial Institutions

Financial institutions operating in Ireland are increasingly exploring and adopting AI technologies across a wide spectrum of activities, driven by the potential for efficiency gains, enhanced risk management, improved customer experiences, and competitive pressures.[29] While adoption maturity varies, with many initiatives still in pilot or testing phases, the trend towards integration is clear.[61]

7.5.1 Common Use Cases (Current and Emerging)

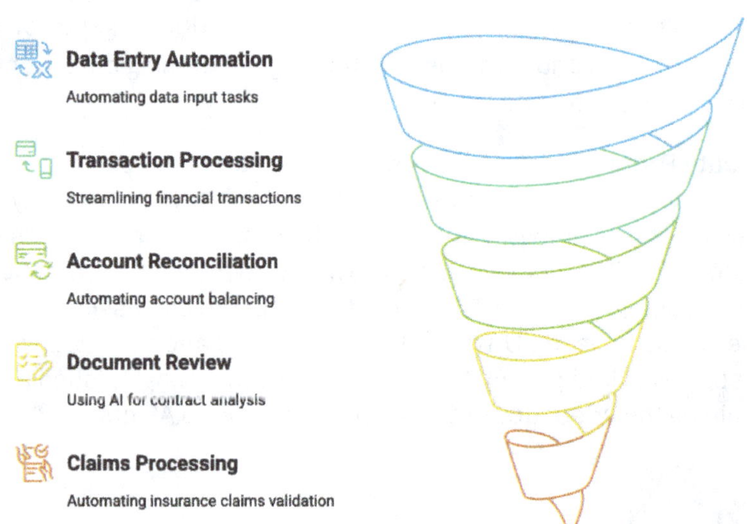

Based on industry reports and observations, key areas of AI application within or relevant to Irish financial institutions include:

- **Operational Efficiency and Automation:** This is currently a primary driver of AI adoption in Ireland.[61] Use cases involve streamlining and automating traditionally manual and labour-intensive back-office functions, such as data entry, transaction processing, account reconciliation, invoice matching and coding, and records management.[28] AI, including Natural Language Processing (NLP) and Generative AI (GenAI), is used for tasks like reviewing lease contracts [45], accelerating the analysis and management of contracts [63], generating summaries of large documents (e.g., policies, reports) [62], and automating aspects of the order-to-cash cycle.[45] In insurance, claims validation and processing are being automated.[42]
- **Risk Management and Compliance:** AI offers powerful tools for managing diverse risks:
    - *Fraud Detection and Anti-Money Laundering (AML):* AI algorithms analyse vast transaction volumes in real-time to identify suspicious patterns indicative of fraud or money laundering, often with greater accuracy and fewer false positives than traditional rule-based systems.[9]
    - *Credit Scoring and Risk Assessment:* AI models leverage broader datasets to provide more nuanced assessments of creditworthiness and predict the probability of default, potentially leading to more accurate lending decisions.[21] This remains a high-risk application under the EU AI Act.[33]
    - *Regulatory Compliance (RegTech):* AI automates the monitoring of activities for compliance adherence, assists in generating regulatory reports, conducts data quality assessments, and helps detect non-compliant behaviour.[13]
    - *Cybersecurity:* AI enhances threat detection by analysing

security logs and network traffic for anomalies, identifying unusual user behaviour (potentially indicating insider threats), and enabling automated responses to incidents.[32]

- **Customer Service and Personalisation:** AI is being used to transform customer interactions:
    - *Chatbots and Virtual Assistants:* Providing 24/7 automated customer support, handling routine inquiries, and potentially assisting with tasks like opening accounts or directing complaints.[11]
    - *Personalisation:* Analysing customer data (transaction history, behaviour) to offer tailored financial advice, personalised product recommendations, and potentially customised pricing or interest rates.[28] Some Irish banks are actively using AI for this.[60]
    - *Enhanced Experience:* Improving efficiency in areas like call centres [32] or using biometrics (facial/voice recognition) for secure and convenient login.[29]
- **Trading and Investment Management:** AI is applied in capital markets and wealth management:
    - *Algorithmic Trading:* Enabling high-speed, automated trading strategies based on real-time market data analysis, aiming to reduce human error and optimise execution.[21] This is utilised by some Irish hedge funds and brokers.[60]
    - *Portfolio Management and Robo-Advisory:* AI-driven platforms provide automated financial planning and investment advice based on client profiles, goals, and risk tolerance, making advice potentially more accessible.[13] AI can also assist in optimising trade execution and identifying arbitrage opportunities.[41]

- **Predictive Analytics and Decision Support:** AI leverages historical and real-time data to generate forecasts and insights, supporting strategic planning and decision-making.[28] This includes forecasting market trends, customer behaviour, revenue, and risks [28], as well as augmenting the capabilities of human experts.[64]

- **Insurance-Specific Applications:** Beyond general financial services, AI is used in insurance for pricing and underwriting (a high-risk area for life/health under the AI Act) [21], claims management automation [42], and risk differentiation.[42]

While AI adoption is widespread in terms of initial exploration (98% of Irish organisations surveyed have started their journey), deployment at scale remains limited (only 6% reported scaled deployment in late 2024).[61] Many institutions are still in the process of testing specific solutions or deploying them in limited areas.[61] The primary value realised so far appears to be in operational efficiencies and productivity gains.[61]

> ***While Ireland is considered well-positioned in AI readiness [65], fully harnessing data at scale for predictive insights is an area still under development for many Irish financial services firms.[60]***

Observing these use cases reveals a distinction between internally focused applications (like back-office automation [28]) and those that are externally facing, directly interacting with or impacting customers (like credit scoring [28], chatbots [11], or personalised offers [28]). This distinction carries significant implications for governance. External-facing applications often entail higher reputational stakes [11] and directly engage consumer protection principles.[12]

They are more likely to fall into higher risk categories under the EU AI Act [38] or trigger specific GDPR rights related to automated decision-making.[56] Consequently, governance frameworks must differentiate, applying potentially more stringent controls, transparency measures, fairness assessments, and human oversight mechanisms to these external-facing systems compared to purely internal tools.

The widespread adoption of similar AI tools across the sector, particularly for critical functions like risk management [28] and trading [28], raises potential systemic considerations.

If many institutions rely on comparable algorithms or data sources, potentially sourced from a concentrated pool of third-party providers [42], it could inadvertently lead to increased homogeneity in market responses.

This could amplify market volatility or create correlated exposures, turning individual firm-level risks into broader financial stability concerns, as flagged by international bodies like the Financial Stability Board (FSB) [30] and the ECB [34], as well as the CBI.[33]

7.6 Analysing Key AI Risks in Irish Financial Services

The deployment of AI in the sensitive and complex environment of financial services introduces a range of significant risks that demand careful management through robust governance structures. These risks span technical, ethical, operational, and regulatory domains.

7.6.1 Algorithmic Bias and Fairness Concerns

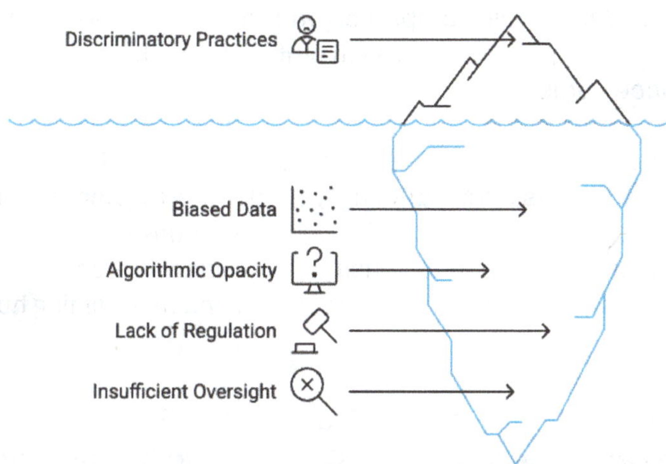

One of the most critical risks associated with AI in finance is the potential for algorithmic bias, leading to unfair or discriminatory outcomes.[6] AI systems learn from data, and if that data reflects existing societal biases or historical inequalities, the AI model can inadvertently learn, perpetuate, and even amplify these biases.[1] Bias can also arise from choices made during model design or from using data that is incomplete or not representative of the population the AI will affect.[9]

In the financial context, this can manifest in discriminatory practices against individuals based on protected characteristics such as race, gender, age, or location.[6]

Examples include AI-driven credit scoring systems unfairly denying loans to qualified applicants from certain demographics [9], biased insurance underwriting or pricing [20], or skewed recruitment tools favouring particular groups.[15] Such outcomes not only violate ethical principles of fairness [5] but can also lead to significant consumer detriment [12], reputational damage [11], and legal challenges under anti-discrimination laws and data protection regulations.[9]

Detecting and mitigating bias is challenging, as it can be subtle and embedded deep within complex algorithms.[12] Effective mitigation requires a multi-pronged approach embedded within the governance framework.

This includes meticulous attention to data quality and representativeness during training [1], conducting regular bias audits using appropriate fairness metrics [1], implementing technical bias mitigation techniques where feasible [8], ensuring diverse perspectives within development teams [66], and maintaining human oversight.[8]

> ***Addressing bias is a key regulatory expectation from the CBI [12], the DPC under GDPR [56], and is explicitly addressed in the EU AI Act's requirements for high-risk systems.[22]***

7.6.2 Transparency and Explainability Challenges

Many powerful AI techniques, particularly those based on machine learning and deep learning, operate as "black boxes," making it difficult to understand precisely how they arrive at a specific output or decision.[9] This lack of transparency and explainability poses significant challenges in the financial sector.

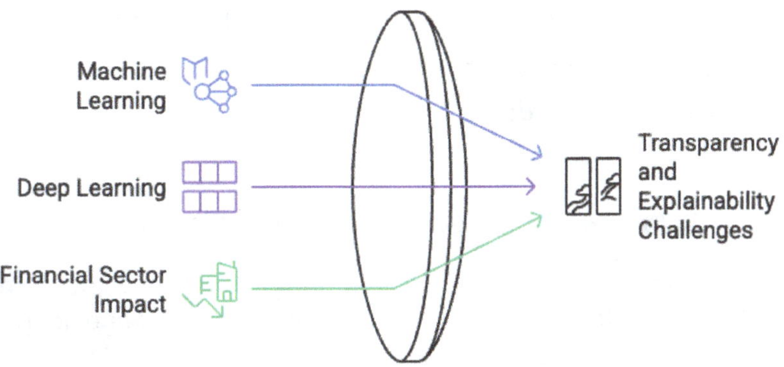

It fundamentally undermines trust among customers, regulators, and internal stakeholders.[2] If an institution cannot explain why an AI system denied a loan or flagged a transaction, it becomes difficult to justify the decision or build confidence in the system's reliability.[9] This opacity also hinders efforts to detect hidden biases [11] or diagnose errors when they occur.

Lack of explainability creates direct compliance challenges, as regulations like GDPR (Article 22) may require explanations for automated decisions, and financial regulators increasingly expect firms to understand and be able to articulate how their critical systems function.[10] The CBI has specifically highlighted the lack of transparency in generative AI models as a downside risk.[33]

Addressing this requires incorporating transparency and explainability considerations throughout the AI lifecycle. This involves maintaining thorough documentation of model design, data used, and decision processes [1]; employing interpretable machine learning techniques where possible [8]; utilising specific Explainable AI (XAI) tools and methods designed to shed light on model behaviour [9]; and ensuring appropriate levels of human monitoring and review.[8]

> ***The EU AI Act explicitly mandates transparency and the provision of user information for high-risk systems [21], and guidance from bodies like ESMA also underscores its importance.[13]***

7.6.3 Data Privacy and Security Vulnerabilities

AI systems are often data-hungry, requiring access to large volumes of information, frequently including sensitive personal and financial data belonging to customers.[5] This inherent reliance on data creates significant privacy and security risks.

Privacy risks include the potential for misuse of personal data [3], accidental or malicious data breaches exposing sensitive information [5], unauthorised access to data used by or generated by AI models [8], and violations of individuals' privacy rights under GDPR.[8]

Specific AI-related privacy threats include 'model inversion' or 'membership inference' attacks, where adversaries attempt to reconstruct sensitive training data or determine if an individual's data was used in training by querying the model.[58]

In the Irish context, concerns also exist regarding the data handling practices of large technology firms providing AI services.[15]

Security vulnerabilities are also amplified by AI. The systems themselves, and the data they rely on, become attractive targets for cyberattacks.[30] Specific threats targeting AI include:

- **Data Poisoning:** Malicious actors intentionally introduce corrupted data into the training set to manipulate the model's behaviour or create hidden backdoors.[58]
- **Input Attacks (Adversarial Attacks):** Attackers subtly modify input data during operation to trick the AI system into making incorrect classifications or decisions.[58]
- **Model Extraction:** Attempts to steal the proprietary AI model itself.[58]

Furthermore, AI itself is being weaponised by attackers to create more sophisticated and convincing attacks, such as highly personalised phishing emails, ransomware messages, or deepfake audio/video for social engineering scams.[17] The increasing use of cloud platforms and third-party AI services also expands the potential attack surface and introduces cloud-specific vulnerabilities like misconfigured storage or insecure APIs.[3]

Mitigating these risks requires a stringent focus on data protection and cybersecurity within the AI governance framework. This includes:

- implementing robust security controls (encryption, access controls, network security) [1]
- adhering strictly to GDPR principles (lawful basis, data minimisation, purpose limitation) [9]
- employing privacy-enhancing techniques like anonymisation, pseudonymisation, or differential privacy where feasible [1]
- establishing secure development lifecycles for AI systems [14]
- having comprehensive incident response plans.[14]

7.6.4 Model Risk and Reliability

Model risk refers to the potential for financial loss or other negative consequences arising from errors in the design, development, implementation, validation, or use of AI models.[30] Given the complexity of many AI systems, ensuring their reliability and robustness is a critical challenge.

AI models are highly sensitive to the quality of the data they are trained on. Inaccurate, incomplete, inconsistent, or biased data will inevitably lead to flawed models that produce unreliable predictions or decisions.[1] Ensuring data integrity is therefore a foundational requirement for managing model risk.[68]

Beyond data quality, models must be robust – capable of performing consistently and accurately across different operating conditions and resilient to unexpected inputs or changes in the environment.[2] They need rigorous testing and validation before deployment to confirm they meet performance requirements.[4]

> ***Crucially, AI models are not static. The relationships they learn from data can become outdated as market dynamics, customer behaviours, or external factors change ('model drift'). This necessitates continuous monitoring of model performance in production environments to detect degradation and trigger recalibration or retraining as needed.***[1]

Stress testing models under extreme conditions is also important to understand their limitations.[13]

A related risk is overreliance on AI systems.[5] If users place undue trust in AI outputs without sufficient critical assessment or human oversight, flawed decisions generated by the model may go unchallenged, leading to negative consequences.

Generative AI models introduce specific reliability risks, such as 'hallucinations' – confidently generating plausible but factually incorrect information.[24]

7.6.5 Cybersecurity Threats Amplified by AI

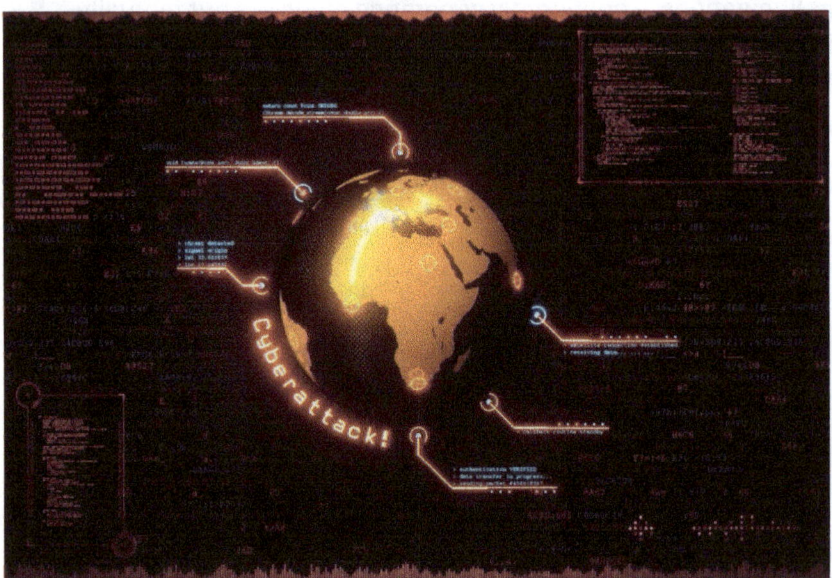

While covered under privacy and security, the amplification effect of AI on cybersecurity warrants specific attention. The relationship is twofold: AI systems themselves are targets, and AI is a tool used by attackers.[32]

Attackers leverage AI to automate and enhance their malicious activities, making attacks more scalable, targeted, and difficult to detect. This includes using AI for reconnaissance, crafting highly convincing phishing messages, generating malware code, and creating deepfakes for impersonation or disinformation campaigns.[17]

Simultaneously, the increasing reliance on complex, often interconnected AI systems within financial institutions creates new vulnerabilities and expands the attack surface.[3] Attacks aimed directly at compromising AI integrity, such as data poisoning or adversarial input attacks [58], pose a novel threat vector that traditional security measures may not adequately address.

This dynamic creates an ongoing "arms race" where both defenders and attackers increasingly employ AI, demanding continuous adaptation of cybersecurity strategies.[32]

7.6.6 Operational and Third-Party Risks

Integrating AI into financial operations introduces specific operational risks. The process of deploying new AI systems, potentially alongside existing legacy systems, can create vulnerabilities and requires careful management to ensure continued operational resilience.[40] Failures in critical AI systems could lead to significant service disruptions. The CBI explicitly expects firms to manage these AI-related operational risks [12], aligning with the broader mandates of DORA.[42]

A major source of operational risk stems from the increasing reliance on third-party vendors for AI models, platforms, data, or infrastructure.[30] This dependency creates several challenges:

- **Concentration Risk:** The market for sophisticated AI capabilities may be dominated by a few large providers. Over-reliance on these few providers across the financial sector could create systemic vulnerabilities; a failure or compromise at one major vendor could impact numerous institutions simultaneously.[30]
- **Vendor Lock-in:** Institutions may become dependent on a specific vendor's ecosystem, making it difficult or costly to switch providers later.[24]
- **Supply Chain Security:** Ensuring the security, reliability, and compliance (e.g., with the AI Act, GDPR) of AI components sourced from third parties requires rigorous due diligence and ongoing monitoring.[69] Obtaining sufficient information from vendors about their models can be challenging due to intellectual property concerns.[69]

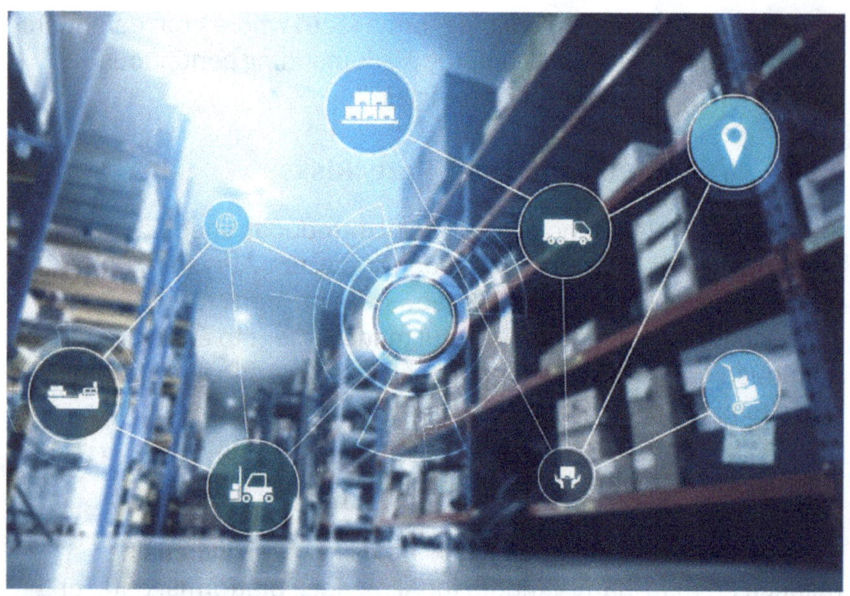

- **Integration Challenges:** Seamlessly integrating third-party AI solutions with existing internal systems and processes can be technically complex.[67]

The convergence of these AI-specific risks (cyber threats targeting AI, model failures causing operational disruption, third-party dependencies) with the core concerns of DORA (ICT risk, resilience, third-party management) is undeniable.

This means that AI governance cannot be treated as a separate silo within Irish financial institutions. It must be intrinsically linked and integrated into the organisation's overall DORA compliance framework and broader ICT risk management strategy.

> ***AI systems must be subject to the same rigorous standards for resilience testing, incident management, and third-party risk assessment mandated by DORA.***

The aggregation of certain risks at the sector level elevates them beyond individual firm concerns to potential financial stability issues. As highlighted by the FSB and ECB, widespread reliance on a few third-party AI providers (concentration risk) [30] and the potential for correlated market behaviour driven by similar AI models reacting in unison [30] represent macroprudential risks.

This necessitates monitoring and potentially regulatory intervention at a systemic level, extending beyond the scope of individual institutional governance frameworks.

7.7 AI Governance Frameworks and Best Practices

To navigate the complexities of AI adoption and effectively mitigate the risks outlined above, financial institutions require structured approaches. AI governance frameworks provide systematic methodologies, standards, and best practices for managing AI responsibly and ethically throughout its lifecycle.[2]

7.7.1 Overview of Relevant Frameworks and Standards

Several frameworks and standards are emerging globally, offering guidance for establishing robust AI governance. Key examples relevant for Irish financial institutions include:

- **ISO/IEC 42001:2023 (AI Management System - AIMS):** This is the first international, certifiable standard specifically for AI management systems, published in December 2023.[47] It provides a comprehensive framework for organisations of all sizes to establish, implement, maintain, and continually improve their governance of AI.[47]
    - *Scope & Focus:* It covers the entire AI lifecycle and emphasizes responsible and ethical development and use, transparency, accountability, risk management (including bias mitigation), privacy, security, and continuous improvement.[47]
    - *Requirements:* It mandates establishing an AI policy, defining roles and responsibilities, conducting AI-specific risk assessments and system impact assessments, implementing controls (often referencing its Annex A control objectives), conducting internal audits, and ensuring management review and leadership commitment.[70]
    - *Relationship with other standards:* It is designed to complement existing management system standards,

particularly ISO/IEC 27001 for information security, by layering AI-specific risk considerations onto established security practices.[48]

- *Benefits:* Adopting ISO 42001 can help build stakeholder trust, provide a competitive advantage, attract investment, demonstrate commitment to responsible AI, and crucially, provide a structured way to prepare for and demonstrate compliance with emerging regulations like the EU AI Act.[47] Some recommend it for governing AI used in financial crime prevention.[5]

- **NIST AI Risk Management Framework (AI RMF):** Developed by the US National Institute of Standards and Technology, this is a voluntary framework providing guidance specifically on managing the risks associated with AI systems.[3]
    - *Scope & Focus:* It aims to promote the development and deployment of trustworthy and responsible AI by focusing on identifying, assessing, and managing risks related to security, bias, transparency, fairness, and reliability.[3]
    - *Structure:* It organises the risk management process into four core functions: **Govern** (establish context and policies), **Map** (identify context and risks), **Measure** (analyse and assess risks), and **Manage** (treat risks).[50]
    - *Applicability:* It is designed to be flexible and applicable across different sectors and AI applications.[50] While not a certifiable management *system* standard like ISO 42001, it provides a detailed process-oriented approach to AI risk management.[50]
- Other Frameworks and Guidance:
    - *EU AI Act:* While primarily a regulation, the Act itself establishes a legally binding framework with specific governance requirements for different risk levels.[50]
    - *Regulatory Guidance:* Specific guidance from financial regulators like the CBI [12] and ESMA [13] sets expectations for governance.
    - *Internal Codes/Principles:* Many organisations develop their own internal AI ethics codes or responsible AI principles aligned with their values.[6]
    - *Foundational Principles:* Frameworks often build upon widely accepted principles like those developed by the OECD.

7.7.2 Best Practices for Implementing AI Governance:

Regardless of the specific framework chosen, effective implementation generally involves several best practices:

- **Clear Governance Structure:** Establish clear roles, responsibilities, and reporting lines for AI governance. Designate specific individuals or committees accountable for overseeing AI initiatives.[2] Securing buy-in and active support from senior leadership is critical for success.[10]
- **Multidisciplinary Collaboration:** AI governance is not solely an IT or compliance function. Effective implementation requires input and collaboration from diverse teams, including technology, legal, ethics, risk management, compliance, internal audit, and relevant business units.[1]
- **Policies and Ethical Guidelines:** Develop clear, actionable AI policies and ethical guidelines that reflect organisational values and regulatory requirements.[1]
- **Lifecycle Integration:** Embed governance checks and controls throughout the entire AI lifecycle, from initial conception and data sourcing to deployment and ongoing monitoring.[1] Where feasible, automate governance checks by embedding them as code within development and deployment workflows.[46]
- **Risk and Impact Assessment:** Implement processes for systematically identifying, assessing, and mitigating AI-specific risks.[6] Conduct impact assessments to understand the potential consequences of AI systems on individuals and society.[70]
- **Data Governance:** Establish robust data governance practices specifically tailored for AI, ensuring data quality, integrity, security, privacy, and appropriate usage rights.[1] Focus on creating 'AI-ready' data.[1]

- **Continuous Monitoring and Auditing:** Implement mechanisms for continuously monitoring the performance, reliability, fairness, and security of AI systems in production. Conduct regular audits to ensure ongoing compliance and effectiveness of governance controls.[2]
- **Training and Awareness:** Invest in training programmes to enhance AI literacy across the organisation, ensuring staff understand the capabilities, risks, ethical implications, and governance requirements related to AI.[2]
- **Adaptability and Evolution:** Recognise that the AI landscape is constantly changing. Governance frameworks should be flexible, adaptable to the needs of different teams and contexts [46], and continuously reviewed and updated to remain relevant.[46]

7.7.3 Aligning Frameworks with Risk Mitigation

A key purpose of adopting AI governance frameworks is to provide a systematic structure for addressing the specific risks associated with AI deployment (as detailed in Section 4). These frameworks translate high-level principles into concrete processes and controls designed for risk mitigation. Table 3 illustrates how elements of common frameworks can map to specific AI risks relevant to financial services.

Table 3: Mapping Key AI Risks to Governance Framework Controls

AI Risk Category (Section 4)	Specific Manifestation in Finance	Relevant Framework Element / Process	Example Control / Best Practice
Algorithmic Bias (4.1)	Discriminatory credit scoring; Unfair insurance pricing	ISO 42001 Risk Assessment & Controls (Annex A); NIST RMF Measure/Manage Functions; EU AI Act Data Quality & Bias Monitoring Reqs.	Regular bias audits using fairness metrics; Validation of training data diversity; Implementation of technical bias mitigation techniques; Human review protocols for sensitive decisions.
Transparency/Explainability (4.2)	"Black box" loan decisions; Inability to explain fraud alerts	ISO 42001 Documentation & Transparency Controls; NIST RMF Govern Function	Maintaining detailed technical documentation; Using interpretable

		(Transparency); EU AI Act Transparency & User Info Reqs.	models where feasible; Implementing XAI tools; Providing clear explanations to customers/regulators upon request.
Data Privacy (4.3)	Misuse of customer data for training; GDPR breaches	ISO 42001 Privacy Controls (builds on ISO 27701); NIST RMF Govern/Manage Functions; GDPR Compliance (DPIAs, Lawful Basis).	Conducting DPIAs for high-risk processing; Implementing robust data anonymisation/ pseudonymisation; Enforcing data minimisation; Ensuring secure data handling protocols; User consent mechanisms.
Security Vulnerabilities (4.3/4.5)	Data poisoning of risk models; Model extraction; AI-enhanced phishing	ISO 42001 Security Controls (builds on ISO 27001); NIST RMF Manage Function; DORA Requirements.	Implementing robust cybersecurity measures (encryption, access controls); Adversarial testing of models; Secure development practices; Staff

			training on AI-specific threats; Incident response plans.
Model Risk/Reliability (4.4)	Inaccurate market forecasts; Model drift leading to poor decisions	ISO 42001 Risk Management & Performance Evaluation; NIST RMF Measure/Manage Functions; EU AI Act Accuracy & Robustness Reqs.	Rigorous model validation before deployment; Continuous performance monitoring in production; Regular model recalibration/retraining; Stress testing; Ensuring high-quality input data.
Operational/Third-Party (4.6)	System disruption due to AI failure; Vendor compliance issues	ISO 42001 Organisational Context & Risk Management; NIST RMF Govern/Map Functions; DORA Third-Party Risk Management.	Integrating AI into operational resilience plans; Rigorous vendor due diligence (incl. AI Act/GDPR compliance checks); Contractual safeguards; Monitoring vendor performance & concentration risk.

The adoption of established frameworks like ISO 42001 or NIST AI RMF serves a purpose beyond internal risk management best practice. It acts as a significant enabler of regulatory compliance.[70] The structured processes, documentation requirements, risk assessments, and control implementations mandated by these frameworks align closely with the expectations of regulators enforcing the EU AI Act and GDPR.

For example, the risk management system required by ISO 42001 [70] directly supports compliance with the AI Act's risk management obligations.[21] Similarly, the documentation generated through framework implementation provides crucial evidence for demonstrating accountability and transparency to supervisors. Therefore, investing in a recognised governance framework can be viewed as a strategic approach to streamlining and demonstrating compliance with mandatory legal requirements.

However, while international frameworks offer valuable blueprints, they cannot be implemented in a vacuum. Effective governance requires contextualisation to the specific operating environment of an Irish financial institution.[6]

This involves tailoring the framework's implementation to align explicitly with the expectations and guidance issued by the Central Bank of Ireland [12], incorporating interpretations of data protection law from the Irish DPC [56], addressing the unique risks posed by the specific AI applications being deployed by the institution (Section 3), and reflecting the institution's own defined risk appetite and ethical values.[6]

> ***A generic, one-size-fits-all application of an international standard is unlikely to adequately address the nuances of the Irish financial regulatory and business landscape.***

7.8 Ethical Considerations for AI in Irish Finance

Beyond technical risks and regulatory compliance, the deployment of AI in financial services raises profound ethical questions that demand careful consideration. These centre on protecting consumers, ensuring fairness, establishing accountability, and promoting responsible practices that align with societal values.

7.8.1 Consumer Protection Issues

The potential impact of AI on consumers is a primary ethical concern and a key focus for regulators like the Central Bank of Ireland.[12] Key issues include:

- **Preventing Detriment:** AI systems, particularly those designed to influence behaviour or make critical decisions, must not be used in ways that exploit consumer vulnerabilities or lead to negative outcomes.[12] This includes avoiding manipulative practices, ensuring advice is suitable, and preventing unfair pricing. The EU AI Act explicitly bans certain manipulative AI systems.[23]
- **Fair Treatment:** As discussed previously, algorithmic bias can lead to unfair discrimination against certain consumer groups in areas like access to credit or insurance.[9] Ensuring fairness is a fundamental consumer protection requirement.
- **Transparency and Redress:** Consumers have a right to understand how AI-driven decisions affecting them are made, especially adverse ones like loan rejections.[9] Lack of transparency erodes trust.[10] Effective mechanisms for explanation, appeal, and redress are needed, aligning with GDPR rights regarding automated decision-making.[56]

- **Financial Inclusion:** There is a risk that AI systems, particularly if trained on data that underrepresents certain populations, could inadvertently exacerbate financial exclusion, denying services to vulnerable groups or those with non-traditional financial histories.[12] Ethically deployed AI should ideally strive to *improve* financial inclusion.[64]
- **Data Privacy:** The use of vast amounts of consumer data by AI systems necessitates stringent adherence to data protection principles to safeguard privacy and prevent misuse.[5]

7.8.2 Ensuring Fairness and Non-Discrimination

While closely linked to consumer protection and algorithmic bias risk, fairness stands as a core ethical principle in its own right.[3] The ethical imperative is to ensure that AI systems treat all individuals and groups equitably and do not perpetuate or amplify existing societal inequalities.[8]

AI Fairness Hierarchy

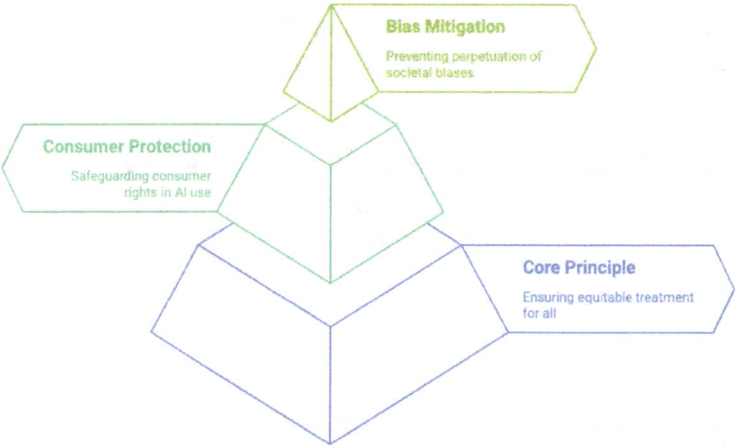

Bias Mitigation
Preventing perpetuation of societal biases

Consumer Protection
Safeguarding consumer rights in AI use

Core Principle
Ensuring equitable treatment for all

Achieving fairness in AI is an active challenge, requiring a conscious and proactive approach throughout the system's lifecycle.[1] It involves not just technical solutions like bias detection algorithms and diverse datasets, but also fostering diversity within AI development teams to bring varied perspectives [66] and establishing governance processes that prioritise fairness assessments.

Fairness considerations are embedded within key regulations like the EU AI Act [21] and underpin broader anti-discrimination legislation.

7.8.3 Accountability in AI-Driven Decisions

Accountability is another cornerstone of ethical AI.[1] When AI systems make decisions, especially those with significant consequences, there must be clarity on who is responsible for the outcomes.

A key ethical challenge is the potential for an "accountability gap," where the complexity or opacity of an AI system makes it difficult to assign responsibility when errors occur or harm is caused.[2] If a self-driving car causes an accident, or an AI trading algorithm triggers a market disruption, determining liability can be complex.[2]

Establishing accountability requires deliberate governance mechanisms. These include defining clear ownership structures for AI systems [8], maintaining detailed audit trails of AI operations and decisions [8], ensuring meaningful human oversight, particularly for critical applications [6], and providing clear channels for users or affected parties to seek redress or appeal decisions.[2]

Regulatory bodies like the CBI explicitly expect firms to demonstrate clarity on accountability [12], and the EU AI Act mandates accountability measures for high-risk systems.[21]

7.8.4 Promoting Responsible AI Principles

Responsible AI serves as an umbrella concept, encapsulating the commitment to developing and deploying AI systems in a manner that is ethical, transparent, accountable, fair, secure, and beneficial to society.[5] It involves proactively embedding these principles throughout the AI lifecycle.[5]

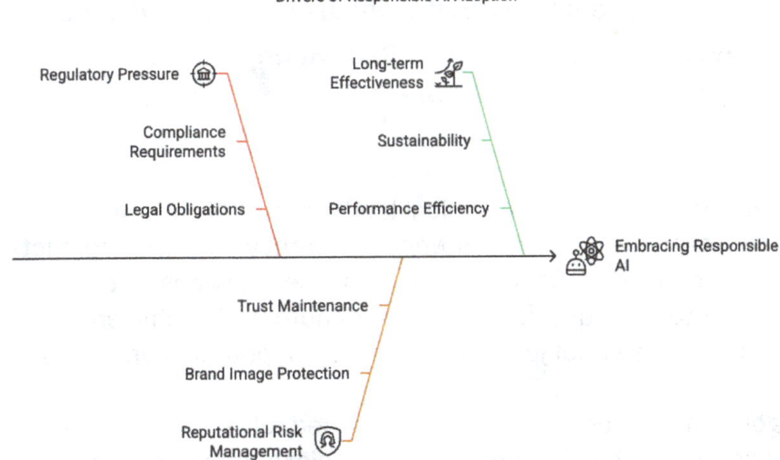

The motivation for embracing Responsible AI stems from multiple drivers: regulatory pressure [25], the need to manage reputational risk and maintain customer trust [11], and the recognition that trustworthy AI is often more effective and sustainable in the long run.[12]

Implementing Responsible AI requires more than just technical fixes; it involves establishing clear organisational principles or codes of ethics [6], fostering a culture where ethical considerations are prioritised [14], ensuring adequate training and awareness [14], engaging with stakeholders on potential impacts [35], and integrating ethical review into development and deployment processes.

Governance frameworks like ISO 42001 and NIST AI RMF are built upon these Responsible AI principles.[47]

Crucially, adhering to Responsible AI principles often requires organisations to go beyond minimum legal compliance.[5]

> ***While regulations set the floor, ethical AI demands a proactive consideration of broader societal impacts [15], potential harms to vulnerable groups [16], and alignment with fundamental human values [3], even in areas not explicitly covered by current laws. It involves asking not just "Can we do this?" or "Is it legal?" but "Should we do this?"***

Furthermore, navigating the ethical landscape of AI inevitably involves confronting dilemmas where different values may conflict – for example, the desire for highly personalised services [28] versus the need to protect privacy [31], or the drive for automation efficiency [28] versus concerns about job displacement [15] or potential unfairness.[9]

AI algorithms, based on data and predefined rules, cannot resolve these complex ethical trade-offs alone. This underscores the indispensable role of human judgement within the governance process.[17]

Effective AI governance must therefore define clear points where human intervention, review, and ethical deliberation are required to make decisions in ambiguous or high-stakes situations, reinforcing the CBI's focus on the 'appropriateness' of AI use.[12]

7.9 Practical Implementation Challenges

Despite the clear need for robust AI governance, financial institutions in Ireland face several practical challenges in implementing effective structures and processes.

7.9.1 Resource Constraints and Skills Gaps

A significant barrier is the shortage of personnel with the necessary expertise in AI development, data science, risk management specific to AI, and AI governance itself.[40]

There is a recognised gap in data literacy skills even among existing finance professionals in Ireland, hindering their ability to effectively understand, use, and oversee AI-driven processes.[74]

Building broad AI literacy across the workforce, as encouraged by the EU AI Act [49] and necessary for responsible adoption [27], requires investment in training.[27]

Implementing and maintaining comprehensive AI governance also demands substantial resources – financial investment in tools and platforms, dedicated personnel time, and technological infrastructure.[10] The high computational requirements of some advanced AI models also raise cost and environmental sustainability considerations.[69] The overall cost of AI ownership, whether building in-house or relying on third parties, can be significant.[17]

7.9.2 Integrating Governance into Existing Processes

Embedding new AI governance requirements into established, often complex, organisational structures and existing risk management frameworks (like those for operational risk or compliance) presents a considerable integration challenge.[1]

AI governance cannot operate in a silo; it requires effective coordination and collaboration across multiple functions – IT, legal, compliance, risk, audit, and business lines – which can be difficult to achieve in practice.[1]

The presence of legacy IT systems further complicates integration, as firms may be running older systems in parallel with new AI-enabled processes.[40] Successfully implementing AI governance often necessitates a cultural shift within the organisation, embedding principles of responsibility and ethical consideration into everyday workflows and decision-making.[10]

> ***This requires more than just policies; it involves changing mindsets and behaviours, demanding a thoughtful change management approach.[10]***

Governance needs to be adapted to fit the way teams work, rather than imposing overly rigid structures that hinder adoption.[46]

7.9.3 Navigating Regulatory Interpretation

The regulatory landscape for AI is new and evolving rapidly.[25] Financial institutions face the challenge of interpreting broad principles and newly enacted legal requirements, like those in the EU AI Act, and applying them to their specific operational contexts.[10] Ambiguity in regulations can create uncertainty, and there is potential for differing interpretations by supervisory authorities across jurisdictions or even within the EU.[27]

Keeping pace with regulatory developments, guidance from bodies like the CBI, DPC, and ESMA, and emerging best practices requires continuous monitoring and dedicated resources.[10] Proactive engagement with regulators can be beneficial in seeking clarity.[22]

7.9.4 Data Management and Quality Issues

As highlighted previously, AI systems are heavily dependent on data. Ensuring the quality, accuracy, completeness, consistency, and relevance of the vast datasets used for training and operating AI models is a persistent and significant challenge for financial institutions.[1]

> ***Data is often siloed across different parts of the organisation, may contain inconsistencies or errors, and may lack consistent definitions.[9] Poor data quality directly translates into unreliable and potentially biased AI outcomes.[9]***

In some cases, the limited availability of high-quality data in sufficient volumes can itself be a barrier to AI adoption.[60] Implementing effective data governance specifically for AI – encompassing data lineage tracking, validation processes, access controls, privacy protection, and clear usage rights – is complex but non-negotiable for trustworthy AI.[1] Managing data distributed across cloud environments adds further complexity.[3]

7.9.5 Other Challenges

- **Third-Party Vendor Management:** Effectively assessing, onboarding, and monitoring third-party AI providers presents unique challenges, including verifying their compliance with regulations like the AI Act and GDPR, managing data security risks, and balancing the need for transparency with vendors' intellectual property concerns.[17]

- **Measuring Governance Effectiveness:** Quantifying the effectiveness of AI governance measures and demonstrating their impact can be difficult. There are challenges in developing meaningful metrics for ethical performance, fairness, or transparency.[66] The quality and effectiveness of AI governance tools themselves may vary and lack independent assessment.[76]

- **Balancing Innovation and Control:** Institutions constantly face the challenge of striking the right balance between rapidly adopting AI to capture its benefits (efficiency, competitiveness) and implementing the necessary controls and ethical guardrails to manage risks.[27] There are concerns, particularly regarding the EU AI Act, that overly stringent regulations might inadvertently stifle innovation.[22]

These implementation challenges are notably interconnected. For instance, the pervasive skills gap [74] makes it harder for institutions to interpret complex regulations [27], design effective controls, validate models accurately, or manage data quality effectively.[9]

Resource constraints [10] impact the ability to invest in necessary technology, hire skilled personnel, or dedicate sufficient time to the complex task of integrating governance across functions.[67]

Data quality problems [9] directly feed into increased model risk and fairness concerns (Section 4).

Addressing these challenges therefore requires a coordinated and holistic strategy, recognising that progress in one area, such as closing the skills gap, can have positive ripple effects across others. Ultimately, successfully implementing AI governance transcends being a purely technical or compliance project; it must be approached as a significant organisational change management initiative.[10]

> ***Success hinges not just on policies and tools, but on fostering a culture of responsibility [27], promoting cross-functional collaboration [1], securing sustained commitment from senior leadership [10], and investing in the upskilling and empowerment of employees.[61]***

Overlooking these critical human and organisational dimensions is a key risk to effective implementation.

7.10 Conclusion

The integration of Artificial Intelligence into the Irish financial services sector offers undeniable potential for transformation, efficiency, and innovation. However, this potential can only be realised sustainably and ethically through the implementation of robust AI governance frameworks. The high-stakes nature of financial services, coupled with an increasingly stringent regulatory environment spearheaded by the EU AI Act and vigilant oversight from the Central Bank of Ireland and the Data Protection Commission, makes effective governance not just advisable, but imperative.

The inherent risks associated with AI – ranging from algorithmic bias and lack of transparency to data privacy breaches, model failures, cybersecurity threats, and emerging systemic concerns – necessitate a proactive and structured approach to mitigation. Core principles of transparency, accountability, fairness, privacy, security, and human oversight must guide the development and deployment of AI systems throughout their lifecycle.

While established frameworks like ISO/IEC 42001 and the NIST AI RMF provide valuable blueprints, their effective implementation faces practical hurdles in Ireland, including significant skills gaps, resource constraints, the complexities of integration with existing systems and processes, and the challenges of navigating a rapidly evolving regulatory landscape.

These challenges are interconnected and require a holistic, strategic response that treats governance implementation as a fundamental organisational change process, demanding leadership commitment, cross-functional collaboration, and investment in people.

Ultimately, AI governance should not be viewed as merely a compliance burden or a barrier to innovation. Instead, it is a critical enabler of trustworthy AI.

By embedding ethical considerations, ensuring transparency, managing risks effectively, and prioritising fairness and consumer protection, Irish financial institutions can build confidence among customers, regulators, and the public.

This trust, in turn, provides the foundation for leveraging AI's full potential responsibly, fostering sustainable innovation, enhancing competitiveness, and contributing positively to the future of the Irish financial system.

> ***The path forward requires proactive engagement, strategic investment in governance capabilities and skills, the cultivation of a strong culture of responsibility, and a commitment to continuous learning and adaptation in the face of ongoing technological and regulatory change.***

7.11 References

- [7] University of San Diego. (n.d.). *What is AI Governance? Principles & Examples Explained*. Retrieved from https://onlinedegrees.sandiego.edu/ai-governance/#:~:text=Principles%20of%20AI%20Governance,they%20work%20easier%20to%20understand.
- [1] Alation. (n.d.). *AI Governance*. Retrieved from https://www.alation.com/glossary/ai-governance/
- [2] Accelirate. (n.d.). *AI Governance*. Retrieved from https://www.accelirate.com/ai-governance/
- [8] Palo Alto Networks. (n.d.). *AI Governance*. Retrieved from https://www.paloaltonetworks.com/cyberpedia/ai-governance
- [6] Modulos AG. (n.d.). *A Comprehensive Guide to AI Governance*. Retrieved from https://www.modulos.ai/guide-to-ai-governance/
- [46] Atlan. (n.d.). *AI Governance Principles: Guidelines for Ethical, Transparent & Accountable AI*. Retrieved from https://atlan.com/know/ai-readiness/ai-governance-principles/
- [4] Duality Technologies. (n.d.). *What is an AI Governance Framework?* Retrieved from https://dualitytech.com/blog/ai-governance-framework/
- [3] Wiz. (n.d.). *What is AI governance?* Retrieved from https://www.wiz.io/academy/ai-governance
- [28] Holistic AI. (n.d.). *AI Governance in Financial Services*. Retrieved from https://www.holisticai.com/blog/ai-governance-in-financial-services
- [10] Crowe. (n.d.). *AI governance in finance*. Retrieved from

https://www.crowe.com/insights/asset/a/ai-governance-in-finance

- [44] World Economic Forum. (2025). *Artificial Intelligence in Financial Services: The Next Frontier*. Retrieved from https://reports.weforum.org/docs/WEF_Artificial_Intelligence_in_Financial_Services_2025.pdf
- [30] Financial Stability Board. (2024, November 14). *The Financial Stability Implications of Artificial Intelligence*. Retrieved from https://www.fsb.org/2024/11/the-financial-stability-implications-of-artificial-intelligence/
- [11] Forbes Finance Council / Kumar, A. (2024, March 28). *The AI Revolution In Financial Services: Governance's Critical Role*. Retrieved from https://www.forbes.com/councils/forbesfinancecouncil/2024/03/28/the-ai-revolution-in-financial-services-governances-critical-role/
- [31] EY Greece. (n.d.). *How artificial intelligence is reshaping the financial services industry*. Retrieved from https://www.ey.com/en_gr/insights/financial-services/how-artificial-intelligence-is-reshaping-the-financial-services-industry
- [29] Deloitte Nigeria. (n.d.). *How Artificial Intelligence is Transforming the Financial Services Industry*. Retrieved from https://www.deloitte.com/ng/en/services/risk-advisory/services/how-artificial-intelligence-is-transforming-the-financial-services-industry.html
- [32] Palo Alto Networks Blog / Earley, S. (2024, October). *Banking on AI to Defend the Financial Services Sector*. Retrieved from https://www.paloaltonetworks.com/blog/2024/10/banking-on-ai-to-defend-the-financial-services-sector/

- [36] Goodwin Procter LLP. (2024, August). *EU AI Act: Key Points for Financial Services Businesses*. Retrieved from https://www.goodwinlaw.com/en/insights/publications/2024/08/alerts-practices-pif-key-points-for-financial-services-businesses#:~:text=In%20this%20context%2C%20the%20AI,respect%20to%20financial%20services%20entities.
- [21] Consultancy.eu / Protiviti. (2024, November 11). *The EU AI Act: The impact on financial services institutions*. Retrieved from https://www.consultancy.eu/news/11237/the-eu-ai-act-the-impact-on-financial-services-institutions
- [22] Smarsh. (n.d.). *EU AI Act*. Retrieved from https://www.smarsh.com/regulations/eu-ai-act
- [49] Goodwin Procter LLP. (2024, August). *EU AI Act: Key Points for Financial Services Businesses*. Retrieved from https://www.goodwinlaw.com/en/insights/publications/2024/08/alerts-practices-pif-key-points-for-financial-services-businesses
- [41] Eurofi. (2024, December). *The EU AI Act: Key measures and implications for financial services*. Retrieved from https://www.eurofi.net/wp-content/uploads/2024/12/ii.2-ai-act-key-measures-and-implications-for-financial-services.pdf
- [38] Deloitte Luxembourg. (n.d.). *European Artificial Intelligence Act adopted by the Parliament*. Retrieved from https://www.deloitte.com/lu/en/Industries/investment-management/perspectives/european-artificial-intelligence-act-adopted-parliament.html
- [26] Protiviti. (2025, February 5). *Understanding the Impact of the*

EU AI Act. Retrieved from https://www.protiviti.com/us-en/insights-paper/understanding-impact-eu-ai-act

- [37] American Bankers Association / Protiviti. (2024, November 11). *Understanding the Impact of the EU AI Act: A Primer for Financial Institutions*. Retrieved from https://www.aba.com/news-research/analysis-guides/understanding-the-impact-of-the-eu-ai-act
- [40] Dillon Eustace. (n.d.). *AI Considerations for Irish Fund Management Companies*. Retrieved from https://www.dilloneustace.com/insights/ai-considerations-for-irish-fund-management-companies/
- [12] Central Bank of Ireland / Kincaid, C. (2024, May 22). *Speech: Financial Consumer Protection and Market Conduct Considerations of AI in Finance*. Retrieved from https://www.centralbank.ie/news/article/speech-colm-kincaid-financial-consumer-protection-and-market-conduct-considerations-of-AI-in-finance-22-may-2024
- [23] Pinsent Masons / Higgins, A. (n.d.). *Businesses urged to review AI policies as Ireland set to implement EU AI Act*. Retrieved from https://www.pinsentmasons.com/out-law/analysis/businesses-urged-review-ai-policies-ireland-implement-eu-ai-act
- [53] Research Ireland. (2024, November 26). *Central Bank of Ireland and Insight Research Ireland Centre at University of Limerick Join Forces to Boost AI Research*. Retrieved from https://www.researchireland.ie/news/central-bank-of-ireland-and-insight-research-ireland-to-boost-ai-research/
- [13] Walkers. (2024, June). *Initial guidance on the use of AI in the provision of investment services*. Retrieved from https://www.walkersglobal.com/Insights/2024/06/Initial-guidance-on-the-use-of-AI-in-the-provision-of-

investment-services

- [33] Maples Group. (2024, April 29). *AI: Risk and Regulatory Considerations for Irish Regulated Firms*. Retrieved from https://maples.com/knowledge/ai-risk-and-regulatory-considerations-for-irish-regulated-firms
- [42] Institute of Directors Ireland / William Fry. (2024, June). *Big Data, Big Change: The new AI Act has Big Implications for the Financial Services Sector*. Retrieved from https://www.iodireland.ie/images/uploads/downloads/8300_IOD_FactSheet_June_Big_Data%2C_Big_Change_The_new_AI_Act_has_Big_Implications_for_the_Financial_Services_Sector.pdf
- [43] Central Bank of Ireland / Cross, G. (2024, June 24). *Speech: Insurance Industry Event on Responsible Use of Big Data and Related Technologies*. Retrieved from https://www.centralbank.ie/news/article/speech-gerry-cross-Insurance-Industry-Event-on-Responsible-Use-of-Big-Data-and-Related-Technologies-24-june-2024
- [25] EY Global. (n.d.). *Responsible AI in financial services*. Retrieved from https://www.ey.com/en_gl/responsible-ai-financial-services
- [14] FS-ISAC. (n.d.). *Responsible AI Principles*. Retrieved from https://www.fsisac.com/hubfs/Knowledge/AI/FSISAC_ResponsibleAI-Principles.pdf
- [68] PwC US. (n.d.). *Responsible AI in finance: Charting the course for CFOs*. Retrieved from https://www.pwc.com/us/en/tech-effect/ai-analytics/responsible-ai-in-finance.html
- [66] Atlassian Blog / Franklin, J. (n.d.). *What is responsible AI? Principles and strategies for safe implementation*. Retrieved from https://www.atlassian.com/blog/artificial-intelligence/responsible-ai

- [5] SymphonyAI. (n.d.). *What is Responsible AI?* Retrieved from https://www.symphonyai.com/resources/blog/financial-services/what-is-responsible-ai/
- [64] Intuit. (n.d.). *Responsible AI*. Retrieved from https://www.intuit.com/privacy/responsible-ai/
- [24] Bain & Company. (n.d.). *Five Principles for Generative AI in Financial Services*. Retrieved from https://www.bain.com/insights/five-principles-for-generative-ai-in-financial-services/
- [35] World Economic Forum / Poss, C. (2024, June 21). *Why every investor should embrace Responsible AI*. Retrieved from https://www.weforum.org/stories/2024/06/why-every-investor-should-embrace-responsible-ai/
- [18] ProfileTree. (n.d.). *Navigating AI and GDPR in Ireland: 6 Pitfalls to Avoid*. Retrieved from https://profiletree.com/navigating-ai-and-gdpr-in-ireland/
- [54] Tech Monitor / Bandhakavi, S. (2024, December 19). *EDPB releases AI data guidance to harmonise GDPR compliance*. Retrieved from https://www.techmonitor.ai/digital-economy/ai-and-automation/edpb-ai-data-guidance-harmonise-gdpr-compliance
- [19] William Fry. (2024, December). *Unwrapping the EDPB's Guidance on AI Models and Data Protection*. Retrieved from https://www.williamfry.com/knowledge/unwrapping-the-edpbs-guidance-on-ai-models-and-data-protection/
- [55] European Data Protection Board. (2024, December 18). *EDPB Opinion on AI models & GDPR principles to support responsible AI*. Retrieved from https://www.edpb.europa.eu/news/news/2024/edpb-opinion-ai-models-gdpr-principles-support-responsible-ai_en

- [56] Pinsent Masons / Barden, N. (n.d.). *Irish DPC flags GDPR risks in developing and using AI*. Retrieved from https://www.pinsentmasons.com/out-law/news/irish-dpc-gdpr-risks-developing-using-ai
- [59] Data Protection Commission Ireland. (2024, December 18). Irish Data Protection Commission welcomes EDPB opinion on the use of personal data for the development and deployment of AI models. Retrieved from http://www.dataprotection.ie/en/irish-data-protection-commission-welcomes-edpb-opinion-use-personal-data-development-and-deployment
- [57] Data Protection Commission Ireland. (n.d.). *AI, LLMs and Data Protection*. Retrieved from http://www.dataprotection.ie/en/dpc-guidance/blogs/AI-LLMs-and-Data-Protection
- [39] 2B Advice / Ailance. (2024, September 12). *Irish Data Protection Commission launches AI proceedings against Google*. Retrieved from https://2b-advice.com/en/2024/09/12/irish-data-protection-commission-initiates-ki-proceedings-against-google/
- [63] EY Ireland. (n.d.). *AI Case studies*. Retrieved from https://www.ey.com/en_ie/services/ai/case-studies
- [45] EY Ireland. (n.d.). *How AI can be leveraged for the finance function*. Retrieved from https://www.ey.com/en_ie/insights/assurance/how-ai-can-be-leveraged-for-the-finance-function
- [67] PwC Ireland. (n.d.). *Artificial Intelligence*. Retrieved from https://www.pwc.ie/services/consulting/technology/artificial-intelligence.html
- [62] KPMG Ireland. (2024, October). *Harnessing AI: Opportunities in the Finance Function for Insurance*. Retrieved from

https://kpmg.com/ie/en/home/insights/2

7.11.1 Works cited

1. What is AI Governance? | Alation Glossary, accessed on April 11, 2025, https://www.alation.com/glossary/ai-governance/
2. 9 Principles of an AI Governance Framework - Accelirate, accessed on April 11, 2025, https://www.accelirate.com/ai-governance/
3. AI Governance: Principles, Regulations, and Practical Tips - Wiz, accessed on April 11, 2025, https://www.wiz.io/academy/ai-governance
4. 9 Principles of an AI Governance Framework - Duality Technologies, accessed on April 11, 2025, https://dualitytech.com/blog/ai-governance-framework/
5. What is responsible AI - how can it address concerns within financial services?, accessed on April 11, 2025, https://www.symphonyai.com/resources/blog/financial-services/what-is-responsible-ai/
6. A Guide to AI Governance: Navigating Regulations, Responsibility, and Risk Management, accessed on April 11, 2025, https://www.modulos.ai/guide-to-ai-governance/
7. onlinedegrees.sandiego.edu, accessed on April 11, 2025, https://onlinedegrees.sandiego.edu/ai-governance/#:~:text=Principles%20of%20AI%20Governance,they%20work%20easier%20to%20understand.
8. What Is AI Governance? - Palo Alto Networks, accessed on April 11, 2025, https://www.paloaltonetworks.com/cyberpedia/ai-governance
9. AI in Finance: How Better Quality and Governance is Crucial

for AI Implementation, accessed on April 11, 2025, https://www.harnham.com/ai-in-finance-how-better-quality-and-governance-is-crucial-for-ai-implementation/

10. AI Governance in Finance | Crowe LLP, accessed on April 11, 2025, https://www.crowe.com/insights/asset/a/ai-governance-in-finance
11. The AI Revolution In Financial Services: Governance's Critical Role - Forbes, accessed on April 11, 2025, https://www.forbes.com/councils/forbesfinancecouncil/2024/03/28/the-ai-revolution-in-financial-services-governances-critical-role/
12. Financial consumer protection and market conduct considerations of AI in finance - Remarks by Colm Kincaid, Director of Consumer Protection - Central Bank of Ireland, accessed on April 11, 2025, https://www.centralbank.ie/news/article/speech-colm-kincaid-financial-consumer-protection-and-market-conduct-considerations-of-AI-in-finance-22-may-2024
13. Initial guidance on the use of AI in the provision of investment services - Walkers Global, accessed on April 11, 2025, https://www.walkersglobal.com/Insights/2024/06/Initial-guidance-on-the-use-of-AI-in-the-provision-of-investment-services
14. Responsible AI Principles - FS-ISAC, accessed on April 11, 2025, https://www.fsisac.com/hubfs/Knowledge/AI/FSISAC_ResponsibleAI-Principles.pdf
15. The Dark Side of AI: 5 Ethical Challenges Facing Governments in Ireland & Germany, accessed on April 11, 2025,

https://www.devcentrehouse.eu/blogs/ai-governments-ireland-germany/

16. Data Ethics Within Insurance | Central Bank of Ireland, accessed on April 11, 2025, https://www.centralbank.ie/docs/default-source/regulation/industry-market-sectors/insurance-reinsurance/solvency-ii/communications/data-ethics-within-insurance.pdf?sfvrsn=54219f1d_4
17. The risks and ethical implications of AI in financial services - FIS, accessed on April 11, 2025, https://www.fisglobal.com/insights/risks-and-ethical-implications-of-ai-in-financial-services
18. Navigating AI and GDPR in Ireland: 6 Pitfalls to Avoid - ProfileTree, accessed on April 11, 2025, https://profiletree.com/navigating-ai-and-gdpr-in-ireland/
19. Unwrapping the EDPB's Guidance on AI models and Data Protection - WILLIAM FRY, accessed on April 11, 2025, https://www.williamfry.com/knowledge/unwrapping-the-edpbs-guidance-on-ai-models-and-data-protection/
20. Understanding the Ethical Risks of AI in Financial Services - HSO, accessed on April 11, 2025, https://www.hso.com/blog/understanding-the-ethical-risks-of-ai-in-financial-services
21. The EU AI Act: The impact on financial services institutions - Consultancy.eu, accessed on April 11, 2025, https://www.consultancy.eu/news/11237/the-eu-ai-act-the-impact-on-financial-services-institutions
22. The EU AI Act: Key Provisions and Impact on Financial Services - Smarsh, accessed on April 11, 2025, https://www.smarsh.com/regulations/eu-ai-act

23. Businesses urged to review AI policies as Ireland prepares to implement EU AI Act, accessed on April 11, 2025, https://www.pinsentmasons.com/out-law/analysis/businesses-urged-review-ai-policies-ireland-implement-eu-ai-act

24. Responsible by Design: Five Principles for Generative AI in Financial Services, accessed on April 11, 2025, https://www.bain.com/insights/five-principles-for-generative-ai-in-financial-services/

25. Responsible AI in Financial Services | EY - Global, accessed on April 11, 2025, https://www.ey.com/en_gl/responsible-ai-financial-services

26. Understanding the Impact of the EU AI Act | Protiviti United States, accessed on April 11, 2025, https://www.protiviti.com/us-en/insights-paper/understanding-impact-eu-ai-act

27. NAVIGATING THE FUTURE OF AI REGULATIONS IN BANKING: CHALLENGES AND SOLUTIONS - Finance Derivative, accessed on April 11, 2025, https://www.financederivative.com/navigating-the-future-of-ai-regulations-in-banking-challenges-and-solutions/

28. AI Governance in Financial Services - Holistic AI, accessed on April 11, 2025, https://www.holisticai.com/blog/ai-governance-in-financial-services

29. How Artificial Intelligence is Transforming the Financial Services Industry - Deloitte, accessed on April 11, 2025, https://www.deloitte.com/ng/en/services/risk-advisory/services/how-artificial-intelligence-is-transforming-the-financial-services-industry.html

30. The Financial Stability Implications of Artificial Intelligence ..., accessed on April 11, 2025, https://www.fsb.org/2024/11/the-financial-stability-implications-of-artificial-intelligence/

31. How artificial intelligence is reshaping the financial services industry | EY - Greece, accessed on April 11, 2025, https://www.ey.com/en_gr/insights/financial-services/how-artificial-intelligence-is-reshaping-the-financial-services-industry

32. Banking on AI to Defend the Financial Services Sector - Palo Alto Networks, accessed on April 11, 2025, https://www.paloaltonetworks.com/blog/2024/10/banking-on-ai-to-defend-the-financial-services-sector/

33. AI: Risk and Regulatory Considerations for Irish Regulated Firms - Maples Group, accessed on April 11, 2025, https://maples.com/knowledge/ai-risk-and-regulatory-considerations-for-irish-regulated-firms

34. The rise of artificial intelligence: benefits and risks for financial stability - European Central Bank, accessed on April 11, 2025, https://www.ecb.europa.eu/press/financial-stability-publications/fsr/special/html/ecb.fsrart202405_02~58c3ce5246.en.html

35. Here's why every investor should embrace Responsible AI | World Economic Forum, accessed on April 11, 2025, https://www.weforum.org/stories/2024/06/why-every-investor-should-embrace-responsible-ai/

36. www.goodwinlaw.com, accessed on April 11, 2025, https://www.goodwinlaw.com/en/insights/publications/2024/08/alerts-practices-pif-key-points-for-financial-services-

businesses#:~:text=In%20this%20context%2C%20the%20AI,respect%20to%20financial%20services%20entities.

37. Understanding the Impact of the EU AI Act: A Primer for Financial Institutions, accessed on April 11, 2025, https://www.aba.com/news-research/analysis-guides/understanding-the-impact-of-the-eu-ai-act

38. EU AI Act adopted by the Parliament: What's the impact for financial ..., accessed on April 11, 2025, https://www.deloitte.com/lu/en/Industries/investment-management/perspectives/european-artificial-intelligence-act-adopted-parliament.html

39. Irish Data Protection Commission initiates AI proceedings against Google - 2B Advice, accessed on April 11, 2025, https://2b-advice.com/en/2024/09/12/irish-data-protection-commission-initiates-ki-proceedings-against-google/

40. AI: Considerations for Irish Fund Management Companies | Commercial Law Firm, accessed on April 11, 2025, https://www.dilloneustace.com/insights/ai-considerations-for-irish-fund-management-companies/

41. AI Act: key measures and implications for financial services | Eurofi, accessed on April 11, 2025, https://www.eurofi.net/wp-content/uploads/2024/12/ii.2-ai-act-key-measures-and-implications-for-financial-services.pdf

42. The new AI Act has Big Implications for the Financial Services Sector - Institute of Directors Ireland, accessed on April 11, 2025, https://www.iodireland.ie/images/uploads/downloads/8300_IOD_FactSheet_June_Big_Data%2C_Big_Change_The_new_AI_

Act_has_Big_Implications_for_the_Financial_Services_Sector.pdf

43. Remarks by Gerry Cross, Director of Financial Regulation - Policy & Risk, accessed on April 11, 2025, https://www.centralbank.ie/news/article/speech-gerry-cross-Insurance-Industry-Event-on-Responsible-Use-of-Big-Data-and-Related-Technologies-24-june-2024

44. Artificial Intelligence in Financial Services - Publications - The World Economic Forum, accessed on April 11, 2025, https://reports.weforum.org/docs/WEF_Artificial_Intelligence_in_Financial_Services_2025.pdf

45. How AI can be leveraged for the finance function | EY - Ireland, accessed on April 11, 2025, https://www.ey.com/en_ie/insights/assurance/how-ai-can-be-leveraged-for-the-finance-function

46. 6 AI Governance Principles for Responsible Deployment & Use - Atlan, accessed on April 11, 2025, https://atlan.com/know/ai-readiness/ai-governance-principles/

47. Understanding ISO 42001 and Demonstrating Compliance - ISMS.online, accessed on April 11, 2025, https://www.isms.online/iso-42001/

48. ISO/IEC 42001:2023 Guide to AI Management & IT Security - Linford & Company LLP, accessed on April 11, 2025, https://linfordco.com/blog/iso-42001-it-security/

49. EU AI Act: Key Points for Financial Services Businesses | Insights & Resources | Goodwin, accessed on April 11, 2025, https://www.goodwinlaw.com/en/insights/publications/2024/08/alerts-practices-pif-key-points-for-financial-

services-businesses

50. Navigating the Future of AI Governance: A Guide to NIST AI RMF, ISO/IEC 42001, and the EU AI Act - ZenGRC, accessed on April 11, 2025, https://www.zengrc.com/blog/navigating-the-future-of-ai-governance-a-guide-to-nist-ai-rmf-iso-iec-42001-and-the-eu-ai-act/

51. The role of ISO/IEC 42001 in AI governance - Osler, Hoskin & Harcourt LLP, accessed on April 11, 2025, https://www.osler.com/en/insights/updates/the-role-of-iso-iec-42001-in-ai-governance/

52. European Commission targeted consultation on AI in finance - KPMG International, accessed on April 11, 2025, https://kpmg.com/ie/en/home/insights/2024/07/artificial-intelligence-in-financial-services-fs-insurance.html

53. Central Bank of Ireland and Insight Research Ireland Centre at University of Limerick Join Forces to Boost AI Research, accessed on April 11, 2025, https://www.researchireland.ie/news/central-bank-of-ireland-and-insight-research-ireland-to-boost-ai-research/

54. EDPB releases AI data guidance to harmonise GDPR compliance - Tech Monitor, accessed on April 11, 2025, https://www.techmonitor.ai/digital-economy/ai-and-automation/edpb-ai-data-guidance-harmonise-gdpr-compliance

55. EDPB opinion on AI models: GDPR principles support responsible AI - European Union, accessed on April 11, 2025, https://www.edpb.europa.eu/news/news/2024/edpb-opinion-ai-models-gdpr-principles-support-responsible-ai_en

56. Irish data protection commission highlights GDPR risks in developing and using AI, accessed on April 11, 2025, https://www.pinsentmasons.com/out-law/news/irish-dpc-

gdpr-risks-developing-using-ai

57. AI, Large Language Models and Data Protection | 18/07/2024, accessed on April 11, 2025, http://www.dataprotection.ie/en/dpc-guidance/blogs/AI-LLMs-and-Data-Protection

58. Powering the Digital Economy: Opportunities and Risks of Artificial Intelligence in Finance in, accessed on April 11, 2025, https://www.elibrary.imf.org/view/journals/087/2021/024/article-A001-en.xml

59. Irish Data Protection Commission welcomes EDPB opinion on the use of personal data for the development and deployment of AI models | 18/12/2024, accessed on April 11, 2025, http://www.dataprotection.ie/en/irish-data-protection-commission-welcomes-edpb-opinion-use-personal-data-development-and-deployment

60. AI and Risk Management in Ireland | Deloitte Ireland, accessed on April 11, 2025, https://www.deloitte.com/ie/en/services/risk-advisory/research/_ai-and-risk-management-in-ireland.html

61. GenAI Business Leaders Survey — Report - PwC Ireland, accessed on April 11, 2025, https://www.pwc.ie/reports/gen-ai-business-leaders-survey.html

62. Insurance Accounting Advisory Quarterly - AI - KPMG Ireland, accessed on April 11, 2025, https://kpmg.com/ie/en/home/insights/2024/10/harnessing-ai-fs-insurance.html

63. AI Case Studies | EY - Ireland, accessed on April 11, 2025, https://www.ey.com/en_ie/services/ai/case-studies

64. Intuit Responsible AI Principles, accessed on April 11, 2025,

https://www.intuit.com/privacy/responsible-ai/

65. Why the Irish financial services sector needs technology-enabled transformation, accessed on April 11, 2025, https://eyfinancialservicesthoughtgallery.ie/why-the-irish-financial-sector-needs-technology-enabled-transformation/
66. Responsible AI: Key Principles and Best Practices - Atlassian, accessed on April 11, 2025, https://www.atlassian.com/blog/artificial-intelligence/responsible-ai
67. Artificial Intelligence — Technology Services - PwC Ireland, accessed on April 11, 2025, https://www.pwc.ie/services/consulting/technology/artificial-intelligence.html
68. Responsible AI in finance: 3 key actions to take now - PwC, accessed on April 11, 2025, https://www.pwc.com/us/en/tech-effect/ai-analytics/responsible-ai-in-finance.html
69. THE IMPACT OF AI IN FINANCIAL SERVICES - UK Finance, accessed on April 11, 2025, https://www.ukfinance.org.uk/system/files/2023-11/The%20impact%20of%20AI%20in%20financial%20services.pdf
70. ISO 42001: Paving the Way Forward for AI Governance - Hyperproof, accessed on April 11, 2025, https://hyperproof.io/iso-42001-paving-the-way-forward-for-ai-governance/
71. ISO 42001 vs NIST AI RMF: Which AI Program Do You Need? - IS Partners, LLC, accessed on April 11, 2025, https://www.ispartnersllc.com/blog/iso-42001-vs-nist-ai-rmf/

72. ISO/IEC 42001 vs. NIST AI RMF: A Comparative Analysis - PECB, accessed on April 11, 2025, https://pecb.com/article/isoiec-42001-vs-nist-ai-rmf-a-comparative-analysis

73. Webinar Recap: Building a Robust AI Governance Framework with ISO 42001 - RSI Security, accessed on April 11, 2025, https://blog.rsisecurity.com/webinar-recap-building-an-ai-governance-framework-with-iso-42001/

74. Transforming Ireland's Financial Industry through AI & Data Literacy - University College Dublin, accessed on April 11, 2025, https://www.ucd.ie/professionalacademy/resources/finance-industry-ai-transformation/

75. AI – HERE FOR GOOD A National Artificial Intelligence Strategy for Ireland - Department of Enterprise, Trade and Employment, accessed on April 11, 2025, https://enterprise.gov.ie/en/publications/publication-files/national-ai-strategy.pdf

76. Report: Risky Analysis: Assessing and Improving AI Governance Tools, accessed on April 11, 2025, https://www.worldprivacyforum.org/2023/12/new-report-risky-analysis-assessing-and-improving-ai-governance-tools/

Bias

In the context of financial services, AI bias is not merely a matter of technical inaccuracy or random error. It refers to systematic and unjustified differences in the predictions, outcomes, or treatment generated by AI systems based on individuals' demographic characteristics (such as gender, ethnicity, age, or location) or other sensitive attributes, leading to unfair, discriminatory, or disadvantageous results.[20] This unfairness is the core concern, distinguishing bias from simple model imperfections.[20]

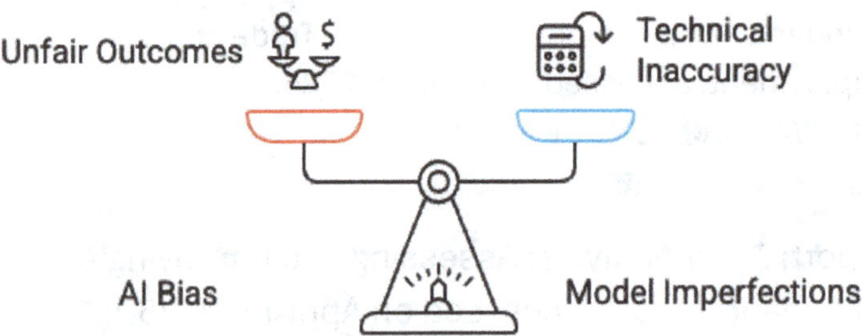

Distinguishing AI Bias from Model Imperfections

Crucially, AI bias can manifest even when there is no explicit programming to discriminate based on protected characteristics.[1] It often arises subtly from patterns learned from data, the design choices made during algorithm development, or the way humans interact with and interpret the AI's outputs.[1] Understanding bias, therefore, requires looking beyond the algorithm itself to consider the data it learns from, the context in which it is deployed, and the potential societal impacts. It demands a socio-technical perspective, recognising that AI systems are embedded within, and can reflect or even amplify, existing societal structures and historical inequalities.[1]

7.12 Why Addressing Bias is Critical

For financial institutions operating in Ireland, proactively addressing AI bias is not optional but a critical imperative driven by multiple interconnected factors:

- **Ethical Imperative:** AI systems increasingly act as gatekeepers to vital economic opportunities, such as access to credit, insurance, housing, and potentially employment within the sector itself.[24] Bias embedded within these systems can unfairly deny opportunities to certain individuals or groups, thereby perpetuating and even amplifying existing societal inequalities and historical discrimination based on characteristics like race, colour, gender, disability, or socio-economic background.[1] The Central Bank of Ireland consistently emphasises the importance of fairness and consumer protection, aligning with this ethical obligation.[15]
- **Legal & Regulatory Compliance:** A robust legal and regulatory framework is rapidly solidifying around AI. The EU AI Act imposes stringent requirements on 'high-risk' AI systems, common in financial services, mandating fairness, non-discrimination, transparency, and human oversight.[18] Non-compliance carries the risk of substantial financial penalties.[18] Furthermore, the General Data Protection Regulation (GDPR) grants individuals rights concerning automated decision-making and mandates the protection of personal data used in AI systems.[26] In Ireland, specific authorities like the Irish Human Rights and Equality Commission (IHREC) and the Financial Services and Pensions Ombudsman (FSPO) are designated to oversee the protection of fundamental rights in the context of AI use, particularly in

sensitive areas like credit and insurance.[32]

- **Reputational Risk:** Incidents of AI bias can severely damage an institution's reputation, leading to public backlash, erosion of customer trust, and negative media attention.[1] Trust is the bedrock of the financial services industry, and deploying systems perceived as unfair fundamentally undermines this foundation.[15] Rebuilding trust once lost can be an arduous and costly process. As highlighted by institutions like Permanent TSB, building and maintaining trust is a core strategic objective.[41]
- **Commercial Impact:** Biased AI systems can lead to tangible negative business consequences. Unfairly excluding potentially creditworthy customers or mispricing insurance risks for certain demographics can result in missed revenue opportunities and reduced market share.[1] Furthermore, customer dissatisfaction stemming from perceived unfairness can lead to reduced loyalty and higher churn rates.[1] Conversely, demonstrating a commitment to fairness and responsible AI can enhance customer satisfaction, build brand loyalty, and potentially serve as a competitive differentiator.[1]

These drivers are not mutually exclusive; they often reinforce each other. An ethical lapse leading to discriminatory outcomes can trigger regulatory action, reputational damage, and ultimately, commercial harm. This convergence provides a compelling rationale for institutions to embed fairness considerations into their AI strategies, aligning risk management with ethical conduct and sustainable business practices.

This chapter serves as a practical guide for staff working across various functions within Irish financial institutions. Its purpose is to equip personnel with the necessary knowledge and tools to understand, recognise, mitigate, and minimise AI bias in their specific operational contexts. It will delve into the different types and sources of bias, explore the relevant regulatory landscape, analyse the potential consequences, detail practical mitigation strategies, provide insights from the Irish context, and offer an implementation framework. Ultimately, this guide aims to foster a shared understanding and a proactive culture of responsible AI development and deployment throughout the organisation.[42]

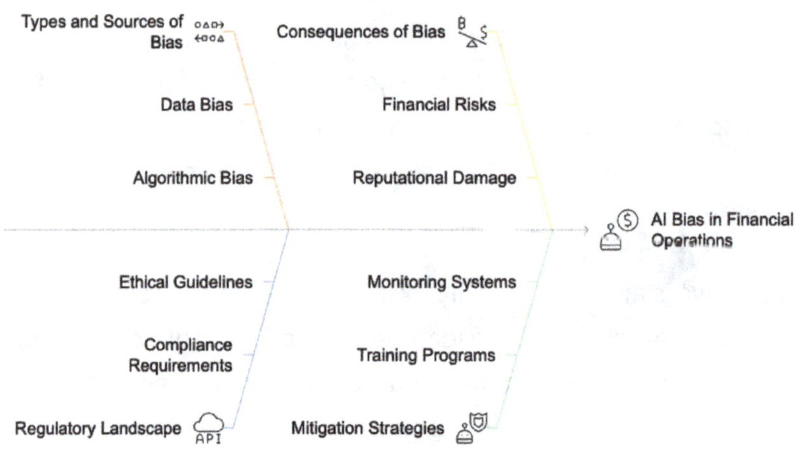

7.13 Unpacking AI Bias: Types, Sources, and Manifestations

Understanding the various forms bias can take and where it originates within the AI lifecycle is crucial for effective recognition and mitigation. Bias is not a monolithic concept; it arises from diverse sources related to data, algorithms, and human factors.

7.13.1 A Taxonomy of Bias in Financial AI

Bias in AI systems used within financial services can be broadly categorised:

- **Data Bias:** This is perhaps the most widely recognised source of bias, stemming from issues within the data used to train and test AI models.

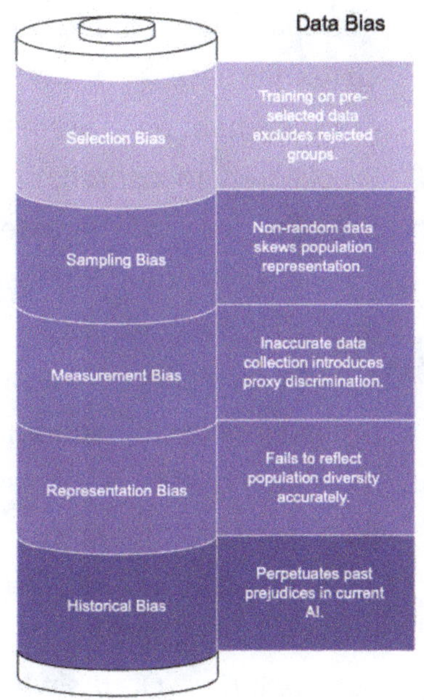

- *Historical Bias:* Occurs when datasets reflect past societal prejudices, discriminatory practices, or inequalities that were prevalent at the time the data was generated.[20] For example, historical loan data might embed past biases in lending decisions, which an AI model could learn and perpetuate, even if current policies are non-discriminatory.[1] Using data collected before the implementation of modern privacy regulations and ethical standards also raises significant concerns.[1]
- *Representation Bias:* Arises when the training data fails to accurately reflect the diversity of the population the AI system will serve in the real world.[1] A credit scoring model trained predominantly on data from high-income individuals may perform poorly or unfairly assess applicants from lower-income backgrounds, reinforcing financial exclusion.[38] Similarly, data collected from users of a specific app might not represent the broader customer base.[20]
- *Measurement Bias:* Stems from inaccuracies in how data is collected, measured, or labelled, often involving the use of proxies for characteristics that are difficult to measure directly.[20] For instance, using postcode as a proxy for credit risk could inadvertently discriminate against residents of certain areas due to historical redlining or socio-economic factors, rather than individual creditworthiness. Using ATM withdrawal frequency or amount as a primary indicator of customer value could disadvantage groups like pensioners or low-income individuals.[20]
- *Sampling Bias:* Occurs when the data collection process

is not random, leading to a sample that is not representative of the target population.[20] Training a model only on data from urban customers might lead to biased outcomes when applied to rural customers.[38]

- *Selection Bias:* A specific type of sampling bias where the selection process itself introduces bias.[20] A common example in credit scoring is training models only on data from applicants who were previously *granted* credit, potentially excluding information about unfairly rejected groups and biasing the model against similar future applicants.[20]

- **Algorithmic Bias:** This type of bias originates from the design and implementation of the AI algorithm itself.[1] It can occur when:
  - The model's architecture or assumptions inherently favour certain outcomes.
  - The algorithm assigns inappropriate weights to specific input variables, leading to skewed results. For example, heavily weighting continuous employment history could unfairly penalise applicants with legitimate career breaks, such as parental leave, which may disproportionately affect women.[23]
  - More complex models, while potentially more accurate overall, might learn to infer protected characteristics (like race or gender) from seemingly neutral data points (like purchasing patterns or online behaviour) and base decisions on these inferences, making bias harder to detect and explain.[20]

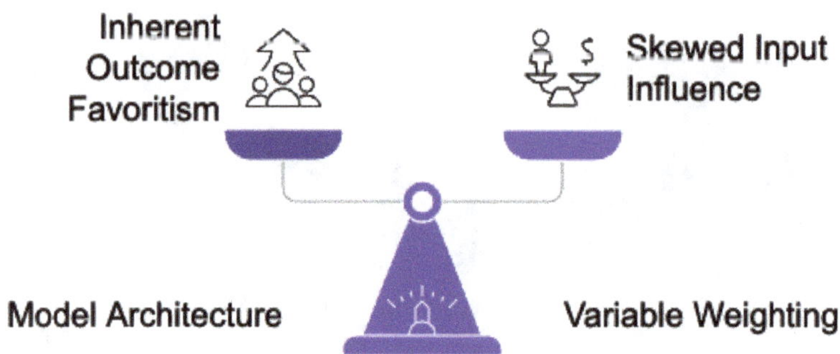

Balancing Algorithmic Bias Sources

- **Human Bias:** Human actions, assumptions, and interpretations play a significant role throughout the AI lifecycle, introducing various forms of bias:

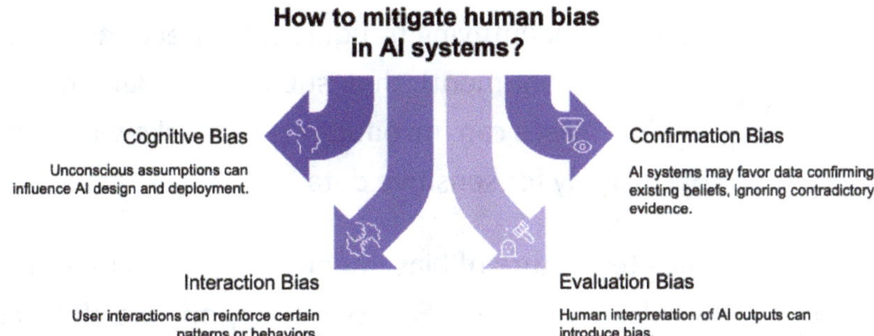

  - *Cognitive Bias:* The inherent biases and assumptions held by developers, data scientists, and business users can unconsciously influence how AI systems are designed, built, trained, and deployed.[1]
  - *Confirmation Bias:* AI systems might be designed (or data selected) in a way that favours information confirming pre-existing beliefs or hypotheses, potentially ignoring contradictory evidence or diverse perspectives.[38] An example is a loan algorithm primarily trained on data from affluent areas continuing to favour applicants from those areas.[38]
  - *Interaction Bias:* Bias introduced through how users interact with an AI system over time, potentially reinforcing certain patterns or behaviours.[26]
  - *Evaluation/Interpretation Bias:* Humans involved in overseeing or using AI outputs may apply their own biases when interpreting results or deciding whether to

override the AI's recommendation.[20] Studies have shown human overrides of algorithmic bail recommendations can sometimes increase racial disparities.[20]

- *Annotation/Label Bias:* When human annotators label data (e.g., identifying fraudulent transactions, classifying customer sentiment), their subjective judgments or implicit biases can introduce errors or skew the dataset, particularly for sensitive data.[42]

This multifaceted nature of bias underscores that addressing it requires a holistic approach. Focusing solely on data cleaning, for instance, is insufficient if algorithmic design choices or human oversight practices remain unexamined.[1]

7.13.2 Tracing the Roots: How Bias Enters the AI Lifecycle

Bias is not introduced at a single point but can creep in at various stages of an AI system's development and deployment:

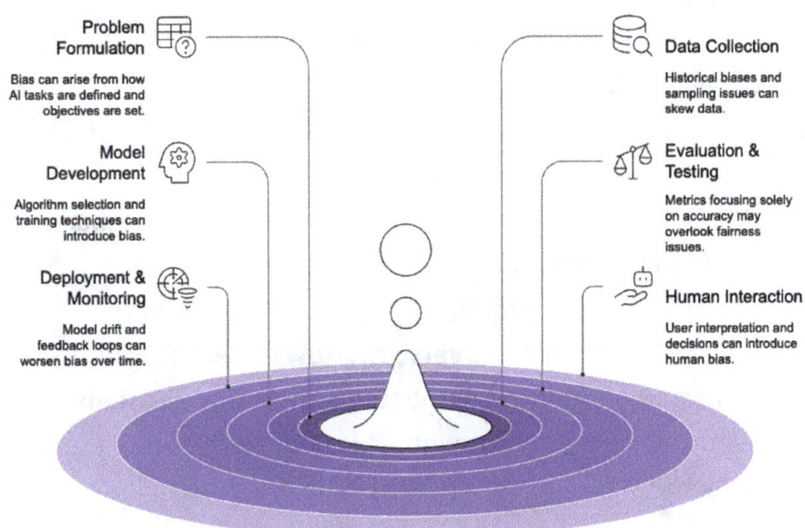

1. **Problem Formulation:** How a business problem is defined and translated into a task for AI can embed bias from the start. The choice of objective function (what the AI is optimised to achieve) and the selection of input features can inadvertently disadvantage certain groups.[20]
2. **Data Collection & Preparation:** As detailed above, historical biases, lack of representation, measurement errors, and sampling issues during data collection are major sources of bias.[1] Data scientists overlooking the societal context of the data can further exacerbate these issues.[1] Pre-processing choices, like how missing data is handled or how data points

are weighted, can also introduce or amplify bias.[20]

3. **Model Development & Training:** Algorithm selection, feature engineering choices, and the specific training techniques used can all introduce or mitigate bias.[20]
4. **Evaluation & Testing:** If evaluation metrics focus solely on overall accuracy without specifically testing for fairness across different demographic subgroups, bias may go undetected.[26]
5. **Deployment & Monitoring:** Bias can emerge or worsen over time due to 'model drift' as the real-world data distribution changes.[20] Feedback loops, where biased outputs influence future inputs, can create self-reinforcing cycles of bias.[20] Lack of continuous monitoring allows such issues to persist.[43]
6. **Human Interaction & Oversight:** How end-users interpret and act upon AI recommendations, including decisions to override the system, can introduce human bias into the final outcome.[20]

A critical takeaway is that seemingly neutral technical decisions made at various stages can have profound and often unintended discriminatory consequences downstream. This highlights the need for technical staff involved in AI development and deployment to possess not only technical expertise but also an awareness of the potential ethical and social implications of their choices.[20]

7.13.3 Real-World Examples

Bias can manifest differently across various financial applications:

- **Credit Scoring/Loan Approvals:** This is a high-profile area where AI bias can lead to individuals from certain ethnic minorities, lower-income groups, specific geographic locations, or other protected categories being unfairly denied credit or offered less favourable terms (e.g., higher interest rates).[1] This risk is explicitly recognised by the EU AI Act, which classifies AI systems used for creditworthiness evaluation of natural persons as 'high-risk'.[19] The potential for AI to use proxies for protected characteristics, even if those characteristics are not direct inputs, is a key concern.[46]
- **Insurance Underwriting/Pricing:** Similar risks exist in insurance, where biased AI could lead to discriminatory pricing (higher premiums) or denial of coverage for certain groups based on factors that are proxies for protected attributes, rather than direct measures of risk.[27] For example, using location data could inadvertently penalise individuals in historically disadvantaged neighbourhoods. The EU AI Act also designates AI systems for risk assessment and pricing in life and health insurance for natural persons as 'high-risk'.[35] The European Commission's binding commitments secured from Insurance Ireland regarding fair access to its data-sharing platform underscore the importance of non-discriminatory data infrastructure in this sector.[49]

- **Fraud Detection:** While aiming to protect both customers and institutions, fraud detection models can exhibit bias. For example, they might generate higher rates of false positives (incorrectly flagging legitimate transactions as fraudulent) for specific demographic groups, leading to inconvenience, blocked accounts, and customer frustration.[1]
- **AML/KYC:** AI used for Anti-Money Laundering and Know Your Customer processes carries risks of bias. Risk-scoring algorithms might unfairly assign higher risk levels to individuals from certain regions or backgrounds. Facial recognition technology used for identity verification has historically shown lower accuracy rates for individuals with darker skin tones and women, potentially leading to exclusion or delays.[1]
- **Customer Service (Chatbots):** AI-powered chatbots might fail to understand or appropriately respond to diverse dialects, accents, or communication styles, leading to frustrating experiences for some customer segments.[13] They could also potentially generate biased or inappropriate responses if trained on skewed data.
- **Recruitment/HR (within FS firms):** Financial institutions using AI tools for screening CVs, assessing candidates, or managing employee performance risk introducing bias if the tools favour certain demographic groups over others, potentially replicating historical patterns of underrepresentation in the sector.[1] An infamous example involved an AI recruitment tool penalising CVs containing terms associated with women.[2]

The designation of credit scoring and insurance pricing/assessment as 'high-risk' under the EU AI Act signifies that firms operating in Ireland using AI for these purposes face the most immediate and stringent regulatory expectations regarding bias identification and mitigation.[19]

7.14 The Regulatory Imperative: Navigating Irish and EU Rules

The increasing use of AI in financial services is occurring alongside the development of a specific and demanding regulatory framework. Irish financial institutions must navigate expectations set by the Central Bank of Ireland (CBI) as well as the comprehensive requirements of the EU AI Act, alongside existing data protection and consumer laws. This regulatory landscape is rapidly becoming concrete, moving beyond high-level principles to specific obligations backed by significant enforcement powers and penalties.[15]

7.14.1 The Central Bank's Expectations for AI Fairness and Responsibility

The CBI plays a crucial role in overseeing Ireland's financial markets, promoting transparency, fairness, and trust, with a strong commitment to financial consumer protection.[29] In the context of AI, the CBI has clearly signalled its focus on ensuring responsible innovation:

- **Supervisory Expectations:** Firms are expected to demonstrate a clear understanding of the AI technologies they deploy.[15] Supervisors will scrutinise the rationale for using AI for specific business challenges and assess its appropriateness.[15] Crucially, firms must ensure AI is not used in ways that exploit consumer behaviours or vulnerabilities, potentially leading to detriment.[15] They must proactively identify and manage new operational risks introduced by AI, including the risk of data or algorithmic bias leading to discriminatory treatment, which may be difficult to detect.[15]

Clear accountability for decisions regarding AI use is paramount.[15]

- **Key Principles:** The CBI, aligning with guidance from European bodies like EIOPA for the insurance sector, emphasizes a risk-based and proportional approach.[14]

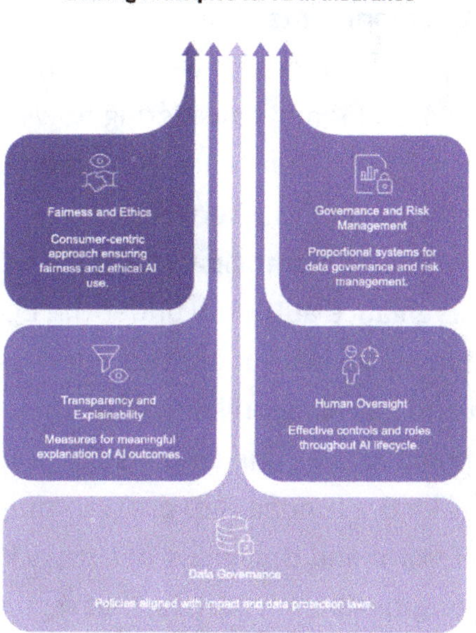

- Expectations centre on:
    - **Fairness and Ethics:** Adopting a consumer-centric approach.[14]
    - **Governance and Risk Management:** Proportional systems covering data governance, documentation, transparency, human oversight, accuracy, robustness, and cybersecurity.[14]
    - **Transparency and Explainability:** Taking necessary measures so AI outcomes can be meaningfully explained;

complexity hindering explainability requires complementary risk management measures.[14]
   - **Human Oversight:** Effective internal controls and defined roles/responsibilities throughout the AI lifecycle.[14]
   - **Data Governance:** Policies aligned with potential impact and data protection laws.[14]
- **Ongoing Developments:** The CBI is actively developing its supervisory expectations for AI use in financial services (during 2024/2025) and considering how AI impacts existing frameworks like the Consumer Protection Code, particularly regarding digital financial services.[15]
- **Regulatory Role:** It is anticipated that the CBI will act as the market surveillance authority under the EU AI Act for the regulated financial institutions it supervises.[46]
- **Research and Capacity Building:** The CBI is investing in understanding AI risks and responsible practices through initiatives like the funded PhD programme with the Insight Research Centre and University of Limerick, focusing on areas including responsible AI, AI risks, and regulation.[54]

7.14.2 Decoding the EU AI Act for Financial Services

The EU AI Act establishes a harmonised legal framework for AI across the Union, aiming to ensure AI systems are safe, trustworthy, and respect fundamental rights, while fostering innovation.[18] It applies extraterritorially, affecting providers and users outside the EU if their AI systems impact individuals within the EU.[31] The Act employs a risk-based approach:

- **Risk Categories:**
  - *Unacceptable Risk:* Practices deemed a clear threat to fundamental rights are prohibited (e.g., social scoring by public authorities, certain manipulative techniques).[18]
  - *High Risk:* Systems posing significant risks to health, safety, or fundamental rights are permitted but subject to strict requirements.[19]
  - *Limited Risk:* Systems requiring specific transparency obligations (e.g., chatbots disclosing they are AI).[19]
  - *Minimal Risk:* Systems with few or no specific obligations beyond potential voluntary codes of conduct.[19]
- **High-Risk Systems in Finance:** The Act explicitly classifies certain financial applications involving natural persons as high-risk:
  - AI systems used to evaluate creditworthiness or establish credit scores.[19]
  - AI systems used for risk assessment and pricing in relation to life and health insurance.[19]
  - Systems impacting access to essential private and public services (which could potentially include other financial services beyond credit/insurance) are also considered high-risk.[28]

- **Key Obligations for High-Risk Systems:** Both providers (developers) and deployers (users) of high-risk AI systems face significant obligations [19]:

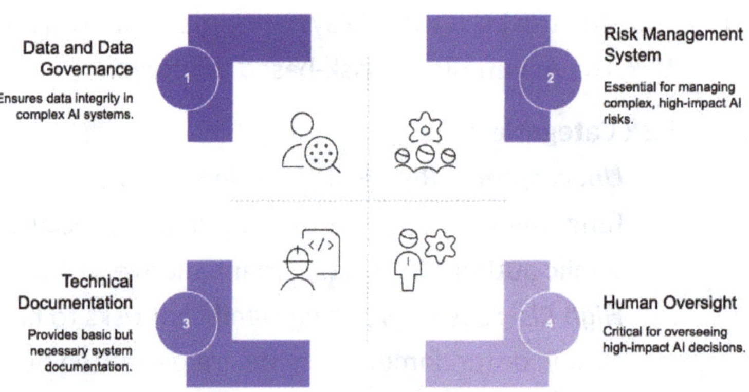

  - *Risk Management System:* Establish, implement, document, and maintain a continuous risk management process throughout the AI system's lifecycle.[16]
  - *Data and Data Governance:* Ensure training, validation, and testing data are relevant, representative, free of errors, and complete. Implement rigorous data governance and management practices, Including examination for potential biases and mitigation strategies.[19] Article 10(5) permits, under strict necessity and safeguard conditions, the processing of special categories of personal data (e.g., ethnicity, health) specifically for bias monitoring, detection, and correction.[27]
  - *Technical Documentation and Record-Keeping:* Maintain comprehensive technical documentation before placing

the system on the market or putting it into service. Ensure automatic logging capabilities for traceability.[14]

- *Transparency and Provision of Information:* Design systems to be sufficiently transparent to allow deployers to interpret outputs and use them appropriately. Provide users with clear and adequate information.[14]
- *Human Oversight:* Design systems to be effectively overseen by humans during their use. Implement appropriate human oversight measures, potentially including the ability to intervene, override, or halt the system.[14]
- *Accuracy, Robustness, and Cybersecurity:* Ensure systems achieve an appropriate level of accuracy, robustness (resilience against errors or inconsistencies), and cybersecurity throughout their lifecycle.[14]
- *Fundamental Rights Impact Assessment (FRIA):* Deployers of high-risk systems are required to conduct an assessment of the system's potential impact on fundamental rights prior to deployment.[31]

- **Irish Implementation:** Ireland is adopting a federated approach, designating existing sectoral regulators as competent authorities.[58] Nine authorities were initially designated to safeguard fundamental rights under Article 77, including the IHREC and FSPO.[32] A further eight were designated as market surveillance authorities under Article 70.[37] The CBI is expected to be the market surveillance authority for regulated financial institutions.[46] Significant investment in resources and expertise will be needed for these bodies to fulfil their roles.[58] Ireland has a specific exemption under EU treaties related to freedom, security, and justice, but this is unlikely to significantly impact standard financial services applications.[37]

- **Timelines:** The AI Act's obligations are being phased in. Prohibitions on unacceptable risk practices took effect shortly after entry into force (around August 2024), with enforcement from early 2025.[18] Obligations for general-purpose AI models apply from mid-2025.[18] The demanding requirements for high-risk systems become fully enforceable in mid-2027.[16]

7.14.3 Interplay with GDPR and the Consumer Protection Code

Balancing AI-Specific and General Data Protection

The AI Act operates alongside, and does not supersede, existing legislation like the GDPR.[27] Key GDPR principles remain fully applicable, including:

- Lawful basis for processing personal data.
- Data minimisation (collecting only necessary data).
- Purpose limitation (using data only for specified purposes).
- Transparency obligations.
- Security requirements.
- Individual rights, including those related to automated decision-making (Article 22), which grants rights to obtain human intervention, express one's point of view, and contest decisions made solely by automated means.[26]

There is potential complexity regarding the AI Act's provision (Article 10(5)) allowing the processing of sensitive 'special category' data for bias detection and correction.[27] This must be reconciled with the strict conditions for processing such data under GDPR Article 9, requiring robust safeguards, strict necessity, and compliance with all GDPR principles.[27]

Furthermore, the CBI's ongoing review of the Consumer Protection Code is considering the implications of digitalisation.[15] Existing Code principles, such as the requirement for firms to act honestly, fairly, and professionally in the best interests of their customers, remain highly relevant in the context of AI deployment.[52]

This complex regulatory web necessitates an integrated compliance approach. Firms cannot address AI Act requirements in isolation from GDPR or existing consumer protection obligations. A unified governance structure is needed to manage these interconnected requirements effectively, ensuring that data governance, risk assessment, transparency measures, and consumer rights are handled coherently across all relevant regulations.[14] The strong regulatory emphasis on *demonstrable* compliance – through comprehensive documentation, risk assessments (including FRIAs), audits, logging, and transparency reports – means that firms must not only *be* compliant but must be able to *prove* their compliance through robust internal processes and verifiable records.[14]

7.15 Consequences of AI Bias in Ireland

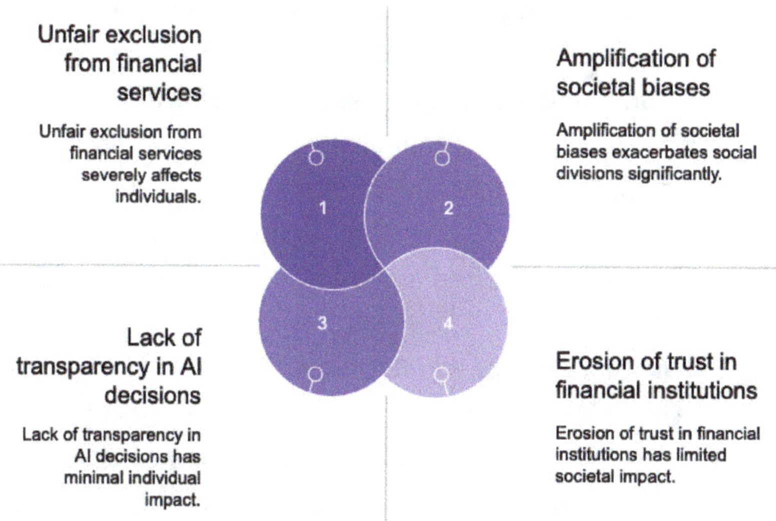

The deployment of biased AI systems within the Irish financial sector carries significant potential consequences, impacting not only individual consumers and broader society but also posing substantial risks to the institutions themselves. These consequences are often interconnected, creating a cascade of negative effects.

7.15.1 Impacts on Irish Consumers and Society

For individuals interacting with the financial system, AI bias can have direct and detrimental effects on their financial well-being and opportunities:

- **Unfair Exclusion and Discrimination:** Biased algorithms can lead to the unfair denial of essential financial products and services, such as loans, mortgages, or insurance policies, or result in individuals being offered significantly less favourable terms (e.g., higher interest rates or premiums) based on their demographic group rather than their individual circumstances.[1] This disproportionately affects vulnerable populations and groups that have faced historical discrimination, thereby reinforcing existing financial inequalities and potentially hindering economic mobility.[38] The potential for exclusion from services they would otherwise have accessed is a specific concern highlighted by the CBI.[15]

- **Lack of Transparency and Recourse:** The 'black box' nature of some complex AI systems can make it difficult, if not impossible, for consumers to understand why a particular decision was made (e.g., why a loan was denied).[3] This lack of transparency hinders their ability to identify potential errors or biases and makes it challenging to seek recourse or contest unfair decisions, undermining fundamental consumer rights.[47] Both GDPR (Article 22) and the EU AI Act (transparency and explainability requirements for high-risk systems) aim to address this challenge.[26]
- **Erosion of Trust:** When AI-driven decisions are perceived as opaque, arbitrary, or unfair, it inevitably erodes consumer trust in the financial institutions deploying these technologies, and potentially in technology itself.[15] Given that trust is fundamental to the financial services relationship, this erosion represents a significant threat.[15]
- **Wider Societal Harm:** Beyond individual impacts, the systematic amplification of societal biases through widely

deployed AI systems can have broader negative consequences, potentially exacerbating social divisions, limiting opportunities for certain communities, and undermining efforts towards greater financial inclusion and social cohesion.[1]

The potential harm is far from abstract; it translates into tangible difficulties for individuals navigating essential financial aspects of their lives within Ireland.[1]

7.15.2 Risks and Liabilities for Financial Institutions

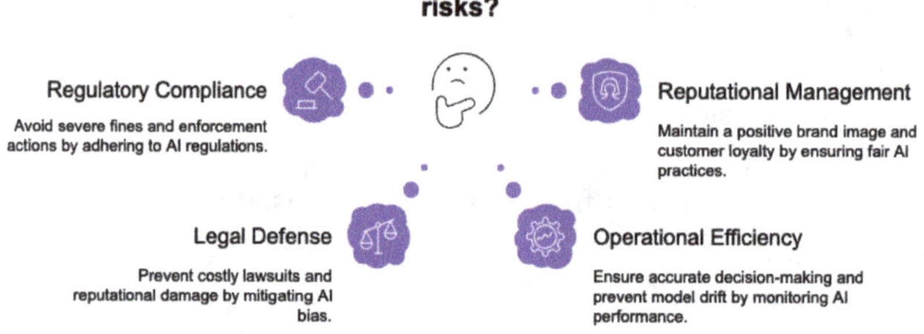

For the institutions deploying AI, failing to adequately address bias creates exposure to a range of significant risks:

- **Regulatory Penalties and Enforcement:** Non-compliance with the EU AI Act can result in severe fines, potentially reaching up to €35 million or 7% of global annual turnover, whichever is higher.[18] GDPR breaches also carry substantial penalties. Financial institutions face enforcement actions from the CBI and other designated national authorities responsible for overseeing AI Act compliance and fundamental rights protection.[32]
- **Reputational Damage:** Public exposure of biased AI systems can lead to significant reputational harm, damaging the institution's brand image and public standing.[1] This can result in loss of customer loyalty, difficulties in attracting and retaining talent, and increased public and political scrutiny.
- **Legal Challenges:** Institutions may face litigation from individuals or consumer advocacy groups alleging discrimination resulting from biased AI decision-making.[51] Such lawsuits can be costly, time-consuming, and further

damage reputation.

- **Operational Risks:** Biased algorithms can lead to flawed decision-making, impacting business outcomes. For example, an overly conservative credit scoring model might reject too many creditworthy applicants, while a poorly calibrated one might underestimate risk. Furthermore, 'model drift' – where a model's performance degrades or becomes more biased over time due to changes in the underlying data patterns – poses an ongoing operational risk if not actively monitored and managed.[20]
- **Reduced Market Access and Competitiveness:** As regulatory expectations and public awareness increase, institutions that fail to demonstrate a commitment to fair and responsible AI may find their ability to deploy these technologies constrained. They may also lose competitiveness compared to peers who successfully build customer trust through demonstrably fair practices.[1]

These risks are interconnected and can create a negative feedback loop. A regulatory fine can trigger negative press, leading to reputational damage, customer attrition, and potentially further legal challenges. This complex risk landscape provides a strong incentive for institutions to move beyond a purely compliance-driven approach towards proactively embedding fairness and ethical considerations into their AI strategies and operations.[1] Ultimately, building and maintaining trust through responsible AI practices is not just an ethical or regulatory requirement, but increasingly a prerequisite for the sustainable adoption and long-term viability of AI in the financial sector.[15]

7.16 A Toolkit for Mitigation: Practical Strategies and Techniques

Recognising the potential for bias and understanding its consequences necessitates the implementation of practical strategies and techniques to mitigate these risks throughout the AI system's lifecycle. Effective mitigation requires a multi-layered approach, combining technical solutions with robust governance, diligent monitoring, and meaningful human oversight. No single technique is sufficient; rather, a combination of measures tailored to the specific application and its associated risks is required.[26]

7.16.1 Proactive Measures: Data Governance and Feature Engineering

Addressing bias often begins with the data used to train and test AI models. Key practices include:

- **Diverse and Representative Data Collection:** Actively work to ensure that data collection processes capture the diversity of the target population. This involves seeking varied data sources and employing techniques like stratified sampling to ensure adequate representation of different demographic groups.[2] Consideration should be given to alternative data sources that might provide a more holistic view of individuals, particularly those underserved by traditional data points.[26]

- **Data Quality and Cleaning:** Rigorous processes are needed to identify and rectify errors, inconsistencies, and outliers within datasets.[3] The provenance and reliability of data sources, especially external or third-party data, must be carefully verified.[60]
- **Bias Detection in Data:** Employ statistical methods and specialised tools to audit datasets before use, specifically looking for imbalances, skewed distributions, or correlations that might indicate potential bias against protected groups.[42]
- **Data Pre-processing Techniques:**
    - *Balancing:* Where datasets exhibit significant underrepresentation of certain groups, techniques like undersampling the majority class, oversampling the minority class, or generating synthetic data points (data augmentation) can be used to create more balanced training sets.[20] These techniques must be applied carefully to avoid introducing other distortions.
    - *Careful Feature Selection/Engineering:* Input features should be critically analysed for their potential to act as proxies for protected characteristics (e.g., postcode, certain types of purchasing behaviour). Problematic features may need to be removed, transformed, or replaced with less discriminatory alternatives, while ensuring that features crucial for achieving fairness are not inadvertently eliminated.[20]

- **Data Governance Framework:**

- Establish comprehensive data governance policies and procedures covering the entire data lifecycle (collection, storage, access, usage, quality control, security, retention, deletion). These frameworks must align with the requirements of the EU AI Act (particularly for high-risk systems) and GDPR.[14] Implementing centralised data management systems, such as data lakes, can facilitate consistency, control, and security.[60]

7.16.2 During Development: Fairness-Aware Modelling and Testing

Choices made during the model development and training phase significantly impact fairness:

- **Algorithm Selection:** Where feasible and appropriate for the task, consider using more inherently interpretable models (e.g., linear regression, decision trees) as they make it easier to understand the decision-making process and identify potential biases.[57] Be mindful that highly complex 'black-box' models can obscure biases, making them harder to detect and rectify.[20]
- **Fairness-Aware Algorithms:** Incorporate techniques designed to explicitly promote fairness during the model training process. These can include:
  - *Pre-processing:* Adjusting the training data before feeding it to the model.
  - *In-processing:* Adding fairness constraints directly into the model's optimisation objective during training (e.g., techniques like adversarial debiasing, which trains the model to make predictions that are simultaneously accurate and non-discriminatory across groups).[38]
  - *Post-processing:* Adjusting the model's outputs after predictions have been made to improve fairness across groups.[38]
- **Fairness Metrics and Testing:** Define clear, contextually appropriate fairness metrics *before* training begins. Regularly test the model's performance against these metrics across relevant demographic subgroups throughout the development process.[26] Common metrics include:

- *Demographic Parity (or Statistical Parity):* Aims for similar rates of positive outcomes (e.g., loan approval) across different groups.[26]
- *Equal Opportunity:* Aims for similar true positive rates (e.g., correctly identifying creditworthy applicants) across groups.[26]
- *Equalized Odds:* Aims for similar true positive rates AND similar false positive rates across groups.[38]
- *Disparate Impact Analysis:* Examines whether the model's outcomes result in significantly different adverse effects for different subgroups.[26] Specialised toolkits like IBM AI Fairness 360, Google's What-If Tool, and Microsoft's Fairlearn can assist in measuring and visualising fairness.[42]

- **Robustness and Stress Testing:** Evaluate the model's performance and fairness under a variety of conditions, including simulated stress scenarios (e.g., market downturns) or using synthetic data designed to specifically challenge potential biases.[42]

7.16.3 Detection and Monitoring: Fairness Metrics and Auditing Tools

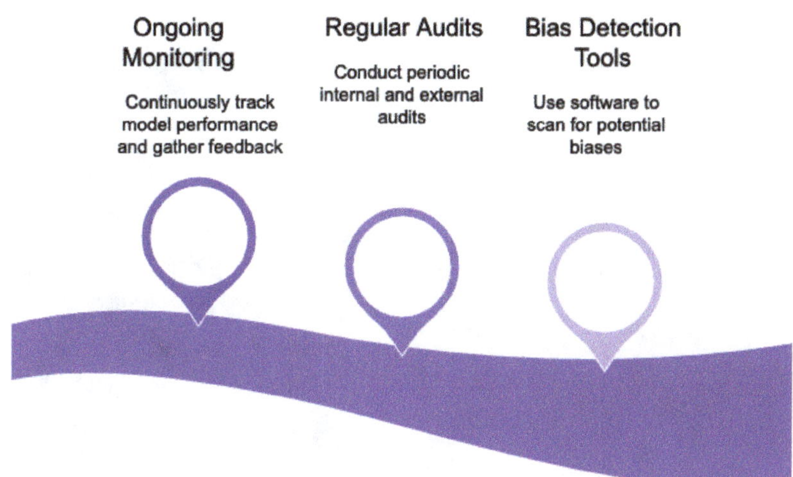

Bias mitigation is not a one-off task; ongoing vigilance is required after deployment:

- **Ongoing Monitoring:** Continuously track the deployed model's performance, including key fairness metrics, to detect any degradation, drift, or emergence of new biases over time.[20] Establish robust feedback loops to capture information about potentially biased outcomes reported by users or identified through other channels.[45]
- **Regular Audits:** Conduct periodic internal audits (and potentially independent external audits) of AI systems to assess their fairness, accuracy, robustness, and compliance with regulations and internal policies.[2] Maintaining a

comprehensive inventory of all AI models, including their risk ratings, is essential for effective auditing and management.[19]

- **Bias Detection Tools:** Leverage software tools designed to automatically scan data and model outputs for statistical indicators of potential bias.[42]

7.16.4 Essential Pillars: Transparency, Explainability (XAI), and Human Oversight

These three elements are increasingly recognised as fundamental components of responsible AI:

- **Transparency:** Be open about how and where AI is being used. Document the development process, data sources, modelling choices, and evaluation results thoroughly.[57] Provide clear, understandable information to deployers, users, regulators, and affected individuals about the AI system's purpose, capabilities, limitations, and how decisions are made.[14] This includes meeting specific disclosure requirements under regulations like the AI Act and GDPR.[26]
- **Explainable AI (XAI):** Employ techniques that make the reasoning behind AI decisions understandable to humans.[2] This can involve using inherently interpretable models or applying post-hoc explanation methods (like SHAP or LIME) to more complex models to identify the key factors driving a specific prediction.[57] Data visualisation tools can also help

reveal patterns and potential biases.[57] Explainability is particularly critical for high-stakes decisions (like loan application denials) to enable meaningful review and challenge.[26] The growing emphasis on XAI from regulators and stakeholders suggests that opaque 'black-box' models will face increasing scrutiny, especially in high-risk areas.[14]

- **Human Oversight:** Ensure meaningful human involvement in the AI lifecycle, particularly for high-risk systems. This doesn't just mean having a human 'in the loop', but designing processes where humans can effectively monitor, understand, question, intervene in, and potentially override AI decisions when necessary.[14] Clear procedures, roles, responsibilities, and training are needed for those performing oversight functions.[14] It is crucial, however, to implement human oversight carefully, with clear guidelines and potentially structured review processes, to avoid merely substituting algorithmic bias with inconsistent or biased human judgment.[20] Techniques like human-in-the-loop monitoring can help correct biased model behaviours in real-time.[42]

7.16.5 Organisational Measures

Technical solutions must be supported by organisational structures and culture:

- **Diverse Teams:** Actively promote diversity (in terms of demographics, expertise, and perspectives) within the teams responsible for developing, testing, and overseeing AI systems. Diverse teams are better equipped to identify potential biases and challenge assumptions.[42]
- **Ethical Guidelines and Culture:** Establish clear, actionable ethical principles or codes of conduct for AI development and deployment, anchored in the organisation's values.[42] Foster an organisational culture that prioritises ethical considerations and encourages open discussion about fairness and potential harms.[42]
- **Training and Awareness:** Provide comprehensive and ongoing training to all relevant staff (developers, data scientists, risk managers, compliance officers, business users, leadership) on AI concepts, ethical considerations, bias detection, mitigation techniques, and regulatory requirements.[16] Organisations like the Institute of Banking (IOB) offer relevant introductory courses.[4]

7.16.6 Mitigation Techniques Mapped to AI Lifecycle Stages

To provide a practical overview, the following table maps key mitigation techniques to the stages of the AI lifecycle where they are most relevant. This illustrates that bias mitigation is an end-to-end process, not a single step.

AI Lifecycle Stage	Data Governance	Algorithmic Techniques	Testing/ Metrics	Transparency/XAI	Human Oversight	Org. Measures
Problem Definition	Define fairness objectives	Consider model interpretability needs	Define fairness metrics		Involve diverse stakeholders	Establish ethical guidelines
Data Collection/Prep	Diverse data sourcing; Stratified sampling; Data quality checks; Bias detection in data; Feature analysis (proxies)	Data balancing (sampling, augmentation); Feature engineering /selection	Audit data for bias	Document data sources/lineage	Review data collection strategy	Diverse data teams
Model Dev/Training	Ensure representative training data	Fairness-aware algorithms (pre-, in-, post-processing) ; Interpretable models	Test fairness during training	Document model design/assumptions	Review modelling choices	Training on fair modelling
Testing/ Validation	Use representative test data		Comprehensive fairness testing	Explainability testing (XAI tools)	Independent model validation	Diverse testing teams

			(metrics, subgroups); Robustness/stress testing			
Deployment	Monitor input data relevance		Pre-deployment fairness checks	Provide user transparency info	Define oversight procedures	User training on limitations
Monitoring/Maintenance	Ongoing data quality monitoring	Model retraining strategies	Continuous bias/fairness monitoring; Regular audits	Monitor explainability drift	Human-in-the-loop review; Feedback mechanisms	Ongoing training; Culture reinforcement

Note: This table provides examples; specific techniques and their applicability may vary based on the AI system and context.

7.17 Addressing AI Bias in Practice

While the principles and techniques for mitigating AI bias are becoming clearer, understanding how these are being applied within the specific context of Irish financial services provides valuable practical insights. Although detailed public disclosures on specific mitigation strategies remain limited, several initiatives and examples signal growing awareness and action within the sector.

7.17.1 Case Study: AIB's Initiative on Algorithmic Fairness

Allied Irish Banks (AIB) has undertaken work focused on algorithmic fairness, notably through a collaboration with Accenture.[39] While specific technical details of the "Algorithmic Fairness Tool" or framework are not publicly available in the reviewed materials [9], reports on the collaboration highlight key organisational factors that enabled progress:

- **Executive Sponsorship:** Strong buy-in and support from senior leadership created an environment conducive to exploring the sensitive and complex issues surrounding bias and fairness.[39]
- **Multidisciplinary Approach:** The initiative involved an internal, cross-functional team working collaboratively with external experts, allowing for diverse perspectives and expertise.[40]
- **Open Culture:** Leadership support fostered a culture where team members felt empowered to ask difficult questions, raise concerns, and thoroughly investigate potential sources of bias without fear of reprisal.[39] This psychological safety is crucial when dealing with ethically charged topics.

- **Practical Framework:** The collaboration reportedly resulted in a Responsible AI playbook designed to translate high-level principles into concrete actions across the project lifecycle, clarifying activities, roles, and responsibilities.[40]
- **Phased Rollout:** AIB piloted its approach to algorithmic fairness modelling and AI, indicating a measured implementation strategy, with plans noted in a 2021 report for wider rollout.[61]
- **Enhanced Governance:** This initiative occurred alongside significant enhancements to AIB's overall Data Governance structure and control environment.[61]

This example, although lacking technical specifics, underscores the critical importance of organisational factors – leadership commitment, cross-functional collaboration, and an open culture – in successfully tackling algorithmic fairness.[39] It suggests that addressing bias effectively requires more than just technical tools; it necessitates significant organisational change and support.

7.17.2 Case Study: Central Bank & Academia Collaboration on Responsible AI

The Central Bank of Ireland has proactively engaged with the academic community to build knowledge and capacity around responsible AI. Its partnership with the Insight Research Centre for Data Analytics at University of Limerick involves funding a dedicated PhD programme.[54]

- **Focus Areas:** The research explicitly targets challenging issues relevant to the financial sector, including responsible AI, AI risks and regulation, financial crime, cyber risk, and climate risk.[54]
- **Objectives:** The collaboration aims to advance research that builds public trust in AI, improves policy outcomes through evidence-based insights, and cultivates the next generation of AI talent in Ireland capable of addressing these complex challenges.[54]
- **Strategic Alignment:** This initiative aligns directly with Ireland's National AI Strategy and reflects the CBI's recognition of AI's importance and associated risks.[54]

This collaboration highlights a strategic approach to addressing AI risks, including bias, by investing in foundational research and talent development. It signifies the value placed on collaboration between regulators, industry, and academia in navigating the complexities of responsible AI adoption within the Irish financial ecosystem.[54]

7.17.3 Case Study: Industry Commitments (e.g., Insurance Ireland)

Regulatory actions can also drive industry-level changes relevant to fairness. The European Commission's decision regarding Insurance Ireland provides an example.[49]

- **Issue:** The case involved access to Insurance Link, an information exchange system used by Irish insurers.
- **Outcome:** The Commission made legally binding the commitments offered by Insurance Ireland to ensure fair, objective, transparent, and non-discriminatory access to the system for all members and applicants.[49]
- **Relevance to AI Bias:** While not directly about AI algorithms, ensuring fair and non-discriminatory access to foundational data infrastructure like Insurance Link is crucial. AI systems trained on or reliant upon such data could inherit biases if access to the underlying data pool is itself discriminatory. This case underscores the importance of fairness considerations extending to the data ecosystem supporting AI applications.

7.17.4 Other Relevant Irish Context/Examples

Beyond specific case studies focused on bias mitigation frameworks, other activities within the Irish financial services landscape are relevant:

- **Innovation Hubs and Fintech Engagement:** Major Irish banks like Bank of Ireland, AIB, and Permanent TSB (along with KBC and Ulster Bank prior to their market exits) have established innovation labs or supported fintech hubs (e.g., Dogpatch Labs, PorterShed).[6] These initiatives foster collaboration with fintechs, which often pioneer the use of newer technologies like AI, potentially including solutions relevant to areas where bias can occur.[6]
- **Activities of Key Firms:**
    - **Stripe:** With significant operations in Ireland [11], Stripe utilises AI and machine learning extensively, particularly for fraud detection (Radar product).[5] Managing bias in fraud models is critical to avoid unfairly impacting legitimate users.
    - **Fexco and TransferMate:** As prominent Irish fintechs involved in payments and international transfers [13], they operate in areas where AI might be used for risk assessment, compliance checks (AML/KYC), or process automation, all carrying potential bias risks.
    - **Inscribe:** Co-founded by Irish entrepreneurs, Inscribe uses AI specifically for fraud detection and risk assessment based on document analysis (bank statements, tax forms), directly engaging with high-risk areas where fairness is paramount.[50]
    - **Permanent TSB:** The bank implemented IBM Business

Automation Workflow technology to streamline its complaints management process.[41] While not explicitly an AI bias mitigation tool, effectively capturing and analysing customer complaints can be a valuable source of feedback for identifying potential systemic issues or perceived unfairness arising from automated processes.[41]

- **Skills Development:** Initiatives like the IFS Skillnet, apprenticeships, and partnerships between industry and educational institutions aim to build the necessary talent pipeline for the future of financial services, which increasingly includes data science and AI skills.[12] Developing talent with an awareness of responsible AI principles is crucial.

While publicly documented examples of specific, implemented bias mitigation frameworks within Irish financial institutions are currently limited, the available evidence points towards growing recognition of the issue. High-level initiatives at major banks, regulatory engagement through research partnerships, and the activities of AI-reliant fintechs operating in Ireland suggest that capability and awareness are building.[39] The focus appears to be on establishing foundational governance structures, understanding the problem space, and building capacity, rather than widespread deployment of specific technical debiasing tools at this stage.

7.18 Building a Foundation: An Implementation Framework for Irish Firms

Given the regulatory imperatives and the potential consequences of AI bias, Irish financial institutions need a structured approach to embed fairness and responsibility into their AI practices. A comprehensive implementation framework, adaptable to the size and complexity of the firm and its AI usage, is essential. This framework should not exist in isolation but should integrate with existing governance, risk management, and compliance structures.[16] Relying solely on technical fixes is insufficient; a holistic organisational approach is required.[16]

7.18.1 Key Pillars of a Responsible AI Framework

Building a Robust Framework for Ethical and Responsible AI Development

Governance & Accountability

Ensures leadership commitment, clear structures, and ethical policies for AI development.

Integration with Risk Management

Identifies, assesses, and categorizes AI risks within existing risk management frameworks.

AI Lifecycle Controls

Implements controls to mitigate bias and ensure data governance throughout the AI lifecycle.

Transparency, Explainability & Oversight

Provides transparency, explainability, and human oversight in AI decision-making.

Capacity Building & Culture

Fosters ethical culture, diversity, and stakeholder engagement in AI development.

A robust framework for managing AI bias and promoting responsible AI can be built upon five key pillars:

- **Pillar 1: Governance & Accountability:**
  - **Leadership Commitment:** Secure explicit buy-in and oversight from the Board and senior management,

demonstrating a clear tone from the top regarding the importance of ethical and fair AI.[44]

  - **Clear Structures:** Establish clear roles, responsibilities, and lines of accountability for AI development, deployment, and oversight. This might involve creating a dedicated AI Ethics Committee or Board, assigning specific responsibilities to existing functions, or establishing a dedicated AI governance/compliance function.[14]
  - **Policies & Standards:** Develop and disseminate comprehensive AI policies and ethical guidelines that explicitly address fairness, non-discrimination, transparency, accountability, and data governance, aligning with company values and regulatory requirements.[14]

- **Pillar 2: Integration with Risk Management:**
  - **AI Risk Identification & Assessment:** Systematically identify and assess the risks associated with AI systems, including bias, discrimination, operational failures, security vulnerabilities, and ethical concerns. Integrate these into the firm's existing Enterprise Risk Management (ERM) framework.[16]
  - **Risk Categorisation:** Classify AI systems based on their potential risk level, paying particular attention to the 'high-risk' definition under the EU AI Act.[19]
  - **Impact Assessments:** Conduct thorough risk assessments, including Fundamental Rights Impact Assessments (FRIAs) for high-risk systems before deployment, evaluating potential harms to individuals and society.[19]

- **Model Inventory:** Maintain a detailed, up-to-date inventory of all AI models in use or development, including their purpose, data sources, risk classification, and validation status.[19]
- **Operational Resilience:** Ensure AI risks are considered within the firm's operational resilience framework, aligning with requirements like the Digital Operational Resilience Act (DORA).[16]

- **Pillar 3: AI Lifecycle Controls:**
  - **End-to-End Mitigation:** Implement specific technical and procedural controls to detect and mitigate bias at each stage of the AI lifecycle – from problem formulation and data handling through model development, testing, deployment, and ongoing monitoring – as detailed in Section 5.[26]
  - **Robust Data Governance:** Enforce strict data governance practices focused on data quality, representativeness, bias detection, and compliance with GDPR and AI Act requirements.[14]
  - **Validation & Testing:** Establish rigorous validation and testing protocols that explicitly include fairness assessments alongside traditional accuracy and performance metrics before any AI system is deployed.[60] Consider parallel running of new and old models during transition.[60]
- **Pillar 4: Transparency, Explainability & Oversight:**
  - **Transparency Measures:** Implement mechanisms to ensure appropriate transparency for different stakeholders (users, customers, regulators) regarding AI system operation and decision-making.[14]

    - **Explainability (XAI):** Deploy XAI techniques suitable for the complexity and risk level of the AI system, enabling meaningful understanding of how outcomes are produced.[26]
    - **Human Oversight:** Design and implement effective human oversight procedures, ensuring humans have the capacity, training, and authority to monitor, interpret, intervene, and override AI systems where necessary, particularly for high-risk applications.[14]
    - **Documentation & Record-Keeping:** Maintain thorough documentation of AI systems, development processes, data lineage, testing results, decisions made, and oversight activities to demonstrate compliance and facilitate audits.[14]
- **Pillar 5: Capacity Building & Culture:**
    - **Training & Awareness:** Invest in continuous training programs to build AI literacy and awareness of ethical considerations, bias risks, and mitigation strategies among all relevant staff.[4]
    - **Ethical Culture:** Foster an organisational culture that values ethical behaviour, encourages critical questioning, and promotes responsibility in AI development and use.[42]
    - **Diversity & Inclusion:** Promote diversity within AI teams to bring broader perspectives and reduce the risk of embedded cognitive biases.[42]
    - **Stakeholder Engagement:** Engage with relevant internal and external stakeholders to understand concerns and expectations regarding AI fairness.[43]

7.18.2 Developing a Tailored Roadmap

Implementing such a framework requires a structured roadmap, tailored to the institution's specific circumstances. A risk-based and proportional approach is key, focusing efforts where the risks are highest.[14] Potential steps include:

1. **AI Inventory & Risk Classification:** Conduct a thorough inventory of all existing and planned AI systems across the organisation. Classify each system according to its potential risk level, using the EU AI Act categories (minimal, limited, high, unacceptable) as a primary guide.[16]
2. **Gap Analysis:** Compare current practices, policies, and controls against the requirements outlined in the Responsible AI framework pillars and relevant regulations (AI Act, CBI expectations, GDPR). Identify key gaps and areas needing improvement.[34]
3. **Prioritisation:** Based on the risk classification and gap analysis, prioritise actions. Focus initial efforts on addressing gaps related to high-risk AI systems and areas posing the greatest potential for consumer harm or regulatory non-compliance. The demanding nature of high-risk requirements under the AI Act makes this prioritisation crucial for efficient resource allocation.[14]
4. **Action Plan Development:** Create a detailed action plan outlining specific, measurable, achievable, relevant, and time-bound (SMART) steps to close the identified gaps. Assign clear ownership for each action and establish realistic timelines, considering regulatory deadlines (e.g., for AI Act compliance).[18]
5. **Implementation & Monitoring:** Execute the action plan,

deploying necessary resources. Establish mechanisms to continuously monitor progress, measure the effectiveness of implemented controls, and adapt the plan as needed based on evolving risks, technologies, and regulations.

7.18.3 Assigning Roles and Responsibilities

Clear allocation of responsibilities is vital for effective implementation. While specific structures will vary, potential roles and their contributions include:

- **Board / Senior Management:** Ultimate oversight, setting strategic direction, ensuring adequate resources, fostering ethical culture.[44]
- **Chief Risk Officer (CRO) / Risk Management Function:** Integrating AI risks into ERM, overseeing risk assessments (including FRIAs), defining risk appetite for AI.[16]
- **Chief Data Officer (CDO) / Data Governance Lead:** Ensuring data quality, representativeness, managing data lineage, overseeing data-related bias checks.[14]
- **Head of AI / Data Science / IT:** Leading model development, implementing technical bias mitigation techniques, ensuring model validation and testing, deploying XAI tools.[23]
- **Compliance Officer:** Ensuring adherence to relevant regulations (AI Act, GDPR, Consumer Protection Code), reviewing policies, monitoring compliance activities.[23]
- **Legal Counsel:** Advising on legal risks, interpreting regulations, reviewing contracts with third-party AI vendors.
- **Human Resources (HR):** Developing and delivering training programs, promoting diversity in AI teams, ensuring fairness in AI used for HR purposes.[42]
- **Internal Audit:** Independently verifying the effectiveness of AI governance, risk management, and control processes.[2]
- **Business Line Owners / Deployers:** Understanding AI system limitations, ensuring appropriate use, providing input for development and testing, participating in human oversight.[19]

Leveraging existing governance committees and risk management structures (e.g., Model Risk Management committees, Data Governance councils, Compliance committees) and adapting their mandates to include AI-specific considerations is generally more effective than creating entirely new, isolated AI governance bodies.[19] This promotes integration and ensures AI risks are managed within the broader organisational context.

7.18.4 Implementation Framework Summary

The following table summarises the key components of the proposed framework and potential lead responsibilities within a typical financial institution.

Framework Pillar	Key Actions/Components	Potential Lead Responsibility
1. Governance & Accountability	Establish AI Ethics Policy/Guidelines; Define Roles & Responsibilities; Set up Oversight Body (e.g., AI Ethics Committee)	Board / Senior Management / Compliance / Legal
2. Integration with Risk Management	Maintain AI Inventory & Risk Classification; Integrate AI into ERM; Conduct Risk Assessments/FRIAs; Align with DORA	Risk Management / CRO / Model Risk

3. AI Lifecycle Controls	Implement Data Governance for AI; Apply Fairness Testing & Mitigation Techniques; Ensure Robust Validation	Data Science / IT / Data Governance / Model Risk
4. Transparency, Explainability & Oversight	Deploy XAI Tools & Techniques; Establish Transparency Protocols; Implement Human Oversight Procedures; Ensure Documentation	IT / Data Science / Business Lines / Compliance
5. Capacity Building & Culture	Develop & Deliver Staff Training; Promote Diverse Teams; Foster Ethical Awareness; Engage Stakeholders	HR / Compliance / Leadership / Communications / All Functions

Note: Lead responsibilities are indicative and may vary based on organisational structure.

7.19 Your Role in Ensuring Fairness: A Practical Guide for Staff

Addressing AI bias is not solely the responsibility of data scientists or compliance officers; it requires collective awareness and action across all relevant roles within a financial institution.[15] Every staff member who interacts with AI systems, the data they use, their outputs, or the policies governing them has a part to play in fostering fairness and responsibility. Practical guidance must be tailored, as the way different roles encounter and can influence bias varies significantly.[26]

7.19.1 Recognising Potential Bias in Day-to-Day Work (Role-Specific Examples)

Developing an awareness of how bias might manifest in specific work contexts is the first step:

- **Data Analysts / Data Scientists:**
  - *Critically evaluate data sources:* Question their origin, collection methods, and potential for historical or representation bias. Look for skewed distributions or missing demographics.[1]
  - *Challenge proxies:* Be sceptical of using features that might indirectly correlate with protected characteristics.[20]
  - *Test for fairness:* Actively test models for disparate outcomes across different demographic subgroups using appropriate fairness metrics, not just overall accuracy.[26]
  - *Document thoroughly:* Record assumptions made, data limitations, feature engineering choices, and fairness testing results.[57]

- **IT / Developers / Engineers:**
    - *Consider design impacts:* Understand how architectural choices, data pipelines, and system integrations might inadvertently introduce or propagate bias.[23]
    - *Ensure robust logging:* Implement comprehensive logging capabilities to enable traceability and auditing of AI system behaviour.[34]
    - *Prioritise security:* Implement strong security measures to protect data integrity and prevent malicious manipulation that could introduce bias.[34]
- **Risk Managers / Compliance Officers:**
    - *Stay informed:* Understand the evolving regulatory landscape (AI Act, CBI guidance, GDPR) and internal policies related to AI bias and fairness.[16]
    - *Scrutinise validation:* Review model validation documentation to ensure fairness assessments were conducted rigorously and appropriately.[38]
    - *Oversee assessments:* Ensure that risk assessments, including FRIAs for high-risk systems, adequately address potential bias and discriminatory impacts.[31]
    - *Monitor adherence:* Check that established policies and procedures for responsible AI are being followed in practice.

- **Business Users / Operations Staff (Interacting with AI Outputs):**
  - *Guard against automation bias:* Do not blindly trust AI outputs. Be prepared to question recommendations that seem counterintuitive, unfair, or lack clear justification.[15]
  - *Identify anomalies:* Flag unexpected patterns or consistently adverse outcomes for certain customer groups based on AI recommendations.
  - *Understand limitations:* Be aware of the known limitations and appropriate use cases for the AI tools being used.
  - *Follow oversight procedures:* Adhere to established protocols for human review, intervention, escalation, or overriding AI decisions.[26]
- **Customer-Facing Staff:**
  - *Listen actively:* Pay attention to customer feedback, complaints, or queries related to perceived unfairness, lack of explanation, or difficulties with automated systems.[41]
  - *Escalate concerns:* Report customer concerns regarding potential bias or unexplained decisions through designated internal channels.
- **Human Resources (HR) Professionals:**
  - *Vet HR Tech:* Ensure any AI tools used for recruitment, screening, promotion, or performance management are rigorously assessed for potential bias before deployment.[1]
  - *Promote diversity:* Champion diversity and inclusion initiatives, particularly within teams involved in AI development, to bring wider perspectives.[42]

- **Leadership / Management:**
    - *Champion responsibility:* Actively promote the importance of ethical and fair AI throughout the organisation.[39]
    - *Allocate resources:* Ensure sufficient funding, time, and personnel are dedicated to bias mitigation and responsible AI initiatives.[44]
    - *Foster ethical culture:* Create an environment where ethical considerations are paramount and staff feel safe to raise concerns.[39]
    - *Ensure accountability:* Hold individuals and teams accountable for adhering to responsible AI policies and practices.[44]

7.19.2 Following Internal Procedures and Best Practices

Adherence to established organisational frameworks is crucial for consistent and effective bias management:

- **Know and Follow Policies:** Familiarise yourself with and strictly adhere to the firm's AI governance framework, specific policies on data usage and model development, and overarching ethical guidelines.[42]
- **Complete Training:** Actively participate in and complete all mandatory training related to AI ethics, bias awareness, data protection, and relevant regulatory requirements.[4]
- **Use Approved Tools:** Utilise the organisation's designated tools and standardised methodologies for tasks like bias detection, fairness measurement, and model explainability.[42]
- **Maintain Records:** Follow all required procedures for documenting work, data sources, testing results, decisions made, and any overrides or interventions related to AI

systems, ensuring traceability and auditability.[14]

7.19.3 Raising Concerns and Contributing to Solutions

Identifying and addressing bias often requires critical thinking and open communication. Creating a psychologically safe environment, as highlighted in the AIB example, is vital so that staff feel comfortable speaking up.[39]

- **Know the Channels:** Understand the established internal mechanisms for reporting potential bias, ethical dilemmas, or compliance concerns related to AI systems. Ensure these channels allow for reporting without fear of negative consequences.
- **Participate Actively:** Engage constructively in team discussions, model reviews, and validation processes where fairness and ethical implications are considered.
- **Offer Diverse Perspectives:** Leverage your unique background, experience, and role-specific knowledge to contribute diverse viewpoints during the design, development, testing, and deployment phases of AI systems.[42]

7.19.4 Conclusion: Fostering a Culture of Responsible AI

Ultimately, mitigating AI bias and ensuring the responsible use of AI in Irish financial services is a shared responsibility that extends across the entire organisation. It requires more than just technical fixes or compliance checklists; it demands a fundamental cultural shift towards embedding ethical awareness and critical thinking into everyday practices.

Continuous learning and vigilance are essential, as AI technologies, data sources, and societal expectations are constantly evolving. By embracing the principles and practices outlined in this guide, staff at all levels can contribute to building AI systems that are not only powerful and efficient but also fair, transparent, and trustworthy. This commitment is crucial for protecting consumers, safeguarding the institution's reputation and stability, complying with regulatory obligations, and ultimately, harnessing the transformative potential of AI for the benefit of the institution, its customers, and the wider Irish society.[1]

7.20 References

1. Mitigating Artificial Intelligence Bias in Financial Systems: A Review of Debiasing Techniques - AWS, accessed on April 21, 2025, https://sdiopr.s3.ap-south-1.amazonaws.com/2024/Dec/20_Dec_24/AJRCOS_127815/Ms_AJRCOS_127815.pdf
2. Mitigating AI bias in financial decision-making: A DEI perspective - World Journal of Advanced Research and Reviews, accessed on April 21, 2025, https://wjarr.com/sites/default/files/WJARR-2024-3894.pdf
3. Discussion Paper: Impact of AI on Financial Services Sector Workforce, accessed on April 21, 2025, https://www.fsunion.org/assets/files/pdf/fsu_impact_of_ai_on_fss_workforce_v2.pdf
4. Skills Certificate - Intro to Responsible AI for Financial Services - Programme | IOB, accessed on April 21, 2025, https://iob.ie/programme/skills-cert-intro-to-responsible-ai-for-financial-services
5. A guide to fintech innovation | Stripe, accessed on April 21, 2025, https://stripe.com/en-jp/resources/more/fintech-innovation-where-financial-technology-is-today-and-where-its-heading
6. Banking on Innovation, accessed on April 21, 2025, https://bpfi.ie/wp-content/uploads/2021/07/Banking-on-Innovation-Report-Final.pdf
7. Bank of Ireland prepares for the Netflix-style future of banking - Silicon Republic, accessed on April 21, 2025, https://www.siliconrepublic.com/enterprise/bank-of-ireland-data-science
8. What is a fintech app? Types and how businesses use them - Stripe, accessed on April 21, 2025, https://stripe.com/ae/resources/more/what-is-a-fintech-app-types-and-how-businesses-use-them

9. Harnessing AI to drive financial services enterprise transformation in Ireland, accessed on April 21, 2025, https://www.irishtimes.com/sponsored/2025/03/25/harnessing-ai-to-drive-financial-services-enterprise-transformation-in-ireland/
10. Banks: are you AI ready?, accessed on April 21, 2025, https://ava-p-001.sitecorecontenthub.cloud/api/public/content/3b317ce855104aa6afc50f1ecf7490b0
11. Global Legal Insights FinTech 2024 Ireland chapter, accessed on April 21, 2025, https://www.walkersglobal.com/Insights/2024/09/Global-Legal-Insights-FinTech-2024-Ireland-chapter
12. Financial Services in Ireland – Skills of the Future, accessed on April 21, 2025, https://www.skillnetireland.ie/uploads/attachments/Financial-Services-in-Ireland-%E2%80%93-Skills-of-the-Future-report_%282%29.pdf
13. Fintech in Ireland: recognising the opportunities and managing risks - businessnews.ie, accessed on April 21, 2025, https://www.businessnews.ie/fintech/what-next-for-the-future-of-fintech/
14. FIG Top 5 at 5 - 13/02/2025 - Matheson, accessed on April 21, 2025, https://www.matheson.com/insights/detail/fig-top-5-at-5---13-02-2025
15. Financial consumer protection and market conduct considerations of ..., accessed on April 21, 2025, https://www.centralbank.ie/news/article/speech-colm-kincaid-financial-consumer-protection-and-market-conduct-considerations-of-AI-in-finance-22-may-2024
16. AI: Considerations for Irish Fund Management Companies | Commercial Law Firm, accessed on April 21, 2025, https://www.dilloneustace.com/insights/ai-considerations-for-irish-fund-management-companies/

17. (PDF) Central Bank Perspectives on AI: A Comparative Analysis of Key Issues, accessed on April 21, 2025, https://www.researchgate.net/publication/388817991_Central_Bank_Perspectives_on_AI_A_Comparative_Analysis_of_Key_Issues
18. The EU AI Act: key implications for regulated financial institutions - fscom uk, accessed on April 21, 2025, https://fscom.co/uk/blog/the-eu-ai-act-key-implications-for-regulated-financial-institutions/
19. The EU AI Act: What it means for your business | EY - Switzerland, accessed on April 21, 2025, https://www.ey.com/en_ch/insights/forensic-integrity-services/the-eu-ai-act-what-it-means-for-your-business
20. www.fca.org.uk, accessed on April 21, 2025, https://www.fca.org.uk/publication/research-notes/literature-review-bias-in-supervised-machine-learning.pdf
21. Research Note: A literature review on bias in supervised machine learning | FCA, accessed on April 21, 2025, https://www.fca.org.uk/publications/research-notes/research-note-literature-review-bias-supervised-machine-learning
22. Public Consultation on National Implementation of EU Harmonised Rules on Artificial Intelligence (AI Act): Submissions received, accessed on April 21, 2025, https://enterprise.gov.ie/en/consultations/consultations-files/public-consultation-on-ai-act-submissions-received.pdf
23. AI Bias in Credit & Loan Processing: Is AI Biased When Assessing Credit Worthiness?, accessed on April 21, 2025, https://www.itmagination.com/blog/credit-loan-processing-ai-biased-when-assessing-credit-worthiness
24. Artificial intelligence bias auditing – current approaches, challenges and lessons from practice | Emerald Insight, accessed on April 21, 2025,

https://www.emerald.com/insight/content/doi/10.1108/raf-01-2025-0006/full/html

25. Tackling the Hidden Artificial Intelligence Bias in the Financial Sector: A Literature Review of the Impacts and Strategies for - Aaltodoc, accessed on April 21, 2025, https://aaltodoc.aalto.fi/server/api/core/bitstreams/fbf38ebf-e590-41b3-a0f4-f2215cec3ee4/content
26. The Ethics of AI in Finance: How to Detect and Prevent Bias, accessed on April 21, 2025, https://corporatefinanceinstitute.com/resources/data-science/ai-ethics-in-finance-detect-prevent-bias/
27. Algorithmic discrimination under the AI Act and the GDPR - European Parliament, accessed on April 21, 2025, https://www.europarl.europa.eu/RegData/etudes/ATAG/2025/769509/EPRS_ATA(2025)769509_EN.pdf
28. AI-based credit default risk assessments require regulation, accessed on April 21, 2025, https://safe-frankfurt.de/news-latest/safe-finance-blog/details/ai-based-credit-default-risk-assessments-require-regulation.html
29. Financial Consumer Protection in Ireland - OECD, accessed on April 21, 2025, https://www.oecd.org/en/publications/financial-consumer-protection-in-ireland_5315c3ca-en.html
30. The EU Commission Guidelines on prohibited AI practices under the AI Act - Arthur Cox, accessed on April 21, 2025, https://www.arthurcox.com/knowledge/the-eu-commission-guidelines-on-prohibited-ai-practices/
31. EU Artificial Intelligence Act - EU AI Act - KPMG Ireland, accessed on April 21, 2025, https://kpmg.com/ie/en/home/insights/2024/01/eu-artificial-intelligence-act-art-int.html
32. Ireland Designates Nine Authorities to Safeguard Fundamental Rights Under the EU AI Act, accessed on April 21, 2025, https://www.williamfry.com/knowledge/ireland-

designates-nine-authorities-to-safeguard-fundamental-rights-under-the-eu-ai-act/

33. The EU AI Act: An Extensive Overview of Europe's Groundbreaking AI Regulation, accessed on April 21, 2025, https://aiireland.ie/2024/07/10/the-eu-ai-act-an-extensive-overview-of-europes-groundbreaking-ai-regulation/
34. The EU AI Act and Its Implications for Credit Risk Models in Banking ..., accessed on April 21, 2025, https://advisense.com/2025/03/19/the-eu-ai-act-and-its-implications-for-credit-risk-models-in-banking/
35. AI in finance - European Commission, accessed on April 21, 2025, https://finance.ec.europa.eu/news/ai-finance-2024-06-19_en
36. 7 data privacy considerations in AI adoption - Grant Thornton Ireland, accessed on April 21, 2025, https://www.grantthornton.ie/insights/factsheets/7-data-privacy-considerations-in-ai-adoption/
37. Decrypting the Craic: The latest updates on data protection, cyber, and AI in Ireland, accessed on April 21, 2025, https://www.hoganlovells.com/en/publications/decrypting-the-craic-the-latest-updates-on-data-protection-cyber-and-ai-in-ireland
38. Mitigating Artificial Intelligence Bias in Financial Systems: A Comparative Analysis of Debiasing Techniques - ResearchGate, accessed on April 21, 2025, https://www.researchgate.net/publication/387252070_Mitigating_Artificial_Intelligence_Bias_in_Financial_Systems_A_Comparative_Analysis_of_Debiasing_Techniques
39. Responsible AI Principles to Practice - Accenture, accessed on April 21, 2025, https://www.accenture.com/us-en/insights/artificial-intelligence/responsible-ai-principles-practice
40. Responsible AI: From Principles to Practice | Accenture, accessed on April 21, 2025,

https://www.accenture.com/content/dam/accenture/final/a-com-migration/pdf/pdf-149/accenture-responsible-ai-final.pdf

41. Permanent TSB - IBM, accessed on April 21, 2025, https://www.ibm.com/case-studies/permanent-tsb-ba
42. Biases in Artificial Intelligence: How to Detect and Reduce Bias in AI Models - Onix-Systems, accessed on April 21, 2025, https://onix-systems.com/blog/ai-bias-detection-and-mitigation
43. AI Bias 101: Understanding and Mitigating Bias in AI Systems - Zendata, accessed on April 21, 2025, https://www.zendata.dev/post/ai-bias-101-understanding-and-mitigating-bias-in-ai-systems
44. CIPL Response to NTIA Request for Comment on AI Accountability Policy, accessed on April 21, 2025, https://www.informationpolicycentre.com/uploads/5/7/1/0/57104281/cipl_response_to_ntia_ai_accountability_policy_june2023.pdf
45. Addressing AI Bias in Financial Forecasting and Cyber Threat Assessments - ResearchGate, accessed on April 21, 2025, https://www.researchgate.net/publication/387099391_Addressing_AI_Bias_in_Financial_Forecasting_and_Cyber_Threat_Assessments
46. Big Data, Big Change: The new AI Act has Big Implications for the Financial Services Sector - IoD Ireland, accessed on April 21, 2025, https://www.iodireland.ie/images/uploads/downloads/8300_IOD_FactSheet_June_Big_Data%2C_Big_Change_The_new_AI_Act_has_Big_Implications_for_the_Financial_Services_Sector.pdf
47. emildai.eu, accessed on April 21, 2025, https://emildai.eu/the-future-of-credit-ai-or-human-judgment/#:~:text=The%20EU%20AI%20Act%20specifically,related%20to%20algorithmic%20credit%20decisions.

48. Algorithmic discrimination in Europe - AI & Equality, accessed on April 21, 2025, https://ai.equineteurope.org/system/files/2021-04/EELN_Algorithmic-discrimination_GERARDS%20and%20XENIDIS_2021.pdf
49. Rising Global Regulation for AI.pdf - Jones Day, accessed on April 21, 2025, https://www.jonesday.com/-/media/files/publications/2022/12/rising-global-regulation-for-artificial-intelligence/files/rising-global-regulation-for-ai/fileattachment/rising-global-regulation-for-ai.pdf?rev=33796f1157824a4eb76e9dc38cfe3dbb
50. Reducing risk with increased intelligence - Threshold VC, accessed on April 21, 2025, https://www.threshold.vc/newsroom/using-ai-to-detect-fraud-assess-risk-and-identify-emerging-trends/
51. A guide to Artificial Intelligence at the workplace - EESC, accessed on April 21, 2025, https://www.eesc.europa.eu/sites/default/files/files/qe-03-21-505-en-n.pdf
52. Remarks by Gerry Cross, Director of Financial Regulation - Policy & Risk, accessed on April 21, 2025, https://www.centralbank.ie/news/article/speech-gerry-cross-Insurance-Industry-Event-on-Responsible-Use-of-Big-Data-and-Related-Technologies-24-june-2024
53. Consumer Protection Code Review Discussion Paper - Central Bank of Ireland, accessed on April 21, 2025, https://www.centralbank.ie/docs/default-source/regulation/consumer-protection/other-codes-of-conduct/consumer-protection-code-review/consumer-protection-code-review-discussion-paper.pdf
54. Central Bank announces funded PhD Programme in AI & Data Science, accessed on April 21, 2025, https://www.centralbank.ie/research-exchange/central-bank-announces-funded-phd-programme-in-ai-data-science

55. Central Bank of Ireland and Insight UL in 'landmark AI collaboration', accessed on April 21, 2025, https://www.insight-centre.org/central-bank-of-ireland-and-insight-ul-in-landmark-ai-collaboration/
56. Irish firms must work to understand ESG obligations under AI Act - Pinsent Masons, accessed on April 21, 2025, https://www.pinsentmasons.com/out-law/analysis/irish-firms-must-understand-esg-obligations-under-ai-act
57. (PDF) Mitigating AI Bias in Financial Decision-Making: A DEI Perspective" - ResearchGate, accessed on April 21, 2025, https://www.researchgate.net/publication/387497792_Mitigating_AI_Bias_in_Financial_Decision-Making_A_DEI_Perspective
58. Ireland's Federated Approach to AI Regulation - Byrne Wallace Shields LLP, accessed on April 21, 2025, https://byrnewallaceshields.com/news-and-recent-work/publications/irelands-federated-approach-to-ai-regulation.html
59. Zooming in on AI - #5: AI under financial regulations in the U.S., EU and U.K. – a comparative assessment of the current state of play: part 1 - A&O Shearman, accessed on April 21, 2025, https://www.aoshearman.com/insights/ao-shearman-on-tech/zooming-in-5-ai-under-financial-regulations-in-the-us-eu-and-uk-a-comparative-assessment-part-1
60. Key Challenges and Regulatory Considerations | FINRA.org, accessed on April 21, 2025, https://www.finra.org/rules-guidance/key-topics/fintech/report/artificial-intelligence-in-the-securities-industry/key-challenges
61. Future-Proof Bank - AIB, accessed on April 21, 2025, https://aib.ie/content/dam/frontdoor/personal/sustainability/04-responding-future-proof-bank.pdf
62. Allied Irish Banks Group (AIB) - business abc, accessed on April 21, 2025, https://businessabc.net/wiki/allied-irish-

banks

63. Building a Better Financial Services Ireland: Accelerate to Elevate, accessed on April 21, 2025, https://eyfinancialservicesthoughtgallery.ie/wp-content/uploads/2025/01/EY-Ireland_FS-Research-Report.pdf
64. When Digitalization Meets Regulation across Borders: An Explainer with Actionable Insights, accessed on April 21, 2025, https://insights.aib.world/api/v1/articles/122505-when-digitalization-meets-regulation-across-borders-an-explainer-with-actionable-insights.pdf
65. When Digitalization Meets Regulation across Borders: An Explainer with Actionable Insights, accessed on April 21, 2025, https://insights.aib.world/article/122505-when-digitalization-meets-regulation-across-borders-an-explainer-with-actionable-insights
66. Kellogg AI ML Certification | Artificial Intelligence and Machine Learning Course for Managers and Executives, accessed on April 21, 2025, https://online.em.kellogg.northwestern.edu/artificial-intelligence/spa/aggregate

8 Microsoft Copilot in the Enterprise

Microsoft Copilot represents a significant advancement in artificial intelligence (AI), offering a suite of tools designed to enhance productivity and augment human capabilities across the enterprise. Integrated primarily within the widely adopted Microsoft 365 ecosystem, Copilot promises substantial benefits for Irish organisations, including those in the highly regulated financial services sector. Potential advantages range from considerable time savings on administrative tasks and accelerated content creation to sophisticated data analysis and improved customer service interactions.[1]

However, the deployment of powerful generative AI tools like Copilot introduces critical risks that demand careful management. For Irish enterprises, these risks are amplified by the stringent European Union (EU) regulatory landscape, encompassing the General Data Protection Regulation (GDPR) and the new EU AI Act, alongside specific oversight from Irish bodies such as the Data Protection Commission (DPC) and the Central Bank of Ireland (CBI).[4] Key concerns centre on data privacy and security, particularly when Copilot accesses sensitive organisational data, the potential for algorithmic bias, the need for transparency and accountability in AI-assisted processes, ensuring the accuracy of generated outputs, and mitigating the risks of misuse or overreliance.[8]

This report concludes that a strategic, phased, and governance-led approach is paramount for Irish organisations seeking to harness Copilot's potential while navigating the associated risks. Key recommendations include prioritising robust data governance within the Microsoft 365 environment *before* widespread deployment, establishing clear AI usage policies and ethical guidelines, implementing comprehensive employee training, ensuring human oversight and validation of AI outputs, and adopting a continuous monitoring and improvement cycle. Successfully integrating Copilot requires a holistic strategy that addresses technology, people, processes, and compliance in unison. This guide provides a detailed analysis of Copilot's offerings, the relevant regulatory framework, practical applications, inherent risks, mitigation strategies, and a tailored implementation roadmap to support Irish enterprises in making informed decisions about adopting this transformative technology responsibly.

8.1 AI and Copilot in the Irish Enterprise

The rapid proliferation of generative AI (GenAI) technologies has marked a pivotal moment for businesses globally, and Ireland is no exception.[12] Tools capable of generating human-like text, analysing complex data, and automating tasks are transitioning from experimental concepts to integrated components of the enterprise toolkit. Microsoft Copilot stands as a prominent example, embedding AI assistance directly into the familiar Microsoft 365 applications used daily by countless organisations.[14]

Ireland, with its strong track record in digital adoption, a highly skilled workforce, and a vibrant, globally connected business ecosystem, appears well-positioned to capitalise on the AI revolution.[17] Forecasts suggest AI could significantly boost Ireland's GDP in the coming decades.[18] However, realising this potential is not guaranteed. A noticeable gap exists between the initial exploration of GenAI tools and their scaled, strategic deployment across organisations, particularly comparing multinational corporations operating in Ireland with indigenous firms.[17]

> ***Microsoft Copilot, leveraging advanced Large Language Models (LLMs) and organisational data via Microsoft Graph, offers compelling productivity enhancements.***[19]

Yet, its adoption presents a duality: the promise of efficiency and innovation runs parallel to significant challenges concerning responsible use, data security, privacy, and regulatory adherence.[6] These considerations are particularly acute for Irish organisations operating under the comprehensive data protection regime of GDPR and the emerging requirements of the EU AI Act, with specific expectations set by the Irish DPC and, for financial institutions, the CBI.[4]

The objective of this report is therefore to provide a comprehensive and actionable guide tailored for Irish enterprises, including those within the financial services sector. It aims to demystify the various Microsoft Copilot offerings, clarify the complex regulatory and ethical landscape, illustrate practical applications within an Irish business context, analyse the inherent risks, propose robust mitigation strategies, and outline a structured framework for responsible implementation. By addressing these facets, this report seeks to empower Irish organisations to navigate the adoption of Microsoft Copilot strategically, maximising its value while upholding ethical standards and ensuring compliance.

8.1.1 Understanding Microsoft Copilot Offerings

Microsoft has developed a diverse portfolio of AI assistants under the Copilot brand, ranging from free consumer tools to deeply integrated enterprise solutions. Understanding the distinctions between these offerings – particularly regarding features, data handling, pricing, and target users – is crucial for organisations considering adoption.

8.1.2 Overview of the Copilot Ecosystem

The Copilot ecosystem encompasses several distinct products.[22] While sharing underlying AI technology, they differ significantly in their integration, capabilities, and governance. Key offerings include the free standard Copilot, the premium consumer-focused Copilot Pro, the enterprise-integrated Copilot for Microsoft 365, and the customisation platform Copilot Studio.[2] Additionally, specialised versions like Copilot for Sales, Copilot for Service, Copilot for Finance, and GitHub Copilot target specific roles and functions.[2] The core concept across the suite is providing AI-powered assistance directly within user workflows, leveraging LLMs to understand context and generate relevant outputs.[14]

8.1.3 Standard Copilot (Free Tier)

The entry-level Copilot offering is available free of charge and accessible via the web, dedicated mobile apps, and integration within Windows and the Microsoft Edge browser.[27]

- **Features:** It provides access to underlying AI models, including recent versions like GPT-4o, although potentially with lower priority during peak usage times compared to paid tiers.[23] It offers web-grounded responses for real-time information and includes image generation capabilities powered by DALL-E, albeit with daily limits (e.g., 15 'boosts').[27]
- **Target Users:** This tier is suited for individuals using Copilot for personal tasks, casual research, or basic content generation, who do not require deep integration with work applications or organisational data.[23]
- **Pricing:** Free.[23]
- **Data Handling:** Primarily interacts with user prompts and public web data. While Copilot Chat used with a work (Entra ID) account offers enterprise data protection [24], the standard free Copilot accessed with a personal account operates under different terms.

8.1.4 Copilot Pro (Premium Consumer/Individual Tier)

Copilot Pro is a subscription-based offering aimed at individual power users, creators, and those seeking enhanced AI capabilities for personal use.[27]

- **Features:** Copilot Pro builds upon the free tier by offering priority access to the latest and most powerful LLMs (like GPT-4 and GPT-4 Turbo), even during peak hours.[27] It significantly increases the daily boosts for faster AI image creation (e.g., 100 boosts) and provides early access to new experimental features.[27] A key feature is its integration with the *free web versions* of Microsoft 365 apps (Word, Excel, PowerPoint, OneNote, Outlook).[27] However, unlocking Copilot features within the *full desktop versions* of these applications requires the user to *also* have an active Microsoft 365 Personal or Family subscription.[27]

- **Target Users:** Individuals who use Copilot frequently for personal projects, content creation, or advanced research and require faster performance and enhanced features.[23]

- **Pricing:** Priced at $20 USD per user per month.[19] Euro pricing is typically comparable but should be verified locally. Some sources indicate free trials may be periodically available [27], although others state no trials exist.[19] It is designed for a single user; individuals sharing a Microsoft 365 Family subscription must each purchase their own Copilot Pro subscription to access its features.[27]

- **Data Handling:** Primarily uses public web data, but when used in conjunction with a Microsoft 365 Personal/Family subscription, it can access and process content stored within that personal account (e.g., OneDrive files, Outlook emails associated with personal Microsoft accounts like @outlook.com).[27] It does not access organisational data within a corporate tenant.

8.1.5 Copilot for Microsoft 365 (Enterprise Integration)

> ***This is the flagship offering for businesses and enterprises, designed to integrate AI deeply within the Microsoft 365 suite and leverage organisational data securely.19***

- **Features:** Copilot functionality is embedded directly within core M365 applications like Word, Excel, PowerPoint, Outlook, Teams, OneNote, Loop, and Whiteboard.[14] It enables users to summarise documents, emails, and meetings; draft text and emails; generate presentations; analyse data and create charts in Excel; and retrieve information from across their work content.[1] It includes Microsoft 365 Copilot Chat, a dedicated conversational interface that provides secure, enterprise-grade AI chat grounded in both web data and the user's organisational data, supporting features like file uploads.[22]

- **Integration:** The defining characteristic is its use of the Microsoft Graph API to access and process organisational data – including emails, documents, chats, calendar entries, and contacts – relevant to the user's prompt and working context.[19] Crucially, Copilot only accesses data that the specific user already has permission to view, respecting existing M365 access controls.[5] This ability to reason over internal, contextual data is what distinguishes it fundamentally from consumer-grade AI assistants.

- **Target Users:** Organisations of all sizes (following the removal of the previous 300-seat minimum purchase requirement [19]) seeking to enhance employee productivity, streamline workflows, and leverage their internal knowledge base through AI, within a secure and compliant framework.[19]

- **Pricing:** Available as an add-on license priced at $30 USD per user per month (with an annual commitment).[19] This requires a prerequisite qualifying Microsoft 365 or Office 365 license (e.g., M365 Business Standard/Premium, M365 E3/E5, O365 E3/E5).[19] No free trial is offered for this enterprise version.[19]

- **Data Handling:** This is a critical aspect for enterprises. Microsoft states that prompts, retrieved organisational data, and generated responses remain within the Microsoft 365 service boundary.[5] The service is designed to comply with existing Microsoft 365 commercial commitments regarding privacy, security, and compliance, including GDPR and the EU Data Boundary.[19] Importantly, customer data (prompts and organisational content accessed) is *not* used to train the underlying foundation LLMs.[19] Data residency commitments are maintained, with EU customer traffic generally processed within the EU Data Boundary, although processing may occur in other regions during periods of high demand.[5] User interaction history (prompts and responses) is logged and can be managed by administrators using tools like Microsoft Purview Content Search and retention policies, and users can delete their own history.[5]

8.1.6 Microsoft Copilot Studio (Customisation and Agent Building)

Copilot Studio is a low-code platform enabling organisations to build custom AI experiences (referred to as 'copilots' or 'agents') and extend the capabilities of Copilot for Microsoft 365.[42]

- **Features:** Provides a graphical interface for designing, building, testing, publishing, and managing custom conversational AI agents.[42] These agents can be deployed across various channels, including websites, mobile apps, Microsoft Teams, SharePoint, and within Copilot for M365 Chat.[42] Studio allows agents to connect to a wide range of data sources through pre-built connectors (over 1,500 mentioned) or custom APIs, enabling interaction with internal knowledge bases (Microsoft

Graph, Dataverse, websites) and line-of-business systems (e.g., CRM, ERP).[15] It supports building agents for specific tasks like automating expense submissions, facilitating employee onboarding, answering HR policy questions, or providing specialised customer support.[15] Advanced features include generative AI plugins, triggering actions based on conversations, and building autonomous agents capable of planning and escalating tasks.[42] A recent addition is the 'computer use' capability, allowing agents to automate tasks by interacting directly with the graphical user interfaces (GUIs) of desktop applications and websites, simulating human actions like clicks and typing.[45] Governance is managed through the Power Platform admin center, offering controls over agent creation, access, data loss prevention (DLP), and providing audit logs via Microsoft Purview and Sentinel.[43]

- **Target Users:** Organisations requiring AI solutions tailored to specific business processes, needing to integrate AI with backend systems, or looking to automate complex workflows beyond the standard capabilities of Copilot for M365.[42] It typically requires developer or power-user skills, or engagement with implementation partners.
- **Pricing:** The primary licensing model is $200 USD per month, which includes 25,000 messages, billed annually.[15] Pay-as-you-go options are also available.[43] A free 30-day trial can be initiated with a work or school email.[23] Note that using custom agents within Copilot for M365 Chat may incur additional metered charges requiring an Azure subscription.[24] Customising Copilot for M365 itself also requires the base Copilot for M365 license.[23]
- **Data Handling:** Operates within the security and compliance framework of the Microsoft Power Platform.[43] Allows connection to various enterprise data sources, but access and data handling are subject to the configurations and governance

controls implemented by the organisation within Studio and the connected systems.[43]

8.1.7 Underlying Technologies

The capabilities of the Copilot suite are powered by a combination of advanced AI models and Microsoft's cloud infrastructure:

- **Large Language Models (LLMs):** Copilot relies heavily on OpenAI's GPT-4 series of models, including variants like GPT-4, GPT-4 Turbo, and the multimodal GPT-4o (which can process text and images).[20] Microsoft fine-tunes these models and integrates them using its proprietary 'Prometheus' architecture.[20] Different Copilot tiers may offer access to different model versions or provide priority access during peak times, with Pro and M365 users typically getting access to the most capable models.[27]

- **Image Generation:** Text-to-image features utilise OpenAI's DALL-E models, specifically DALL-E 3 is often cited.[2]

- **Microsoft Graph:** This API is fundamental to Copilot for Microsoft 365's operation. It acts as the secure gateway to the organisation's data residing within the Microsoft 365 tenant (emails, files, chats, calendar, contacts, etc.), allowing Copilot to retrieve relevant information and understand the user's context while respecting established permissions.[19] The effectiveness and safety of Copilot for M365 are therefore intrinsically linked to the quality and governance of data accessible via Microsoft Graph within the organisation.

- **Responsible AI Infrastructure:** Microsoft incorporates safety layers designed to filter harmful content, detect copyrighted material, and prevent malicious use like prompt injection attacks ('jailbreaking').[5] Services like Azure AI Content Safety provide tools for detecting harmful user-generated and AI-generated content, which can be integrated into AI applications.[48]

The distinct features, pricing, and particularly the data access mechanisms across the Copilot family reflect a deliberate market segmentation by Microsoft. For enterprises, the crucial element is Copilot for Microsoft 365's ability to securely interact with internal organisational data via Microsoft Graph, a capability absent in the consumer tiers.[19] This integration justifies the premium pricing and prerequisite licensing but also underscores the critical importance of robust data governance within the M365 environment before deployment. Furthermore, Copilot Studio is positioned not merely as a standalone product but as a vital extensibility layer, enabling organisations to tailor Copilot's capabilities to specific business needs and integrate AI more deeply into custom workflows and line-of-business applications, potentially requiring further investment in development or partner expertise.[15]

8.1.8 Table 1: Comparison of Microsoft Copilot Versions

Feature	**Standard Copilot (Free)**	**Copilot Pro**	**Copilot for Microsoft 365**	**Microsoft Copilot Studio**
Key Features	Web search, basic content/image gen, chat	Priority model access, more image boosts, M365 Web App integration	Deep M365 App integration (Word, Excel, Teams etc.), M365 Chat, Summarisatio n, Content Gen, Data Analysis (Org Data)	Build/customise AI agents, Low-code interface, Connectors, Workflow automation, UI automation, Governance tools
Target User	Casual personal users	Power users, creators, individuals needing	Businesses & Enterprises (all sizes)	Organisations needing custom AI solutions, process

		enhanced personal AI		automation, LOB integration
Pricing Model	Free	Subscription ($20/user/month USD)	Add-on Subscription ($30/user/month USD) + Prerequisite M365/O365 License	Subscription ($200/month/25k messages USD) or Pay-as-you-go. Trial available.
Organisational Data Access	No (except Copilot Chat w/ Entra ID uses EDP)	No (unless linked to M365 Personal/Family account for personal data)	Yes, via Microsoft Graph (respects user permissions) [19]	Yes, via configurable connectors & agents (subject to governance) [43]
Customisation Level	None	Limited (via Copilot GPTs)	Limited (User prompts, settings). Extendable via Copilot Studio.[23]	High (Build custom agents, workflows, integrations) [15]
Key Tech Access	GPT-4o (non-peak) [24], DALL-E (limited) [23]	Priority GPT-4/Turbo/4o [27], DALL-E (higher limits) [27]	Priority GPT-4/Turbo/4o [24], DALL-E, Microsoft Graph [19]	Access to underlying models, plus custom logic, connectors, UI automation [43]
Governance/Security	Basic privacy settings. EDP for Copilot Chat w/ Entra ID.	Personal account security.	Enterprise-grade; inherits M365 policies; GDPR/EUDB compliant;	Governed via Power Platform Admin Center; DLP, Access Controls, Auditing available [43]

			Data not used for training [5]	

8.2 The Regulatory and Ethical Framework for AI in Ireland

The deployment of AI technologies like Microsoft Copilot within Irish enterprises occurs within a complex and evolving regulatory and ethical landscape. Key frameworks include overarching EU legislation (the AI Act and GDPR), specific guidance from Irish regulatory bodies (DPC and CBI), and the responsible AI principles advocated by technology providers like Microsoft. Navigating this landscape is crucial for compliant and trustworthy AI adoption.

8.2.1 EU AI Act

The EU AI Act represents the world's first comprehensive legal framework specifically regulating artificial intelligence.[4] It applies broadly to providers, deployers (users), importers, and distributors who place AI systems on the EU market, put them into service within the EU, or whose AI system outputs are used within the EU, regardless of their geographic location.[49] The Act employs a risk-based approach, categorising AI systems into tiers with varying levels of obligation.[4]

- **Risk Categories:**
  - **Unacceptable Risk:** Certain AI practices deemed a clear threat to safety, livelihoods, or fundamental rights are prohibited outright. Examples include social scoring by public authorities, manipulative or exploitative AI techniques, untargeted scraping of facial images to create databases, and certain uses of emotion recognition (e.g., in workplaces).[4]
  - **High Risk:** This category captures AI systems that could pose significant risks to health, safety, or fundamental rights. It includes AI used as safety components in products already subject to EU safety legislation (e.g., medical devices, machinery, toys) and AI systems

employed in specific sensitive areas listed in Annex III of the Act.[4] For financial services, critical examples in Annex III include systems used for evaluating creditworthiness or credit scores (except for fraud detection) and systems used for risk assessment and pricing in life and health insurance.[51] Other Annex III examples relevant to enterprises include AI in recruitment, worker management, access to essential public and private services, law enforcement, and administration of justice.[4] High-risk systems face stringent requirements *before* market placement and throughout their lifecycle, including robust risk management systems, high-quality data governance, detailed technical documentation, activity logging for traceability, human oversight mechanisms, and high standards for accuracy, robustness, and cybersecurity.[49] They generally require conformity assessments and registration in an EU database.[51] Some AI systems performing narrow procedural tasks or merely improving human activities may be exempt.[53]

- **Limited Risk (Transparency Risk):** AI systems where the primary risk relates to transparency must meet specific disclosure obligations. For instance, users interacting with chatbots must be informed they are dealing with an AI system.[51] AI-generated content, particularly deepfakes or text intended to inform the public, must be identifiable as such.[4]
- **Minimal Risk:** The vast majority of AI systems are expected to fall into this category, facing no mandatory obligations under the Act, although adherence to voluntary codes of conduct is encouraged.[4]

- **Generative AI / General-Purpose AI (GPAI):** Foundation models like OpenAI's GPT series that power tools like Copilot are subject to specific rules, primarily focused on transparency.[4] Providers must disclose that content is AI-generated, design models to prevent the generation of illegal content, and publish summaries of copyrighted data used for training.[4] More powerful "high-impact" GPAI models with potential systemic risks (potentially including models like GPT-4) face additional obligations, such as thorough model evaluations and reporting serious incidents to the European Commission.[4] While the GPAI models themselves may not be classified as high-risk, their *application* in a specific high-risk context (e.g., using Copilot to assist significantly in credit scoring) would subject the *deployer* (the financial institution) to the high-risk obligations for that specific deployment.[51]

- **Obligations for Deployers (Users):** Organisations deploying AI systems, particularly high-risk ones, have specific responsibilities. These include using the system according to the provider's instructions, ensuring the input data they use is relevant and appropriate, implementing human oversight, monitoring the system's operation, maintaining logs generated by the system, and informing individuals when they are subject to a high-risk system.[50] If a deployer substantially modifies a high-risk system or adapts a non-high-risk system for a high-risk purpose, they may take on the more extensive obligations of a provider.[49]
- **Timeline:** The AI Act entered into force in mid-2024. Its provisions apply incrementally: the ban on unacceptable-risk systems takes effect around December 2024 / February 2025; rules for GPAI models apply around June 2025; and the comprehensive requirements for high-risk systems become mandatory around June 2026.[4]

8.2.2 General Data Protection Regulation (GDPR)

GDPR remains the foundational regulation for processing personal data in the EU and is fully applicable whenever AI systems like

Copilot process data relating to identifiable individuals.[5] Microsoft explicitly designs Copilot for Microsoft 365 with GDPR compliance in mind, leveraging existing M365 security and privacy commitments.[5]

- **Core Principles in the AI Context:**
  - **Lawfulness, Fairness, Transparency:** Processing personal data via AI requires a valid legal basis (e.g., legitimate interests, potentially consent depending on context). The processing must be fair, and individuals must be clearly informed about how AI uses their data.[8] Using legitimate interests requires careful documentation of a balancing test (LIA).[55]
  - **Purpose Limitation:** The specific purpose(s) for using AI to process personal data must be defined and documented *before* processing begins.[8] This is crucial for both training data collection and operational use.
  - **Data Minimisation:** Only personal data necessary for the defined purpose should be processed.[8] This can be challenging for LLMs that often benefit from large datasets, requiring careful justification.[8]
  - **Accuracy:** Organisations must ensure the accuracy of personal data input into AI systems and have processes to address potential inaccuracies or biases generated by the AI.[8]
  - **Storage Limitation:** Clear retention periods must be set for personal data processed by AI, including prompts, outputs containing personal data, and any training data snippets.[5]
  - **Integrity and Confidentiality (Security):** Appropriate technical and organisational measures (e.g., encryption, access controls, security monitoring) must protect personal data processed by AI systems.[5]

   - **Accountability:** Organisations must be able to demonstrate compliance with GDPR principles through documentation, policies, DPIAs, audits, and clear governance structures.[54]

- **Data Subject Rights:** Individuals retain their GDPR rights (access, rectification, erasure, restriction, objection) concerning their personal data processed by AI systems.[6] Organisations must have processes to facilitate these rights, which can be technically complex, especially regarding data embedded within trained models. Copilot for M365 allows users to delete their interaction history.[5]

- **Data Protection Impact Assessments (DPIAs):** Deploying AI systems, particularly those involving new technologies, large-scale processing of personal data, processing sensitive data, or automated decision-making with significant effects, will likely trigger the requirement to conduct a DPIA under GDPR Article 35.[6] This involves systematically analysing the processing, identifying risks to data subjects' rights and freedoms, and defining measures to mitigate those risks.

8.2.3 Irish Regulatory Guidance

Irish organisations must pay close attention to the perspectives and expectations of domestic regulators, primarily the Data Protection Commission (DPC) and, for financial entities, the Central Bank of Ireland (CBI).

- **Data Protection Commission (DPC):** The DPC is actively engaged in the AI space, issuing guidance and participating in European-level discussions via the European Data Protection Board (EDPB).[6] Key points from DPC guidance include:

   - Emphasis on applying GDPR principles rigorously to all AI processing involving personal data, including data scraped from public sources for training.[6]

  - Organisations using AI tools must understand the data flows, third-party involvement, retention practices, and how to facilitate data subject rights.[8]
  - Highlighted risks include unanticipated processing, security vulnerabilities (e.g., filter circumvention), model memorisation leading to data regurgitation, inherent inaccuracies and biases in LLMs, and risks associated with automated decision-making.[8]
  - Organisations developing or providing AI tools need to consider DPIAs, lawful basis, transparency notices, data sharing agreements, and storage limitation from the outset.[6]
  - The DPC sought an EDPB opinion to harmonise approaches on key issues like AI model anonymity and the use of legitimate interest as a legal basis for training and deployment.[55]
- **Central Bank of Ireland (CBI):** The CBI views AI as a technology with significant transformational potential for the financial sector but also one that introduces profound challenges and risks.[7] Its expectations for regulated financial institutions using AI are becoming clearer:
  - **Strategic Rationale:** Firms must clearly articulate the business need for AI and justify why the chosen AI solution is appropriate.[9]
  - **Risk Management:** Firms are responsible for identifying, assessing, managing, and mitigating all risks associated with AI use, including operational resilience impacts, data quality issues, algorithmic bias, and cybersecurity threats.[7] Existing risk management frameworks should be adapted.

- **Governance and Accountability:** Clear governance structures and unambiguous accountability for AI systems and the decisions informed by them are essential.[7]
- **Consumer Protection:** AI must be used in the best interests of consumers, avoiding exploitative practices, ensuring fairness (mitigating bias that could lead to financial exclusion), and maintaining transparency.[7]
- **Regulatory Alignment:** Firms must ensure AI use complies with existing financial services regulations (e.g., MiFID II, Solvency II) and the incoming EU AI Act.[7] The CBI anticipates being designated as a Market Surveillance Authority under the AI Act for specific financial use cases (creditworthiness, insurance risk/pricing) and is preparing for this role.[7]
- **Supervisory Focus:** The CBI is actively developing its supervisory approach to AI, engaging with industry, and exploring the use of AI within its own supervisory functions.[7] Its Innovation Hub and Sandbox Programme aim to foster responsible innovation, including AI applications for areas like combating financial crime.[66]

8.2.4 Microsoft's Responsible AI Standard

Complementing the legal and regulatory requirements, Microsoft promotes its own framework for responsible AI development and deployment, embodied in its Responsible AI Standard and operationalised through internal governance bodies like the Aether Committee and the Office of Responsible AI.[18] This framework is built on six core principles:

- **Fairness:** AI systems should treat all individuals equitably and avoid unfair bias based on characteristics like gender, ethnicity, or other demographics.[48]

- **Reliability and Safety:** AI systems should perform reliably and safely as intended, across different operating conditions and contexts.[48]
- **Privacy and Security:** AI systems must protect personal and confidential information, respect user privacy, and be resilient against security threats.[48] This aligns directly with the security commitments for Copilot for M365.[5]
- **Inclusiveness:** AI systems should be designed to empower and engage people from all backgrounds and abilities, considering potential barriers to access or use.[48]
- **Transparency:** The workings and decision-making processes of AI systems should be understandable to users and stakeholders, allowing them to comprehend how outcomes are reached.[48]
- **Accountability:** Individuals and organisations developing and deploying AI systems should be accountable for their operation and impact. Humans should remain in control.[48]

These principles provide a valuable ethical overlay to the legal requirements. They directly support compliance efforts; for example, the Fairness principle addresses non-discrimination requirements in the AI Act and GDPR, while Privacy and Security are central to GDPR adherence. Transparency aids compliance with AI Act disclosure rules, and Accountability underpins the governance expectations of both frameworks.[40] Microsoft also provides tools and resources, such as the Responsible AI Dashboard and Azure AI Content Safety services, to help organisations implement these principles in practice.[48] The Copilot Copyright Commitment further offers customers indemnity against certain intellectual property claims arising from Copilot outputs.[25]

The confluence of GDPR, the AI Act, specific Irish regulatory expectations (especially from the DPC and CBI), and industry principles like Microsoft's creates a demanding environment for AI adoption. Compliance cannot be an afterthought; it requires an integrated strategy that embeds data protection, fairness, transparency, and accountability into the entire lifecycle of AI deployment. The proactive stance of Irish regulators, particularly the CBI's focus on financial services and its anticipated role under the AI Act, signals that organisations in this sector face heightened scrutiny and must demonstrate robust governance from the outset.[7] Furthermore, while core Copilot functions might seem low-risk, the *application* of Copilot or custom agents built with Copilot Studio in sensitive areas like credit assessment or insurance pricing could potentially trigger the stringent obligations associated with high-risk AI systems under the AI Act, necessitating careful, use-case-specific risk classification.[7]

8.3 Practical Applications of Copilot Across the Irish Enterprise

Microsoft Copilot, particularly Copilot for Microsoft 365, offers a wide array of potential applications across various business functions, aiming to enhance productivity, streamline workflows, and unlock creativity. While many use cases are horizontal, applying across industries, specific examples can be contextualised for the Irish enterprise environment, including the financial services sector.

8.3.1 Enhancing Productivity and Collaboration

At its core, Copilot aims to reduce the time employees spend on routine, administrative tasks, freeing them up for higher-value work.[1] Common cross-functional benefits include:

- **Information Retrieval:** Quickly finding files, data points, or relevant passages within documents, emails, and chat histories across the Microsoft 365 tenant.[25]
- **Summarisation:** Condensing long documents, email threads, or meeting transcripts into concise summaries with key points and action items.[1]
- **Content Drafting:** Generating first drafts of emails, reports, presentations, proposals, and other documents based on prompts or existing materials.[1]
- **Meeting Support:** Assisting with setting agendas, capturing discussion points, identifying agreements/disagreements, generating real-time summaries, and suggesting action items during Teams meetings.[2]
- **Data Analysis & Visualisation:** Helping users in Excel analyse data, identify trends, generate formulas, and create charts and graphs through natural language prompts.[1]

Early adopter studies and reports indicate tangible time savings, with users reporting saving significant amounts of time daily or weekly on tasks like searching for information and handling mundane administrative work.[3]

8.3.2 Role-Specific Use Cases

Copilot's capabilities can be applied to enhance the effectiveness of specific roles within an organisation:

- **Sales Teams:** Copilot, especially when integrated with CRM systems (like Salesforce via plugins or the dedicated Copilot for Sales), can assist with identifying and researching high-quality leads [1], drafting tailored proposals and responses to Requests for Proposals (RFPs) [22], generating personalised sales pitches and presentations [22], summarising customer interactions from emails and meetings [2], updating CRM records directly from Outlook [16], and automating follow-up reminders.[75]
    - *Irish/Financial Services Context:* Assisting relationship managers in Irish banks or insurance companies to prepare for client meetings by summarising past interactions and relevant internal data [76], drafting compliant communication templates, or quickly generating responses to standard client queries.
- **Project Managers:** Copilot can streamline project management by automatically summarising project meetings and identifying action items [33], assisting in the creation of project status reports and documentation [3], accelerating the preparation of kick-off presentations [3], and helping track tasks mentioned in communications.[1]
    - *Irish/Financial Services Context:* Supporting project managers overseeing technology implementations in financial institutions, managing regulatory change projects,

or coordinating construction projects (potentially integrating with systems like 4PS ERP via Copilot Studio [15]).

- **Marketing Professionals:** Copilot aids in brainstorming ideas and generating content for various channels, including blog posts, social media updates, newsletters, and website copy.[1] It can help analyse marketing campaign performance data [1], create social media content calendars [36], summarise customer survey results [1], and generate ideas for personalised marketing campaigns.[75]
    - *Irish/Financial Services Context:* Assisting marketing teams in Irish financial institutions to create compliant marketing materials for regulated products, tailoring campaigns for the Irish market, or analysing customer feedback specific to Irish operations.
- **Human Resources:** Copilot can support various HR functions, including drafting job descriptions [36], assisting with initial candidate screening or search [25], enhancing employee onboarding by drafting plans and surfacing relevant policies or training materials [15], creating self-service options for common employee queries via custom agents built with Copilot Studio [15], generating drafts for internal communications or training guides [36], and analysing employee survey data or feedback.[3]
    - *Irish/Financial Services Context:* Helping HR teams in Irish companies ensure recruitment materials align with Irish employment law, drafting internal policies reflecting local regulations, or supporting multilingual communications for diverse workforces common in Ireland.
- **Finance and Actuarial Teams:** This is a potentially high-impact area. Copilot can significantly accelerate data analysis within Excel and Power BI [1], helping to identify trends, anomalies, and generate visualisations.[35] It assists in drafting financial reports, budgets, and forecasts.[1] It can automate repetitive tasks like

data reconciliation [78] and support collections processes by summarising past interactions and drafting communications.[73] For risk management, it can help identify patterns or analyse data for potential risks.[73] It can also support compliance activities by summarising regulations or checking data against requirements.[73] Actuarial teams might use it for preliminary analysis, exploring scenarios (e.g., long-term care insurance modelling [80]), or potentially accelerating coding tasks in R/Python for modelling.[65] The dedicated Copilot for Finance aims to streamline these processes further.[22]

  - *Irish/Financial Services Context:* Supporting the preparation of regulatory returns for the CBI, assisting with Solvency II calculations or reporting in insurance firms, performing analysis for IFRS reporting, checking compliance with Irish financial regulations, or accelerating the analysis required for anti-money laundering (AML) investigations.

- **IT/Developers (including GitHub Copilot):** GitHub Copilot, often considered part of the broader Copilot family, provides significant assistance to developers by suggesting code completions, generating entire functions or boilerplate code, assisting with debugging, and translating code between languages.[34] It can automate repetitive coding tasks, such as creating database interaction methods or utility functions.[78] Copilot for M365 can also assist IT teams with generating documentation, summarising technical discussions, or drafting internal communications.[3] Copilot Studio enables IT teams to build custom agents for internal support or process automation.[43]
  - *Irish/Financial Services Context:* Accelerating software development within Ireland's significant fintech sector, supporting internal IT teams in banks and insurance companies maintaining legacy systems or developing new

digital platforms (e.g., Itaú Bank, Raiffeisen Bank International, Neon Bank examples globally show developer productivity gains [83]), or aiding software companies based in Ireland like ESW.[78]

- **Legal Professionals:** Copilot can assist legal teams by summarising lengthy contracts, policies, or case files [65], drafting initial clauses or standard legal documents [72], performing preliminary reviews of documents for specific terms or compliance issues [72], and assisting with internal knowledge management by finding relevant information within the firm's document repositories.[72]
    - *Irish/Financial Services Context:* Helping in-house legal teams at Irish companies review contracts for compliance with Irish and EU law, summarising complex regulatory guidance from the CBI, DPC, or EU bodies, or drafting initial responses based on internal legal precedents.
- **Customer Service:** Copilot for M365 can help agents draft email responses or summarise previous interactions.[76] Copilot Studio allows for the creation of sophisticated customer-facing chatbots or internal agent assistants.[15] These agents can handle FAQs, provide product information, guide users through processes, access backend systems (like CRM) for context [15], and escalate complex issues to human agents.[75] The dedicated Copilot for Service offering provides further specialised capabilities.[2] Analysing customer feedback and sentiment is another application.[89]
    - *Irish/Financial Services Context:* Developing chatbots for Irish banks to handle common queries about accounts or loans [16], assisting insurance agents in processing claims [76], supporting customer service teams in utilities or retail sectors operating in Ireland, potentially offering support in the Irish language if models are trained appropriately.

Capitec Bank is cited as using Azure OpenAI/Copilot to assist service consultants.[76]

- **Executives/Management:** Copilot assists leaders by summarising lengthy reports, market analyses, or internal documents [1], drafting emails, speeches, or presentations [33], synthesising information from multiple sources to provide strategic insights [36], preparing for board meetings or client presentations [76], and staying updated on team communications and project progress.[3]
    - *Irish/Financial Services Context:* Enabling executives in Irish firms to quickly digest regulatory updates from the CBI or DPC, understand market trends specific to Ireland, or summarise performance data across different business units operating locally.

The breadth of these use cases demonstrates that Copilot's potential impact spans from incremental efficiency gains in daily tasks (like email drafting via M365 Copilot) to more transformative process automation achievable through Copilot Studio or specialised Copilots (like integrating with CRM for sales or building custom finance reconciliation tools). This suggests that organisations can adopt Copilot progressively, starting with foundational productivity enhancements and potentially evolving towards more complex, integrated AI solutions as they gain experience and identify higher-value opportunities.[2] Furthermore, while many applications are horizontal, the emergence of industry-specific examples, particularly in regulated fields like financial services, highlights the growing trend of tailoring AI capabilities to meet sector-specific needs and compliance requirements.[34]

8.4 Navigating Responsible and Ethical AI Considerations with Copilot

While Microsoft Copilot offers compelling benefits, its deployment, particularly Copilot for Microsoft 365 which interacts with sensitive organisational data, necessitates careful consideration of responsible and ethical AI principles. Failure to address these considerations can lead to privacy breaches, biased outcomes, eroded trust, and non-compliance with regulations like GDPR and the EU AI Act, especially critical within the Irish financial services context.

8.4.1 Data Privacy and Security: Leveraging Organisational Data Safely

The core value proposition of Copilot for Microsoft 365 – its ability to reason over organisational data accessed via Microsoft Graph – is also its primary source of privacy and security risk.[19] While Microsoft provides assurances that data processing occurs within the M365 service boundary, inherits existing user permissions, complies with GDPR, and that organisational data is not used to train foundation LLMs [19], significant risks remain for the deploying organisation:

- **Data Exposure through Permissions:** Copilot respects existing user permissions within M365.[5] However, if these permissions are overly broad ('permission sprawl') due to inadequate governance of SharePoint sites, Teams channels, or OneDrive sharing, users might inadvertently use Copilot to surface or summarise sensitive information they technically have access to but perhaps shouldn't be seeing or sharing widely.[10] This 'permissions paradox' means that Copilot's safety feature relies heavily on the organisation's pre-existing M365 data governance maturity. Poorly managed permissions represent a significant vulnerability.[10]

- **Prompt Content Sensitivity:** Users might include sensitive personal or confidential business information directly within their prompts to Copilot. Clear policies and training are needed to guide users on what information is appropriate to include in prompts.[8]
- **Compromised Accounts:** If a user's M365 account is compromised, an attacker could potentially leverage Copilot with that user's permissions to exfiltrate sensitive data through carefully crafted prompts.[10] Robust identity and access management (IAM) practices are therefore essential.
- **Third-Party Plugins:** Enabling Copilot plugins that connect to external services introduces additional data sharing pathways that need to be assessed and governed.[5]
- **Data Residency:** While Microsoft commits to the EU Data Boundary for EU customers, processing may occur outside the EU during high utilisation periods, requiring awareness and assessment against data transfer requirements.[5]

For Irish financial institutions handling highly sensitive customer financial data, transaction records, and market-sensitive information, these risks are particularly acute. Demonstrating robust control over data access and processing via Copilot is essential to meet the stringent expectations of the CBI and comply with GDPR.[7]

8.4.2 Mitigating Bias in Inputs and Outputs

AI systems, including LLMs powering Copilot, can inherit and amplify biases present in the data they are trained on or interact with.[11] Sources of bias can include historical societal biases reflected in datasets, skewed data representation, or choices made during algorithm design.[11]

- **Copilot Context:** Since Copilot for M365 learns from and generates responses based on an organisation's internal data (documents, emails, etc.) [93], any biases present in that internal content could be reflected or even magnified in Copilot's outputs. For example, if internal documents historically use biased language or reflect skewed decision-making patterns, Copilot might replicate these.

- **Potential Impacts:** Biased outputs could lead to unfair or discriminatory outcomes in sensitive areas like HR (recruitment screening, performance summaries influenced by biased input data [96]), customer service (differential treatment based on inferred demographics), or financial analysis (skewed interpretations based on biased historical data).
- **Mitigation Strategies:** Addressing bias requires a multi-faceted approach. While Microsoft is responsible for fairness in the underlying models [48], organisations deploying Copilot must:
    - Strive for fairness and representation in the organisational data Copilot accesses where possible (though this is often existing data).
    - Implement processes to detect bias in Copilot's outputs through regular auditing and testing.[11]
    - Train employees to be aware of potential bias and to critically evaluate Copilot's suggestions.[96]
    - Ensure human oversight in decision-making processes where bias could have significant impact.[11]
- **Financial Services Context:** Bias mitigation is critical due to strict anti-discrimination regulations in lending, insurance, and employment. The CBI explicitly identifies bias as a key risk area for AI in finance.[7] Financial institutions may need to implement specific fairness metrics and conduct bias audits for AI-assisted processes.[62]

8.4.3 Ensuring Transparency and Explainability

Understanding how AI systems arrive at their conclusions is crucial for trust, accountability, debugging, and regulatory compliance, yet LLMs are often described as 'black boxes'.[62]

- **The Need for Transparency:** Users and stakeholders need to understand the basis for Copilot's outputs, especially when they inform important decisions.[48] The EU AI Act mandates transparency for certain AI systems, particularly high-risk ones.[4]
- **Copilot's Approach:** Copilot for M365 enhances transparency by providing citations that link its responses back to the specific source documents, emails, or chats within the user's M365 environment from which information was drawn.[5] This allows users to verify the grounding of the information. Copilot Chat also provides citations for web search results used.[28] Some modes may offer insights into the 'reasoning' process.[80]
- **Limitations:** This provides traceability to sources but doesn't fully explain the internal workings of the LLM itself. The focus is on input/output transparency rather than algorithmic transparency.[62]
- **Financial Services Context:** Traceability and the ability to explain the basis for AI-assisted outputs are vital for audit trails, regulatory reporting (meeting CBI expectations [7]), and resolving customer disputes.

8.4.4 Establishing Accountability for AI-Assisted Decisions

A key ethical question is determining responsibility when an AI system contributes to an error or negative outcome.[48]

- **Microsoft's Stance:** Microsoft's Responsible AI principle of Accountability places responsibility firmly with the humans developing and deploying the AI.[48] Copilot is positioned as an assistant to augment human capabilities, not replace human judgment or accountability.[96]
- **Organisational Imperative:** Organisations must establish clear governance structures and policies that define:
    - The role of Copilot in specific workflows (e.g., assistant, first draft generator, data summariser vs. autonomous decision-maker).
    - The level of human review and oversight required for different types of AI-assisted tasks.[53]
    - Who is ultimately accountable for decisions made with Copilot's assistance.[61]
- **Financial Services Context:** Accountability is non-negotiable. Regulators like the CBI demand clear lines of responsibility for all processes, including those involving AI.[7] Robust audit trails are needed to demonstrate that human judgment was appropriately applied in AI-assisted decisions.

8.5 Validating Accuracy and Reliability of Copilot Outputs

Generative AI models are known to sometimes produce inaccurate, misleading, or entirely fabricated information ('hallucinations').[8] The reliability of Copilot's output is directly dependent on the quality, accuracy, and relevance of the data it accesses – both public web data and the organisation's internal M365 content.[93]

- **The Risk of Inaccuracy:** Blindly trusting Copilot's output without verification can lead to the propagation of errors, poor decision-making, and reputational damage.[41]
- **Mandatory Human Verification:** It is essential to treat Copilot outputs as drafts or suggestions that require critical human review and validation before being used for significant purposes or shared externally.[8]
- **Verification Procedures:** Organisations need to implement processes for:
    - Fact-checking claims or data points generated by Copilot.[99]
    - Cross-referencing information against original sources, using Copilot's citation features.[5]
    - Applying subject matter expertise and critical judgment to evaluate the plausibility and appropriateness of the output.[99]
- **Financial Services Context:** Accuracy is paramount in financial services due to the potential for significant financial loss, regulatory penalties, and damage to customer trust resulting from errors in reporting, analysis, or advice. Rigorous validation processes are indispensable.

8.5.1 Addressing Potential Misuse and Overreliance

Beyond technical risks, human factors play a significant role in the responsible use of AI.

- **Misuse:** Employees might use Copilot for purposes that violate company policy, generate inappropriate content (despite built-in filters [5]), infringe copyright, or attempt to circumvent security controls.
- **Overreliance:** Users, particularly those less experienced or less critical, might accept Copilot's outputs without sufficient scrutiny, leading to the adoption of flawed information, a decline in critical thinking skills, or a failure to develop expertise.[82]
- **Mitigation:** Requires a combination of:
    - Clear Acceptable Use Policies (AUPs) defining boundaries.[96]
    - Training that explicitly covers limitations, the potential for errors, and the importance of human judgment.[96]
    - Fostering a culture that encourages critical evaluation and questioning of AI outputs.[96]
- **Financial Services Context:** Overreliance on AI in areas like compliance checks, risk modelling, or investment recommendations could lead to serious errors with significant consequences. Maintaining strong human oversight and professional judgment is crucial.

Effectively managing these multifaceted risks requires a shift in perspective. Governance for AI like Copilot cannot be merely a technical checklist; it must be a socio-technical endeavour.[61] Technical controls over data access and security are necessary but insufficient without parallel efforts to shape user understanding and behaviour through clear policies, comprehensive training, and the cultivation of a responsible AI culture within the organisation. Furthermore, the very feature that makes Copilot for M365 secure – its respect for existing permissions – creates a direct dependency on the health of the organisation's M365 data governance.[5] Adopting

Copilot responsibly often necessitates a prior or concurrent effort to clean up and tighten M365 access controls to prevent unintended data exposure.

8.5.2 Implementing Robust Mitigation Strategies and Governance

To navigate the risks outlined previously and ensure the responsible and effective deployment of Microsoft Copilot, Irish organisations, particularly financial institutions, must implement a robust set of mitigation strategies and establish strong governance frameworks. This involves a combination of clear policies, technical controls, procedural safeguards, comprehensive training, and defined accountability structures.

8.5.3 Developing Clear AI Usage Policies and Guidelines

Establishing clear rules of engagement for employees using Copilot is fundamental.[71] An AI Usage Policy (AUP) or equivalent set of guidelines should be developed, communicated, and enforced.

- **Essential Content:** The policy should explicitly address:
    - **Scope:** Which Copilot tools are covered (e.g., M365 Copilot, Studio agents, GitHub Copilot).
    - **Permitted Uses:** Clearly define approved use cases aligned with business objectives and roles.
    - **Prohibited Uses:** Outline activities that are not allowed (e.g., generating harmful content, infringing copyright, processing highly sensitive data without specific approval, using for personal gain).
    - **Data Handling:** Provide specific guidance on inputting personal or confidential data into prompts, emphasizing data minimisation and sensitivity awareness.[8]

    - **Output Verification:** Mandate the requirement for human review and validation of Copilot outputs, especially before external sharing or use in critical decision-making.[99] Define the level of scrutiny required based on risk.
    - **Transparency:** Specify when the use of AI assistance should be disclosed (e.g., in certain reports or communications).
    - **Ethical Considerations:** Reinforce principles of fairness, avoiding bias, and respecting privacy.[96]
    - **Security:** Remind users of their responsibilities regarding account security and reporting suspicious activity.
    - **Reporting Concerns:** Establish a clear process for employees to raise concerns or report issues related to AI use or outputs.[61]
- **Alignment and Review:** The policy must align with the organisation's overall code of conduct, values, legal obligations (GDPR, AI Act, employment law), and relevant regulatory requirements (e.g., CBI rules for financial institutions).[96] It should be treated as a living document, subject to regular review and updates as technology and regulations evolve.[59]

8.6 Strengthening Data Governance and Access Controls

Given Copilot for M365's reliance on organisational data via Microsoft Graph, robust data governance within the M365 environment is a non-negotiable prerequisite for safe adoption.[10] Weak data governance translates directly into increased risk of data leakage or misuse via Copilot.

- **Key Technical and Procedural Controls:**
  - **Data Discovery and Classification:** Systematically identify where sensitive data resides across SharePoint Online, OneDrive for Business, Teams, and Exchange Online.[93]
  - **Sensitivity Labelling:** Implement and enforce Microsoft Purview Information Protection sensitivity labels to classify data (e.g., Public, Internal, Confidential, Highly Confidential).[92] These labels can underpin protection policies (like encryption or access restrictions) and potentially inform Copilot's behaviour (though direct restriction based purely on labels needs verification).
  - **Access Control Remediation:** Conduct thorough audits of permissions on SharePoint sites, Microsoft Teams, and M365 Groups. Remediate overly broad access rights, enforce the principle of least privilege, and establish clear ownership and review processes for access management.[10] Pay particular attention to guest and external sharing settings.[92]
  - **Data Loss Prevention (DLP):** Configure Microsoft Purview DLP policies to monitor and block the inappropriate sharing of sensitive information, including potentially via Copilot interactions.[101]

- **Management of ROT Data:** Implement strategies to identify and manage Redundant, Obsolete, and Trivial (ROT) data. Reducing ROT improves the quality of information Copilot accesses and reduces the attack surface.[93]
- **Data Retention and Deletion:** Enforce clear data retention schedules across M365 using Purview policies to ensure data is not kept longer than necessary, aligning with GDPR's storage limitation principle and reducing the volume of legacy data Copilot might access.[5] Ensure policies cover Copilot interaction history logs.[5]

8.6.1 Establishing Procedures for Verification and Human Oversight

Because AI-generated content can be inaccurate or biased, formal procedures for human review and oversight are essential.[8]

- **Workflow Integration:** Define specific points in workflows where Copilot outputs must be reviewed and approved by a human before proceeding. This is particularly crucial for content intended for external audiences, regulatory submissions, financial reporting, legal documents, or decisions with significant impact on individuals (e.g., HR, credit).
- **Responsibility:** Clearly assign responsibility for verification to individuals with the appropriate subject matter expertise and authority.
- **Verification Standards:** Provide guidance on *how* to verify outputs, encouraging critical assessment, fact-checking against reliable sources (using Copilot's citations where available [5]), and checking for potential bias or ethical concerns.[99]

- **Risk-Based Oversight:** The level of required oversight should be proportionate to the risk associated with the task or decision being supported by Copilot.

8.6.2 Comprehensive Employee Training Programs

Effective training is critical to ensure employees understand how to use Copilot productively, responsibly, and safely.[21]

- **Target Audience:** Training should be provided to all potential Copilot users, potentially tailored to different roles or levels of usage. Managers also need specific training on overseeing their teams' use of AI.[100]
- **Key Training Content:**
  - **Capabilities and Limitations:** Realistic overview of what Copilot can and cannot do effectively; understanding the probabilistic nature of LLMs.
  - **Data Interaction:** How Copilot accesses and uses organisational data; the importance of permissions.
  - **Policies and Ethics:** Detailed review of the AI Usage Policy, ethical guidelines, fairness, and bias awareness.
  - **Privacy and Security:** Best practices for handling sensitive data in prompts; recognising phishing or social engineering attempts leveraging AI.
  - **Accuracy and Verification:** Emphasising the need for critical evaluation and fact-checking of outputs.
  - **Prompt Engineering:** Basic skills for writing effective prompts to get better results.[2]
  - **Reporting Issues:** How to report technical problems, inaccurate outputs, biased results, or ethical concerns.

- **Format and Frequency:** Training should be an ongoing effort, not a one-time event, given the rapid evolution of AI.[13] Utilize a mix of formats like interactive e-learning modules, workshops, practical exercises, Q&A sessions, and readily accessible resources (e.g., FAQs, best practice guides).[98]

8.6.3 Defining Roles, Responsibilities, and Accountability

Clear allocation of roles and responsibilities is essential for effective AI governance and accountability.[9]

- **Governance Structure:** Establish a formal AI Governance Committee or Council comprising representatives from key functions (IT, Security, Legal, Compliance, Risk, HR, relevant Business Units).[59] This body should oversee policy development, risk management strategy, ethical reviews, and compliance monitoring.
- **Defined Roles:** Clearly document the responsibilities of:
    - **Data Owners/Stewards:** Accountable for the quality, classification, and access controls for data within their domains.
    - **IT/Security:** Technical implementation, platform security, monitoring infrastructure, managing licenses.
    - **Legal & Compliance:** Ensuring adherence to regulations (GDPR, AI Act), internal policies, advising on legal risks.
    - **Risk Management:** Assessing and mitigating AI-related risks within the organisation's overall risk framework.
    - **Human Resources:** Developing and delivering training, managing change, addressing workforce impacts, ensuring fairness in HR applications of AI.

- **Business Unit Leaders/Managers:** Ensuring appropriate use within their teams, overseeing workflow integration, providing feedback on AI effectiveness and risks.[100]
- **End Users:** Adhering to policies, using Copilot responsibly, verifying outputs, reporting issues.

Implementing these strategies requires a proactive and holistic approach. Strong governance is not merely a constraint but an essential enabler for building the necessary trust – among employees, customers, and regulators – to confidently scale the use of Copilot and realise its full potential benefits.[93] Without addressing the foundational elements of data governance, security, user education, and clear accountability, organisations risk encountering significant pitfalls that could outweigh the productivity gains.

8.6.4 Table 2: Checklist for Responsible AI Controls for Copilot Deployment

Control Area	Specific Control/Action	Status/Owner (Example)	Notes/Evidence Link (Example)
Policy & Guidelines	AI Usage Policy Developed & Communicated	Completed / Legal Dept	Link to Policy Document v1.2
	Ethical Guidelines Established & Integrated	Completed / AI Gov Com	Link to Ethics Framework
Data Governance	Sensitive Data Discovery Exercise Completed (M365)	In Progress / IT Sec	Link to Discovery Report Q3
	Sensitivity Labels Deployed & Policy Enforced	Completed / Compliance	Link to Purview Label Policy
	M365 Access Control Review & Remediation Plan	In Progress / IT Ops	Link to Remediation Tracker
	ROT Data Identification &	Planned / Data Gov Team	Link to Data Lifecycle Policy

	Management Process		
Security	DLP Policies Configured for Key Sensitive Data Types	Completed / IT Sec	Link to DLP Policy Rules
	Multi-Factor Authentication (MFA) Enforced for All M365 Users	Completed / IT Sec	IAM Policy Document
Verification/Oversight	Output Review Process Defined (Risk-Based)	Completed / AI Gov Com	Link to Verification SOP
	Human Oversight Mandated for External Comms/Financial Reporting	Completed / Policy	Section 4.b in AI Usage Policy
Training & Awareness	Role-Based Training Content Developed	Completed / HR & L&D	Link to Training Modules
	Initial User Training Delivered / Schedule	In Progress / HR	Link to Training Schedule

	Communicated		
Accountability	AI Governance Committee Established & Chartered	Completed / Exec Sponsor	Link to Committee Charter
	Roles & Responsibilities Documented	Completed / AI Gov Com	Link to R&R Matrix
Monitoring	Usage Monitoring Plan & Tools Identified	Planned / IT Ops	Decision Log - Monitoring Tools
	Audit Log Review Process (Security & Compliance) Defined	Planned / Compliance	Draft Audit Procedure

9

9.1 Microsoft Copilot in Action: Irish Case Studies

Understanding how organisations are practically implementing Microsoft Copilot, the challenges they face, and the benefits they realise provides valuable context for Irish enterprises considering adoption. While detailed, publicly documented case studies specifically focusing on *Copilot for Microsoft 365* deployment within Irish organisations are still emerging – partly due to the recency of its broad availability following the removal of the 300-seat minimum purchase requirement [19] – several examples and partner activities offer relevant insights.

9.1.1 Introduction to Case Examples

The following examples illustrate early adoption patterns, motivations, and the critical role of governance and partnerships in the Irish context. It is important to note the difficulty in finding publicly verified case studies detailing specific financial institutions in Ireland implementing Copilot for M365 at this stage. The examples below are drawn from available information on Irish companies or prominent partners operating within Ireland.

9.1.2 Case Study 1: Musgrave Group (Retail)

- **Context:** Musgrave Group, a major Irish family-owned retail, wholesale, and foodservice company, has initiated the deployment of Microsoft Copilot tools among its staff.[18]
- **Implementation:** The rollout is overseen by the company's Head of IT, indicating a structured approach.[18] The specific Copilot tools are likely Copilot for Microsoft 365, given the enterprise context and focus on staff productivity.
- **Motivation:** Key drivers appear to be boosting employee productivity and ensuring the secure and governed use of AI within the organisation. An interesting factor mentioned was the desire to manage and potentially mitigate the risks associated with uncontrolled or 'shadow AI' usage by employees (i.e., staff using external AI tools without organisational oversight).[18]
- **Challenges:** The Head of IT acknowledged that the implementation journey was not without its difficulties, describing it as potentially "bumpy along the way," although specific details of these bumps were not provided.[18] This suggests that even large organisations face hurdles in deployment, potentially related to technical integration, user adoption, or change management.
- **Benefits:** The primary anticipated benefits are enhanced productivity and improved security posture regarding AI use.[18] Quantitative results were not detailed in the source.
- **Responsible AI Measures:** The focus on security and addressing shadow AI implies that governance and responsible use were key considerations from the outset.[18]

9.1.3 Case Study 2: KPMG Ireland (Professional Services / Advisory Role)

- **Context:** KPMG Ireland, a major professional services firm, is actively involved in the AI space, collaborating with Microsoft. This includes establishing an AI readiness hub designed to help clients, including those in Ireland, navigate responsible AI implementation and prepare for the EU AI Act.[102]
- **Implementation:** While specific details of KPMG Ireland's *internal* use of Copilot are not provided, firms like KPMG typically adopt such technologies internally to enhance their own operations (e.g., research, analysis, report generation, document review – aligning with general finance and professional services use cases [65]) and build expertise for client advisory. Their primary documented role is advising clients on AI strategy, implementation, risk management, and compliance.[102] They utilise tools like Cranium AI to provide clients with visibility into AI usage.[102]
- **Challenges Addressed (for clients):** KPMG helps organisations overcome common hurdles in AI adoption, such as understanding where to start, navigating security and compliance complexities (particularly the EU AI Act), assessing readiness, and integrating AI effectively into existing processes.[65] They note that the effort required for integration is often underestimated.[65]
- **Benefits Offered (to clients):** KPMG aims to accelerate clients' responsible AI adoption journeys, provide clarity on compliance requirements, enhance efficiency within functions like finance and insurance through AI (e.g., automating analysis, accelerating coding conversion for legacy models), and ensure AI initiatives align with overall business strategy.[65]
- **Responsible AI Measures:** KPMG's advisory services explicitly focus on responsible AI frameworks, governance, security,

ethical considerations, and readiness for regulations like the EU AI Act, advocating for a measured, strategic approach to adoption.[65]

9.1.4 Case Study 3: Other Relevant Irish Examples & Partner Activity

While specific, detailed case studies on Copilot for M365 in Irish financial institutions were not found in the provided materials, several other data points illustrate activity and adoption trends in Ireland:

- **ESB (Energy) & ESW (eCommerce):** An Post presentation slides mention ESB deploying Copilot for Microsoft 365 to enhance employee efficiency and collaboration, and Irish eCommerce company ESW using GitHub Copilot to automate repetitive coding tasks for developers.[78] This confirms adoption in major Irish organisations across different sectors.
- **Partner Sales & Services:**
  - **Bytes Technology Group:** This major IT solutions provider, with a likely presence serving Irish clients, reported selling over 130,000 Copilot licenses (presumably M365 Copilot given the volume and enterprise context) since its launch, generating substantial recurring revenue. They also use Copilot extensively internally and are developing associated services to support customer readiness and adoption.[103] This indicates significant market uptake facilitated through partners.
  - **PwC Ireland:** Actively collaborates with Microsoft on generative AI, offering clients a responsible use toolkit and audit controls.[72] PwC highlights Copilot's productivity benefits across M365 apps and specific business functions [33], suggesting both advisory capacity and likely internal use to build expertise.
  - **Accenture Ireland:** Has a significant presence and focuses on the potential (and challenges) of generative AI for Irish businesses, publishing research on the topic.[17]

Their deep global partnership with Microsoft [105] suggests they are a key player in AI implementations in Ireland.

- **Local Irish IT Partners (HCS, Storm Technology, IT.ie):** These Irish-based Microsoft partners are actively marketing and providing guidance on Copilot for M365, producing eGuides and insights detailing features, use cases (including HR, Finance, Legal, Customer Service), security aspects, and the differences between Copilot products.[14] This demonstrates engagement and capability within the local partner ecosystem.

- **Microsoft Ireland:** Actively promoting AI adoption, highlighting the potential economic benefits for Ireland (€250bn GDP increase forecast [18]), running AI skills initiatives [106], and emphasizing their commitment to responsible AI development and deployment, with engineering work happening locally.[18]

9.1.5 Synthesis of Learnings from Irish Context

Drawing from these examples and activities, several themes emerge regarding Copilot adoption in Ireland:

- **Active Adoption:** Irish organisations across various sectors (retail, energy, eCommerce, professional services) are actively deploying Copilot tools, primarily Copilot for M365 and GitHub Copilot.[18]
- **Productivity Focus:** The main driver appears to be enhancing employee productivity and efficiency by automating routine tasks and streamlining workflows.[18]
- **Governance is Key:** Security, compliance, and responsible use are prominent concerns and integral parts of the implementation strategy for early adopters like Musgrave and advisory firms like KPMG and PwC.[18] Addressing potential 'shadow AI' use is also a factor.[18]
- **Implementation Challenges:** Deployment is not always straightforward, with potential "bumps" related to integration, adoption, or change management.[18]
- **Partner Ecosystem Role:** Both global SIs (KPMG, PwC, Accenture) with strong Irish operations and local Irish IT providers (Bytes, HCS, Storm, IT.ie) are playing a crucial role in facilitating adoption. They provide readiness assessments, implementation services, governance advice, and ongoing support.[14] This reliance on partners is likely essential for many Irish organisations, especially given the complexities around governance, security configuration, and potential customisation via Copilot Studio.

9.2 A Practical Implementation Framework for Irish Organisations

Adopting Microsoft Copilot, especially Copilot for Microsoft 365, requires more than simply purchasing licenses. A structured, strategic implementation framework is essential to maximise benefits, mitigate risks, ensure regulatory compliance (particularly within the Irish/EU context), and foster user adoption.[101] Rushing deployment without adequate preparation can lead to security vulnerabilities, privacy breaches, user frustration, and failure to achieve desired outcomes. This framework outlines key phases for a responsible and effective rollout, tailored for Irish organisations, including financial institutions.

9.2.1 Phase 1: Assessment and Planning

This foundational phase involves understanding the organisation's context, defining goals, and assessing readiness.

- **Define Clear Business Objectives:** Articulate specific, measurable goals for Copilot adoption. Examples include: "Reduce time spent by finance team on monthly reporting by 15%," "Improve first-call resolution rate in customer service by 10%," or "Accelerate software development cycles by 20%." Align these objectives with broader organisational strategy.[9]
- **Identify and Prioritise Use Cases:** Based on objectives, identify potential Copilot use cases across different departments and roles (referencing Section 5). Prioritise based on potential value, feasibility, and risk level.[16] For initial phases, focus on high-value, lower-risk scenarios (e.g., internal content summarisation, drafting assistance) before tackling more complex or sensitive applications.
- **Conduct Comprehensive Risk Assessment:** Perform a thorough assessment covering:
    - **Data Privacy (GDPR):** Identify personal data likely to be processed, determine lawful basis, assess risks to data subjects' rights. A Data Protection Impact Assessment (DPIA) is highly likely necessary, especially for financial institutions or processing involving sensitive data.[6]
    - **Security:** Analyse potential vulnerabilities related to data exposure, compromised accounts, prompt injection, and third-party plugins.[10]
    - **Bias and Fairness:** Evaluate potential for biased outputs based on organisational data and use case context.[11]

    - **Accuracy and Reliability:** Assess risks associated with potential hallucinations or inaccurate outputs for prioritised use cases.[93]
    - **Ethical Concerns:** Consider broader ethical implications aligned with organisational values.
    - **EU AI Act:** Classify intended use cases against the Act's risk tiers. If any use case potentially falls into the 'high-risk' category (e.g., assisting credit scoring, insurance pricing, recruitment filtering), plan for the associated compliance obligations.[51]
- **Assess Organisational Readiness:** Evaluate preparedness across multiple dimensions:
    - **Technical:** Verify prerequisite M365 licenses [19], assess M365 tenant health, network capacity, and IAM maturity.
    - **Data:** Critically assess the state of data governance within M365. Are permissions well-managed? Is sensitive data identified and labelled? Is there significant ROT data? Address critical gaps *before* proceeding.[10]
    - **People & Culture:** Gauge digital literacy, openness to change, and existing AI skills within the workforce.[17]

9.2.2 Phase 2: Policy Development and Governance Setup

Based on the assessment, establish the necessary governance structures and policies.

- **Establish AI Governance Body:** Formally constitute a cross-functional committee (e.g., AI Council, Responsible AI Taskforce) with representatives from IT, Security, Legal, Compliance, Risk, HR, and key business units. Grant this body clear authority and mandate.[59]
- **Develop/Update Policies:**
  - Create a comprehensive AI Usage Policy (AUP) as detailed in Section 7.1.[71]
  - Review and update existing Data Governance, Data Classification, Access Control, Data Retention, and Security policies to explicitly address AI tools like Copilot.[57]
  - Define or adopt an organisational Ethical AI Framework.[61]
- **Define Roles and Responsibilities:** Clearly document who is responsible for specific aspects of Copilot governance, management, and oversight (as per Section 7.5).[59]

9.2.3 Phase 3: Pilot Programs and Testing

Before widespread rollout, conduct controlled pilot programs to test assumptions, gather feedback, and refine the approach.[16]

- **Scope Pilot:** Select specific departments, teams, or use cases identified in Phase 1 for the initial pilot. Choose participants representing different roles and technical aptitudes. Consider a team-based nomination process for fairness and collaboration.[92]
- **Deploy to Pilot Group:** Provision licenses and deploy Copilot to the selected pilot users. Provide initial training and support.
- **Test and Validate:** Encourage users to test Copilot for the prioritised use cases. Systematically evaluate its effectiveness, accuracy, usability, and performance.[71] Validate outputs rigorously, especially in sensitive areas.
- **Collect Feedback:** Use surveys, interviews, and focus groups to gather detailed feedback from pilot users on their experience, perceived benefits, challenges encountered, usability issues, and any observed risks or unexpected behaviours.
- **Analyse and Iterate:** Analyse pilot results and feedback. Identify successes, areas for improvement, necessary policy adjustments, additional training needs, and technical refinements. Use these findings to inform the broader rollout strategy.

9.2.4 Phase 4: Technical Integration and Security Configuration

Prepare the technical environment for broader deployment based on pilot learnings.

- **Licensing and Provisioning:** Procure the required number of Copilot licenses (M365 add-on, potentially Studio) and establish a process for assigning them to eligible users or teams.[19]
- **M365 Environment Hardening:** Implement necessary configurations identified during readiness assessment and pilot phases. This includes ensuring prerequisite applications are deployed [34], finalising sensitivity label policies [92], implementing refined access controls [10], configuring DLP rules [101], and ensuring robust IAM (e.g., MFA).[59]
- **Plugin Governance:** If applicable, establish and implement the process for reviewing, approving, deploying, and monitoring any Copilot plugins.[5]

9.2.5 Phase 5: Training and Change Management

Prepare the workforce for the change and equip them with necessary skills.

- **Develop Comprehensive Training:** Create role-based training materials covering capabilities, limitations, policies, ethics, security, verification, and effective prompting (as per Section 7.4).[71] Include specific guidance relevant to the Irish regulatory environment (GDPR awareness, data sensitivity).
- **Deliver Training:** Roll out mandatory training to all users scheduled to receive Copilot access *before* or concurrently with deployment. Establish ongoing learning resources and opportunities (e.g., champion networks, regular tips, advanced sessions).[92]
- **Implement Communication Plan:** Execute a clear and transparent communication strategy.[100] Explain the rationale for adoption, expected benefits, timelines, policies, support channels, and how employee concerns will be addressed. Manage expectations realistically.
- **Provide User Support:** Establish clear channels for users to get help, ask questions, and report technical or ethical issues (e.g., dedicated helpdesk support, internal forums, AI champions).[61]

9.2.6 Phase 6: Monitoring, Auditing, and Continuous Improvement

Adoption is not a one-time event; ongoing monitoring and adaptation are crucial.[59]

- **Monitor Usage and Adoption:** Track key metrics like license utilisation, active usage across different Copilot features and M365 apps, user sentiment, and reported issues.[22] Identify areas where adoption is lagging or where users are excelling.
- **Measure Impact and ROI:** Evaluate the extent to which the initial objectives (Phase 1) are being met. Quantify benefits where possible (e.g., time saved, productivity improvements, cost reductions).[22]
- **Monitor Risks:** Continuously monitor for security events, potential data leakage incidents (using DLP alerts, audit logs), instances of biased or inaccurate outputs, and policy violations.[11] Review Copilot interaction logs (via Purview) as needed for investigations.[5]
- **Conduct Regular Audits:** Perform periodic audits focusing on:
    - Compliance with the AI Usage Policy.
    - Effectiveness of data governance controls (permissions, labels).
    - Adherence to verification and oversight procedures.
    - Training completion and effectiveness.[59]
- **Review and Adapt:** The AI Governance Committee should regularly review monitoring data, audit findings, user feedback, evolving AI capabilities, and changes in the regulatory landscape (e.g., AI Act implementation milestones, new DPC/CBI guidance). Use this information to update policies,

refine governance controls, enhance training, and adjust the overall Copilot strategy.[59]

This phased approach should be viewed as an iterative cycle rather than a strictly linear process. Learnings from the monitoring phase should feed back into earlier phases, leading to continuous refinement of policies, controls, training, and technical configurations. Such an adaptive strategy is essential for navigating the dynamic nature of AI technology and ensuring long-term, responsible value creation from Microsoft Copilot within the specific context of Irish enterprises. A visual representation of this framework might depict these phases in a circular or spiral diagram to emphasize the ongoing nature of assessment, implementation, and improvement.

9.3 Conclusion and Recommendations

Microsoft Copilot presents a compelling proposition for Irish enterprises, offering the potential to significantly enhance productivity, streamline complex processes, and unlock new insights from organisational data. Its integration within the familiar Microsoft 365 suite lowers the barrier to entry for AI adoption across various roles, from finance and HR to sales and IT.[1] However, this potential is intrinsically linked with significant responsibilities and risks, particularly concerning data privacy, security, accuracy, bias, and ethical use.[8]

For organisations operating in Ireland, these considerations are magnified by a stringent regulatory environment governed by GDPR and the forthcoming EU AI Act, with active oversight from the DPC and, for financial institutions, the CBI.[4] The ability of Copilot for Microsoft 365 to access and process vast amounts of internal organisational data via Microsoft Graph is both its greatest strength and its most critical vulnerability.[19] Successful and responsible adoption is therefore contingent on a proactive, strategic, and governance-led approach.

Based on the analysis presented in this report, the following actionable recommendations are provided for Irish enterprises, including financial institutions, considering or embarking on their Microsoft Copilot journey:

1. **Prioritise Strategy and Governance Over Speed:** Resist the urge to deploy Copilot rapidly without a clear strategy. Define specific business objectives, identify high-value, lower-risk initial use cases, and conduct thorough risk assessments (including DPIAs where necessary) *before* widespread rollout.[9] Establish a cross-functional AI governance body and develop clear AI usage policies from day one.[59]

2. **Treat M365 Data Governance as Foundational:** Copilot's safety and effectiveness depend heavily on the health of your existing Microsoft 365 environment. Prioritise data discovery, classification (using Purview sensitivity labels), access control remediation (enforcing least privilege), and management of ROT data *before* granting Copilot broad access to organisational content.[10] This is not optional; it is a prerequisite for responsible deployment.

3. **Adopt a Phased and Iterative Rollout:** Begin with controlled pilot programs involving representative user groups and use cases.[16] Gather detailed feedback on usability, benefits, challenges, and risks. Use these learnings to iteratively refine policies, training, technical configurations, and the broader deployment strategy. Avoid a 'big bang' approach.

4. **Invest in Comprehensive and Continuous Training:** Equip all users with a clear understanding of Copilot's capabilities *and* limitations, the organisation's usage policies, ethical considerations (including bias awareness), data privacy responsibilities, and the critical need for verifying outputs.[96] Training must be ongoing to keep pace with technological evolution and reinforce responsible practices.[13]

5. **Mandate Human Oversight and Critical Evaluation:** Reinforce that Copilot is an assistant, not a replacement for human judgment and accountability.[48] Implement clear procedures requiring human review and validation of Copilot outputs, especially for decisions with significant consequences, external communications, or regulatory submissions.[53] Foster a culture of critical thinking, not blind acceptance of AI suggestions.

6. **Stay Engaged with the Regulatory Environment:** Actively monitor guidance from the DPC, CBI (for financial institutions), and developments related to the EU AI Act's implementation.[4]

Participate in industry discussions and adapt governance frameworks as requirements evolve. Proactive engagement demonstrates due diligence.

7. **Leverage the Partner Ecosystem:** Recognise that successful implementation often requires external expertise. Engage with trusted Microsoft partners (global SIs or local Irish specialists) for readiness assessments, technical implementation, data governance remediation, policy development, training support, and potentially customisation using Copilot Studio.[14]

Microsoft Copilot offers a powerful toolkit with the potential to reshape how work is done within Irish enterprises. However, unlocking this potential safely and sustainably requires more than technological deployment; it demands a deliberate commitment to responsible innovation, underpinned by robust governance, continuous learning, and unwavering human oversight. By adopting a measured, informed, and ethically grounded strategy, Irish organisations can navigate the complexities of AI adoption and harness Copilot's capabilities to drive meaningful value while maintaining trust and ensuring compliance.

9.4 References

1. How to Boost Your Productivity and Creativity with Copilot for Microsoft 365 - Lantern, accessed on April 21, 2025, https://lanternstudios.com/insights/blog/how-to-boost-your-productivity-and-creativity-with-copilot-for-microsoft-365/
2. ChatGPT vs Microsoft Copilot vs Copilot for M365: What Sets Them Apart?, accessed on April 21, 2025, https://www.doherty.co.uk/blog/chatgpt-vs-microsoft-copilot-vs-copilot-for-m365/
3. How real-world businesses are transforming with AI — with more than 140 new stories, accessed on April 21, 2025, https://blogs.microsoft.com/blog/2025/03/10/https-blogs-microsoft-com-blog-2024-11-12-how-real-world-businesses-are-transforming-with-ai/
4. EU AI Act: first regulation on artificial intelligence | Topics | European ..., accessed on April 21, 2025, https://www.europarl.europa.eu/topics/en/article/20230601STO93804/eu-ai-act-first-regulation-on-artificial-intelligence
5. Data, Privacy, and Security for Microsoft 365 Copilot, accessed on April 21, 2025, https://learn.microsoft.com/en-us/copilot/microsoft-365/microsoft-365-copilot-privacy
6. Irish data protection commission highlights GDPR risks in developing and using AI, accessed on April 21, 2025, https://www.pinsentmasons.com/out-law/news/irish-dpc-gdpr-risks-developing-using-ai
7. www.centralbank.ie, accessed on April 21, 2025, https://www.centralbank.ie/docs/default-source/publications/regulatory-and-supervisory-outlook-reports/regulatory-supervisory-outlook-report-2025.pdf?sfvrsn=e185651a_9

8. AI, Large Language Models and Data Protection | 18/07/2024 | Data ..., accessed on April 21, 2025, http://www.dataprotection.ie/en/dpc-guidance/blogs/AI-LLMs-and-Data-Protection

9. Financial consumer protection and market conduct considerations of ..., accessed on April 21, 2025, https://www.centralbank.ie/news/article/speech-colm-kincaid-financial-consumer-protection-and-market-conduct-considerations-of-AI-in-finance-22-may-2024

10. Microsoft Copilot Security Risks: Are Your M365 Settings Leaving You Exposed?, accessed on April 21, 2025, https://www.channelpronetwork.com/2025/03/26/copilot-security-risks-from-your-microsoft-365-settings/

11. What is AI Bias? - Understanding Its Impact, Risks, and Mitigation Strategies, accessed on April 21, 2025, https://www.holisticai.com/blog/what-is-ai-bias-risks-mitigation-strategies

12. AI Insights: Opportunities and Risks| BMO Capital Markets, accessed on April 21, 2025, https://commercial.bmo.com/en/us/insights/ai-insights-opportunities-and-risks/

13. Artificial intelligence will mean job losses - but more job gains - The Irish Times, accessed on April 21, 2025, https://www.irishtimes.com/special-reports/2024/07/19/artificial-intelligence-will-mean-job-losses-but-more-job-gains/

14. Introducing Copilot for Microsoft 365 - HCS, accessed on April 21, 2025, https://www.hcs.ie/wp-content/uploads/2024/10/Microsoft-Copilot-eGuide-1.pdf

15. Copilot for M365 Vs Copilot Agents Vs Copilot Studio - Storm Technology, accessed on April 21, 2025,

https://www.storm.ie/insights/insights/difference-between-copilot-for-m365-copilot-studio-copilot-agents-/

16. Copilot for Banks - What is It and 7 Steps Before Considering, accessed on April 21, 2025, https://southstatecorrespondent.com/banker-to-banker/innovation/copilot-for-banks-7-steps-before-integrating-generative-ai/
17. Accelerating the Ireland's generative AI reinvention - Accenture, accessed on April 21, 2025, https://www.accenture.com/content/dam/accenture/final/accenture-com/document-3/Accelerating-Irelands-Generative-AI-Reinvention.pdf
18. "Not just a set of interesting science fair projects": Demystifying AI's risks and opportunities, accessed on April 21, 2025, https://thecurrency.news/articles/183411/not-just-a-set-of-interesting-science-fair-projects-demystifying-ais-risks-and-opportunities/
19. Microsoft 365 Copilot: License, Cost, Download, More! [2024-09] - schneider it management, accessed on April 21, 2025, https://www.schneider.im/microsoft-365-copilot-the-future-of-productivity/
20. Microsoft Copilot - Wikipedia, accessed on April 21, 2025, https://en.wikipedia.org/wiki/Microsoft_Copilot
21. Initial guidance on the use of AI in the provision of investment services - Walkers Global, accessed on April 21, 2025, https://www.walkersglobal.com/Insights/2024/06/Initial-guidance-on-the-use-of-AI-in-the-provision-of-investment-services
22. AI for Enterprise Productivity | Microsoft 365 Copilot, accessed on April 21, 2025, https://www.microsoft.com/en-us/microsoft-365/copilot/enterprise

23. Which Copilot Plan Is Right for You? - Microsoft, accessed on April 21, 2025, https://www.microsoft.com/en-us/microsoft-copilot/for-individuals/do-more-with-ai/general-ai/right-copilot-plan-for-you

24. AI Productivity Tools for Microsoft 365, accessed on April 21, 2025, https://www.microsoft.com/en-us/microsoft-365/copilot

25. AI for Enterprise Productivity | Microsoft 365 Copilot, accessed on April 21, 2025, https://www.microsoft.com/en-ie/microsoft-365/copilot/enterprise

26. Microsoft Copilot 101: What It Is and How to Use It - Grammarly Blog, accessed on April 21, 2025, https://www.grammarly.com/blog/ai/what-is-microsoft-copilot/

27. Copilot Pro Plan & Pricing – Premium AI Features & Latest Models | ..., accessed on April 21, 2025, https://www.microsoft.com/en-us/store/b/copilotpro

28. Microsoft 365 Copilot Chat Privacy and Protections, accessed on April 21, 2025, https://learn.microsoft.com/en-us/copilot/privacy-and-protections

29. Microsoft 365 Copilot - Service Descriptions, accessed on April 21, 2025, https://learn.microsoft.com/en-us/office365/servicedescriptions/office-365-platform-service-description/microsoft-365-copilot

30. Copilot for Microsoft 365 – Plans and Pricing, accessed on April 21, 2025, https://www.microsoft.com/en-us/microsoft-365/copilot-for-microsoft-365?trk=test

31. Welcome to the Microsoft 365 Copilot app, accessed on April 21, 2025, https://www.office.com/?ref=tabor%22target%3D%22_blank

32. Data Protection Impact Assessment (DPIA) – Microsoft CoPilot 365 - Information Commissioner's Office, accessed on April 21, 2025, https://ico.org.uk/media2/ob4ncmpz/ic-359252-x5s0-copilot-dpia.pdf

33. Greater employee productivity with Copilot - PwC Germany, accessed on April 21, 2025, https://www.pwc.de/en/strong-alliances/pwc-and-microsoft/greater-employee-productivity-with-copilot.html

34. Microsoft Copilot Support, accessed on April 21, 2025, https://www.uscloud.com/microsoft_support/microsoft-copilot-support/

35. Guiding Your Business to AI Success with Microsoft 365 Copilot | PwC Switzerland, accessed on April 21, 2025, https://www.pwc.ch/en/insights/digital/microsoft-365-copilot.html

36. Unlock more business potential - Managed IT Services | IT.ie, accessed on April 21, 2025, https://it.ie/wp-content/uploads/2024/10/Ebook-Unlock-more-business-potential_Token_24092017593461.pdf

37. Anyone using Copilot for M365? What gains does it bring you? : r/sysadmin - Reddit, accessed on April 21, 2025, https://www.reddit.com/r/sysadmin/comments/1i3du6f/anyone_using_copilot_for_m365_what_gains_does_it/

38. Data Protection Impact Assessment (DPIA) – Microsoft CoPilot 365 | Steiger Legal, accessed on April 21, 2025, https://steigerlegal.ch/wp-content/uploads/2024/12/uk-ico-dpia-microsoft-copilot-365-draft-01-1.pdf

39. Microsoft unveils Copilot Pro to bring more AI services to consumers - Silicon Republic, accessed on April 21, 2025, https://www.siliconrepublic.com/machines/microsoft-copilot-pro-ai-consumers-enterprise

40. GDPR & Generative AI - Microsoft Public Sector Center of Expertise, accessed on April 21, 2025, https://wwps.microsoft.com/wp-content/uploads/2024/04/GDPR-and-Generative-AI-A-Guide-for-the-Public-Sector-FINAL.pdf

41. Microsoft Copilot: Compliance and ethical considerations for the AI tool - @theU, accessed on April 21, 2025, https://attheu.utah.edu/facultystaff/microsoft-copilot-compliance-and-ethical-considerations-for-the-ai-tool/

42. Official Microsoft Copilot Studio documentation, accessed on April 21, 2025, https://learn.microsoft.com/en-us/microsoft-copilot-studio/

43. Customize Copilot and Create Agents | Microsoft Copilot Studio, accessed on April 21, 2025, https://www.microsoft.com/en-us/microsoft-copilot/microsoft-copilot-studio

44. Copilot Studio overview - Learn Microsoft, accessed on April 21, 2025, https://learn.microsoft.com/en-us/microsoft-copilot-studio/fundamentals-what-is-copilot-studio

45. Announcing new computer use in Microsoft Copilot Studio for UI automation, accessed on April 21, 2025, https://www.microsoft.com/en-us/microsoft-copilot/blog/copilot-studio/announcing-computer-use-microsoft-copilot-studio-ui-automation/

46. Microsoft Introduces 'Computer Use' Automation in Copilot Studio - Redmondmag.com, accessed on April 21, 2025, https://redmondmag.com/articles/2025/04/16/microsoft-introduces-computer-use-automation-in-copilot-studio.aspx

47. Azure OpenAI Service models - Learn Microsoft, accessed on April 21, 2025, https://learn.microsoft.com/en-us/azure/ai-services/openai/concepts/models

48. AI Considerations for Your Cloud Strategy - Cloud Adoption Framework | Microsoft Learn, accessed on April 21, 2025, https://learn.microsoft.com/en-us/azure/cloud-adoption-framework/strategy/inform/ai

49. The EU AI Act: What Businesses Need To Know | Insights - Skadden Arps, accessed on April 21, 2025, https://www.skadden.com/insights/publications/2024/06/quarterly-insights/the-eu-ai-act-what-businesses-need-to-know

50. EU AI Act Compliance Checker, accessed on April 21, 2025, https://artificialintelligenceact.eu/assessment/eu-ai-act-compliance-checker/

51. The EU AI Act: What it means for your business | EY - Switzerland, accessed on April 21, 2025, https://www.ey.com/en_ch/insights/forensic-integrity-services/the-eu-ai-act-what-it-means-for-your-business

52. AI Act | Shaping Europe's digital future - European Union, accessed on April 21, 2025, https://digital-strategy.ec.europa.eu/en/policies/regulatory-framework-ai

53. EU AI Act: Key Points for Financial Services Businesses | Insights & Resources | Goodwin, accessed on April 21, 2025, https://www.goodwinlaw.com/en/insights/publications/2024/08/alerts-practices-pif-key-points-for-financial-services-businesses

54. A concise EU AI Act summary for in-scope organizations | Vanta, accessed on April 21, 2025, https://www.vanta.com/resources/eu-ai-act-guide

55. EDPB opinion on AI models: GDPR principles support responsible AI - European Union, accessed on April 21, 2025, https://www.edpb.europa.eu/news/news/2024/edpb-opinion-ai-models-gdpr-principles-support-responsible-ai_en

56. AI system development: CNIL's recommendations to comply with the GDPR, accessed on April 21, 2025, https://www.cnil.fr/en/ai-system-development-cnils-recommendations-comply-gdpr

57. Practical Solutions for Harmonized Compliance with GDPR and AI, accessed on April 21, 2025, https://gdprlocal.com/practical-solutions-for-harmonized-compliance-with-gdpr-and-ai/

58. Ireland: DPC publishes blog on AI, LLMs, and data protection | News - DataGuidance, accessed on April 21, 2025, https://www.dataguidance.com/news/ireland-dpc-publishes-blog-ai-llms-and-data-protection

59. Top 9 AI Data Governance Best Practices for Security, Compliance, and Quality, accessed on April 21, 2025, https://www.pmi.org/blog/ai-data-governance-best-practices

60. How does GDPR fit into the data governance framework? - Secoda, accessed on April 21, 2025, https://www.secoda.co/blog/gdpr-and-data-governance-framework

61. Responsible AI: Key Principles and Best Practices - Atlassian, accessed on April 21, 2025, https://www.atlassian.com/blog/artificial-intelligence/responsible-ai

62. (PDF) Mitigating AI Bias in Financial Decision-Making: A DEI Perspective" - ResearchGate, accessed on April 21, 2025, https://www.researchgate.net/publication/387497792_Mitigating_AI_Bias_in_Financial_Decision-Making_A_DEI_Perspective

63. DPC casts gimlet eye on AI - Lewis Silkin LLP, accessed on April 21, 2025,

https://www.lewissilkin.com/insights/2024/09/23/dpc-casts-gimlet-eye-on-ai-102jjy1

64. Irish Data Protection Commission welcomes EDPB opinion on the use of personal data for the development and deployment of AI models | 18/12/2024, accessed on April 21, 2025, http://www.dataprotection.ie/en/irish-data-protection-commission-welcomes-edpb-opinion-use-personal-data-development-and-deployment
65. Insurance Accounting Advisory Quarterly - AI - KPMG Ireland, accessed on April 21, 2025, https://kpmg.com/ie/en/home/insights/2024/10/harnessing-ai-fs-insurance.html
66. Innovation Sandbox Programme | Central Bank of Ireland, accessed on April 21, 2025, https://www.centralbank.ie/regulation/innovation-hub/innovation-sandbox-programme
67. Innovation Hub 2023 Update - Central Bank of Ireland, accessed on April 21, 2025, https://www.centralbank.ie/docs/default-source/regulation/innovation-hub/innovation-hub-2023-update.pdf?sfvrsn=360b601a_5
68. Responsible AI Principles and Approach | Microsoft AI, accessed on April 21, 2025, https://www.microsoft.com/en-gb/ai/principles-and-approach
69. Empowering responsible AI practices | Microsoft AI, accessed on April 21, 2025, https://www.microsoft.com/en-us/ai/responsible-ai
70. Apply responsible AI principles in learning environments - Training | Microsoft Learn, accessed on April 21, 2025, https://learn.microsoft.com/en-us/training/modules/apply-responsible-ai-principles/

71. Best practices for responsible AI implementation - Box Blog, accessed on April 21, 2025, https://blog.box.com/responsible-ai-implementation-best-practices

72. From general counsel to chief executive - Law Society of Ireland Gazette, accessed on April 21, 2025, https://www.lawsociety.ie/gazette/in-depth/2024/june/from-general-counsel-to-chief-executive/

73. Using Copilot in Finance (Copilot Scenario Library) - Microsoft Adoption, accessed on April 21, 2025, https://adoption.microsoft.com/en-us/copilot-scenario-library/finance/

74. 3 Examples of Microsoft Copilot for financial planning and analysis (FP&A) - Beebole, accessed on April 21, 2025, https://beebole.com/blog/microsoft-copilot-for-financial-planning-and-analysis/

75. Top 10 Use Cases for Microsoft Copilot Studio in 2025 - QServices, accessed on April 21, 2025, https://www.qservicesit.com/top-10-use-cases-for-microsoft-copilot-studio-in-2025

76. Using Copilot in Financial Services - Microsoft Adoption, accessed on April 21, 2025, https://adoption.microsoft.com/en-us/copilot-scenario-library/financial-services/

77. Bechtle AG · Annual Report 2024, accessed on April 21, 2025, https://www.bechtle.com/dam/jcr:f7605839-67f3-4064-a1ea-e109b3f7c2ce/bechtle_ag_annual_report_2024.pdf

78. Annual Technology Conference - Chartered Accountants Ireland Events, accessed on April 21, 2025, https://charteredaccountantsevents.com/wp-

content/uploads/2025/01/Annual-technology-Conference-2025-Slide-Pack.pdf

79. AI Governance in Financial Services - Holistic AI, accessed on April 21, 2025, https://www.holisticai.com/blog/ai-governance-in-financial-services
80. Conversation Modes: Quick, Think Deeper, Deep Research - Microsoft Support, accessed on April 21, 2025, https://support.microsoft.com/en-us/topic/conversation-modes-quick-think-deeper-deep-research-575efe12-eb34-4437-885a-440f7623cffb
81. From Concept to Code: Using GitHub Copilot to Bring Your Ideas to Life - Lantern Studios, accessed on April 21, 2025, https://lanternstudios.com/insights/blog/from-concept-to-code-using-github-copilot-to-bring-your-ideas-to-life/
82. AI on Guardrails: the boost all financial institutions need to innovate - Genesis Global, accessed on April 21, 2025, https://genesis.global/blog/ai-on-guardrails/
83. Itaú · GitHub, accessed on April 21, 2025, https://github.com/customer-stories/itau
84. How an AI Copilot Can Lift the Expertise of Agents, Bankers & Branch Staff, accessed on April 21, 2025, https://interface.ai/how-an-ai-copilot-can-lift-the-expertise-of-your-agents-bankers-and-branch-staff/
85. The changing nature of actuarial departments: Adapting to new challenges and innovations - Milliman Dublin, accessed on April 21, 2025, https://ie.milliman.com/en-gb/insight/changing-nature-of-actuarial-departments
86. Raiffeisen Bank International · GitHub, accessed on April 21, 2025, https://github.com/customer-stories/raiffeisen-bank

87. Neon Bank tackles financial exclusion in Brazil with GitHub Enterprise., accessed on April 21, 2025, https://github.com/customer-stories/neon-bank

88. Top 30 Real-Life Use Cases for Microsoft Copilot - Redress Compliance, accessed on April 21, 2025, https://redresscompliance.com/30-real-life-use-cases-for-microsoft-copilot-in-organizations/

89. Using Copilot in Customer Service (Copilot Scenario Library) - Microsoft Adoption, accessed on April 21, 2025, https://adoption.microsoft.com/en-us/copilot-scenario-library/customer-service/

90. 2024 - Teletimes International, accessed on April 21, 2025, https://teletimesinternational.com/2024/TT_July24.pdf

91. Banking financial advisory support system - Microsoft Adoption, accessed on April 21, 2025, https://adoption.microsoft.com/en-us/copilot-scenario-library/financial-services/banking-financial-advisory-support-system/

92. Microsoft 365 Copilot governance: Managing AI volume and preventing oversharing, accessed on April 21, 2025, https://sharegate.com/blog/microsoft-365-copilot-governance

93. 4 Data Governance Best Practices for Microsoft 365 Copilot - Securiti.ai, accessed on April 21, 2025, https://securiti.ai/copilot-governance-best-practices/

94. Navigating Responsible AI: Best Practices for Implementation - Informatica, accessed on April 21, 2025, https://www.informatica.com/resources/articles/navigating-responsible-ai.html

95. Mitigating Artificial Intelligence Bias in Financial Systems: A Comparative Analysis of Debiasing Techniques - Asian Journal of Research in Computer Science, accessed on April 21, 2025, https://journalajrcos.com/index.php/AJRCOS/article/view/536

96. Ethics and AI: Building Trust in the Workplace - Emtrain, accessed on April 21, 2025, https://emtrain.com/blog/ethics-and-compliance/ethics-and-ai-building-trust-in-the-workplace/

97. The Importance of Validating AI Content - RTInsights, accessed on April 21, 2025, https://www.rtinsights.com/the-importance-of-validating-ai-content/

98. AI at Work: AI Training for Employees - NAVEX, accessed on April 21, 2025, https://www.navex.com/en-us/courses/ai-employee-training/

99. 4 Steps to Take to Ensure the Accuracy of Your AI Content | PRSA, accessed on April 21, 2025, https://www.prsa.org/article/4-steps-to-take-to-ensure-the-accuracy-of-your-ai-content

100. Expert Advice on How to Ethically Implement AI in HR - Senior Executive, accessed on April 21, 2025, https://seniorexecutive.com/ethical-ai-implementation-in-hr-best-practices/

101. Navigating Copilot Adoption: Key Legal Considerations for Data Governance | Epiq, accessed on April 21, 2025, https://www.epiqglobal.com/en-au/resource-center/advice/navigating-copilot-adoption-key-legal-considerations-for-data-governance

102. KPMG EU AI Hub - YouTube, accessed on April 21, 2025, https://www.youtube.com/watch?v=Z_jGZyf1cUc

103. Bytes Technology Group plc ('BTG', 'the Group') Results for the six months ended 31 August 2024, accessed on April 21, 2025, https://www.bytesplc.com/media/2jdh2nqc/btg_interim_results_31_aug_24.pdf

104. Interim Results – Company Announcement - FT.com - Markets data, accessed on April 21, 2025, https://markets.ft.com/data/announce/detail?dockey=1323-16714293-3CSATQNC47F6D320CMQI0PN553

105. Accenture boosts SAP HANA agility and performance by migrating to Azure | Microsoft Customer Stories, accessed on April 21, 2025, https://www.microsoft.com/en/customers/story/709295-accenture-partner-professional-services-azure

106. microsoft - AI Ireland, accessed on April 21, 2025, https://aiireland.ie/tag/microsoft/

107. Copilot Practical Applications and Success Stories with Sarah Miller - Apple Podcasts, accessed on April 21, 2025, https://podcasts.apple.com/us/podcast/copilot-practical-applications-and-success-stories/id1663682415?i=1000697832382&l=zh-Hans-CN

108. AI Archives - Page 3 of 7 - Executive Platforms: Thought Leader Series, accessed on April 21, 2025, https://epthoughtleaders.com/tag/ai/page/3/

109. RunAs Radio - Simplecast, accessed on April 21, 2025, https://feeds.simplecast.com/cRTTfxcT

110. What Is Driving the Global Common Data Capability at RGA, accessed on April 21, 2025, https://www.rgare.com/knowledge-center/article/what-is-driving-the-global-common-data-capability-at-rga

111. M365 Copilot - MnCCC, accessed on April 21, 2025, https://mnccc.gov/assets/pdf3/pdf4/mnccc-shi-copilot.pdf

112. Enjoy AI Assistance Anywhere with Copilot for PC, Mac, Mobile, and More - Microsoft, accessed on April 21, 2025, https://www.microsoft.com/en-ie/microsoft-copilot/for-individuals

113. Delivering greater impact with Copilot and the power of agents | Microsoft Education Blog, accessed on April 21, 2025, https://www.microsoft.com/en-us/education/blog/2025/01/delivering-greater-impact-with-copilot-and-the-power-of-agents/

114. 2024 Annual Report - Investor Relations, accessed on April 21, 2025, https://ir.amd.com/financial-information/sec-filings/content/0001193125-25-067185/0001193125-25-067185.pdf

115. Are AI Summaries, Copilot Insights, and Meeting Transcriptions Discoverable? A Record Keeping Guide for SEC-Registered Advisers - Steel Eye, accessed on April 21, 2025, https://www.steel-eye.com/news/are-ai-summaries-copilot-insights-and-meeting-transcriptions-discoverable

116. AI Insights with Sean Blanchfield on Startup Success - TikTok, accessed on April 21, 2025, https://www.tiktok.com/@aiawards_irl/video/7480900267328720150

117. Generative AI Market worth $136.7 billion by 2030 - Exclusive Report by MarketsandMarkets™, accessed on April 21, 2025, https://www.prnewswire.com/news-releases/generative-ai-market-worth-136-7-billion-by-2030---exclusive-report-by-marketsandmarkets-302129818.html

118. OpenAI - The Irish Times, accessed on April 21, 2025, https://www.irishtimes.com/tags/openai/

119. The Impact of AI in Advancing Accessibility for Learners with Disabilities, accessed on April 21, 2025, https://er.educause.edu/articles/2024/9/the-impact-of-ai-in-advancing-accessibility-for-learners-with-disabilities

120. Microsoft is bringing Copilot to the cybersecurity frontline - Silicon Republic, accessed on April 21, 2025, https://www.siliconrepublic.com/enterprise/microsoft-copilot-for-security-generative-ai-pricing

10 Glossary of Terms

Accountability (AI)
The obligation for organisations and individuals involved in the AI lifecycle (development, deployment, oversight) to justify and take responsibility for AI-related decisions, actions, and outcomes.

Accuracy (AI)
The degree to which an AI system's predictions or decisions correspond to the true or correct values. While important, accuracy alone does not guarantee fairness or reliability.

AI Act (EU Artificial Intelligence Act)
A landmark EU regulation establishing harmonised rules for Artificial Intelligence across member states. It uses a risk-based approach (classifying AI into unacceptable, high, limited, and minimal risk categories) and imposes specific obligations on providers and deployers, particularly for high-risk systems prevalent in finance.

AI Advisory Council (Ireland)
A council established by the Irish government intended to provide guidance on national AI policy and engage with the public on AI implications.

AI Ambassador (Ireland)
An appointed representative (Dr. Patricia Scanlon mentioned) responsible for promoting trustworthy AI and raising public awareness about its societal and economic implications in Ireland.

AI Governance
The comprehensive framework of policies, regulations, principles, standards, and practices designed to ensure that AI systems are developed, deployed, and managed responsibly, ethically, securely, and in compliance with legal requirements.

AI Governance Frameworks
Structured approaches, methodologies, or standards (e.g., ISO/IEC 42001, NIST AI RMF) that organisations can use to implement and manage AI governance effectively.

AI Lifecycle
The entire process of an AI system's existence, from initial conception, problem formulation, data collection

and preparation, model development and training, testing and validation, deployment, ongoing monitoring, and maintenance, through to eventual retirement or decommissioning.

AI Literacy
The ability to understand the basic concepts of AI, its capabilities and limitations, its potential impacts, and to interact with AI systems effectively and critically. Promoted as part of Ireland's national digital literacy strategy.

AI Risk Management
The systematic process of identifying, assessing, evaluating, mitigating, monitoring, and reporting the risks associated with the development, deployment, and use of AI systems.

AI Risk Management Framework (AI RMF) (NIST)
A voluntary framework developed by the US National Institute of Standards and Technology providing guidance on managing AI-specific risks, structured around Govern, Map, Measure, and Manage functions.

Algorithmic Bias
Systematic and repeatable errors in an AI system that create unfair outcomes, such as privileging one arbitrary group of users over others. Bias can emerge from biased training data, algorithm design, or human interaction.

Algorithmic Consumer
Refers to consumers whose interactions with financial services are primarily mediated through AI-powered platforms and automated decision-making systems.

Algorithmic Trading
The use of computer programs and AI algorithms to execute trading orders automatically at high speeds based on predefined rules or learned market patterns.

AML (Anti-Money Laundering)
Practices, laws, and regulations aimed at preventing money laundering. AI is increasingly used to enhance AML processes, such as transaction monitoring and customer due diligence.

Anonymisation
The process of altering personal data so that the data subject is no longer

identifiable. Achieving true and robust anonymisation, especially for complex AI models, is technically challenging and subject to strict legal standards under GDPR.

Artificial Intelligence (AI)

The theory and development of computer systems able to perform tasks normally requiring human intelligence, such as visual perception, speech recognition, decision-making, and translation between languages. In the context of the book, often refers to machine learning and deep learning systems.

Auditability

The capability of an AI system and its surrounding processes to allow for independent review and examination of its operations, data usage, decision-making logic (where possible), and outcomes to verify compliance, accuracy, and fairness.

Automated Decision-Making (GDPR Article 22)

Decisions based solely on automated processing, including profiling, which produce legal effects concerning an individual or similarly significantly affect them. GDPR provides specific rights for individuals subject to such decisions.

Bias (AI)

(See Algorithmic Bias). Refers to systematic prejudice in AI outputs resulting from various factors including flawed data or algorithm design. Key types discussed include Data Bias (Historical, Representation, Measurement, Sampling, Selection), Algorithmic Bias, and Human Bias (Cognitive, Confirmation, Interaction, Evaluation/Interpretation, Annotation/Label).

Black Box Problem

Refers to the difficulty in understanding the internal workings and decision-making processes of complex AI models (like deep neural networks), making them opaque even to their developers.

Central Bank of Ireland (CBI)

Ireland's central bank and primary financial services regulator. It sets supervisory expectations for AI use by regulated firms, focusing on risk management, consumer protection, operational resilience, and accountability, and is expected to be a key authority under the EU AI Act for the financial sector.

Chatbots
AI programs designed to simulate conversation with human users, often used in customer service applications within financial institutions. Subject to transparency requirements under the EU AI Act.

Compliance
Adherence to relevant laws, regulations, standards, and internal policies. Key regulations discussed include the EU AI Act and GDPR.

Concentration Risk (AI)
The risk arising from over-reliance on a small number of third-party providers for critical AI models, platforms, or data, potentially creating systemic vulnerabilities if a major provider fails.

Consent Management
Processes and systems for obtaining, recording, and managing individuals' consent for the processing of their personal data, a key requirement under GDPR, especially for customer-facing AI applications.

Consumer Protection
Measures and regulations designed to safeguard consumers from unfair, deceptive, or harmful practices, a key focus for the CBI regarding AI deployment in financial services.

Consumer Protection Code (Ireland)
A code issued by the Central Bank of Ireland setting out requirements for regulated firms when dealing with consumers. Its application in the context of digital services and AI is under review.

Copilot for Microsoft 365
An AI assistant integrated into Microsoft 365 applications (Word, Excel, Teams, etc.) that uses Large Language Models and Microsoft Graph to access and reason over an organisation's internal data (emails, documents, chats) to enhance productivity.

Copilot Studio (Microsoft)
A low-code platform allowing organisations to build, customise, and manage their own AI agents ('copilots') that can connect to various data sources and automate workflows.

Counterfactual Fairness
A fairness concept ensuring that an AI system's decision would remain the same even if an individual's sensitive attributes (like race or gender)

were different, all else being equal.

Credit Scoring
The process of evaluating an individual's creditworthiness based on their financial history and other relevant data. AI is increasingly used, making it a high-risk application under the EU AI Act.

Cybersecurity
The practice of protecting systems, networks, and data from digital attacks, damage, or unauthorised access. Robust cybersecurity is crucial for AI systems due to the sensitive data they process and their potential vulnerabilities.

Data Bias
Bias originating from the data used to train AI models, including historical biases, lack of representation, measurement errors, or sampling issues.

Data Governance
The overall management of the availability, usability, integrity, and security of the data employed in an organisation. Essential for ensuring the quality and compliance of data used in AI systems.

Data Minimisation
A GDPR principle requiring that personal data collected and processed should be adequate, relevant, and limited to what is necessary for the specified purpose.

Data Poisoning
A type of attack where malicious data is intentionally introduced into an AI model's training set to compromise its performance or security.

Data Portability (GDPR)
The right for individuals under GDPR to receive their personal data from a controller in a structured, commonly used, machine-readable format and to transmit that data to another controller.

Data Protection Act 2018 (Ireland)
The Irish legislation that implements and supplements the GDPR.

Data Protection Commission (DPC)
Ireland's independent national supervisory authority responsible for monitoring and enforcing data protection law (GDPR and Data Protection Act 2018).

Data Protection Impact Assessment (DPIA)

A process required under GDPR for data processing activities likely to result in a high risk to individuals' rights and freedoms (often triggered by AI deployment). It helps identify and mitigate data protection risks.

Data Quality
The degree to which data is accurate, complete, consistent, timely, and fit for its intended purpose. Poor data quality is a major source of AI model unreliability and bias.

Data Subject Rights (GDPR)
Rights granted to individuals under GDPR concerning their personal data, including rights of access, rectification, erasure, restriction, portability, and objection to automated decision-making.

Data Transparency
Understanding the origin, characteristics, quality, potential biases, and processing of the data used to train and operate AI systems.

Deep Learning
A subset of machine learning based on artificial neural networks with multiple layers (deep architectures), capable of learning complex patterns from large datasets. Often associated with 'black box' models.

Deepfakes
AI-generated synthetic media (images, audio, video) where a person's likeness is replaced with someone else's, often used maliciously. Subject to transparency requirements under the EU AI Act.

Digital Operational Resilience Act (DORA)
An EU regulation establishing requirements for the security of network and information systems of companies operating in the financial sector, including ICT risk management and third-party risk management, relevant for AI system resilience.

Discrimination (Non-Discrimination)
The principle that individuals should not be treated unfairly or disadvantageously based on protected characteristics (e.g., race, gender, age). A key goal of AI fairness mitigation.

DORA (Digital Operational Resilience Act)
(See Digital Operational Resilience Act).

DPC (Data Protection Commission)
(See Data Protection Commission).

DPIA (Data Protection Impact Assessment)
(See Data Protection Impact Assessment).

Due Diligence (Vendor)
The process of investigation and assessment performed by an organisation before entering into an agreement with a third-party vendor (e.g., an AI provider) to evaluate their capabilities, security, compliance, and risks.

Ethical Considerations (AI)
The process of evaluating AI development and deployment against moral principles and values, considering potential impacts on individuals, society, and human rights, often going beyond strict legal compliance.

EU AI Act
(See AI Act).

Explainability (XAI)
The capability of an AI system to provide human-understandable explanations for its decisions or predictions. Techniques and methods designed to achieve this are referred to as Explainable AI (XAI).

Fairness (AI)
The principle and practice of ensuring that AI systems do not produce discriminatory outcomes or perpetuate existing biases, treating individuals and groups equitably. Key types include group fairness (equal outcomes across groups) and individual fairness (similar treatment for similar individuals).

Fairness Metrics
Quantitative measures used to assess the fairness of an AI model's outcomes across different demographic subgroups (e.g., demographic parity, equal opportunity, equalized odds).

Fairness-Aware Modelling
Techniques used during AI model development that explicitly incorporate fairness objectives or constraints into the training process to mitigate bias.

False Positives
Instances where an AI system incorrectly identifies a condition or event as present when it is not (e.g., flagging a legitimate transaction as fraudulent).

Feature Engineering
The process of selecting, transforming, or creating input variables (features) used by an AI model, which can influence model performance

and potentially introduce or mitigate bias.

Federated Approach (AI Regulation)
An approach where the supervision and enforcement of AI regulations (like the EU AI Act) are distributed among existing national sectoral regulators (e.g., financial authorities, data protection authorities) rather than creating a single new AI authority.

Financial Consumer Protection
Regulatory and supervisory activities aimed at protecting consumers engaging with financial services, ensuring they are treated fairly and receive clear information.

Financial Inclusion
Efforts to ensure that individuals and businesses have access to useful and affordable financial products and services that meet their needs. AI bias poses a risk to financial inclusion.

Financial Services and Pensions Ombudsman (FSPO)
An independent body in Ireland that investigates complaints from consumers about financial service providers and pension providers. Designated as an authority under the EU AI Act regarding fundamental rights.

Fintech
Technology-enabled innovation in financial services. Companies operating in this space often leverage AI.

Foundation Models
Large AI models (often LLMs) trained on vast amounts of broad data that can be adapted or fine-tuned for a wide range of downstream tasks (e.g., GPT-4).

Fraud Detection
The use of processes and technologies, increasingly including AI, to identify and prevent fraudulent activities in financial transactions.

FRIA (Fundamental Rights Impact Assessment)
An assessment required under the EU AI Act for deployers of high-risk AI systems to evaluate the potential impact of the system on fundamental rights before putting it into service.

FSPO (Financial Services and Pensions Ombudsman)
(See Financial Services and Pensions Ombudsman).

Fundamental Rights

Basic rights and freedoms protected under EU law (e.g., Charter of Fundamental Rights), including dignity, privacy, non-discrimination, freedom of expression. The EU AI Act aims to ensure AI systems respect these rights.

GDPR (General Data Protection Regulation)
The primary EU law regulating the processing of personal data, setting out principles, rights, and obligations for organisations handling such data. Fully applicable to AI systems processing personal data.

General Data Protection Regulation (GDPR)
(See GDPR).

General-Purpose AI (GPAI)
AI systems, such as large foundation models, designed for a wide range of possible uses and which can be integrated into various downstream systems. Subject to specific transparency rules under the EU AI Act.

Generative AI (GenAI)
AI systems capable of creating new content (text, images, code, etc.) based on the patterns and information learned from their training data (e.g., ChatGPT, DALL-E).

Governance (AI)
(See AI Governance).

GPAI (General-Purpose AI)
(See General-Purpose AI).

GPT-4 / GPT-4 Turbo / GPT-4o
Specific versions of Large Language Models developed by OpenAI, used to power tools like Microsoft Copilot.

Group Fairness
A category of fairness metrics aiming to ensure that an AI model's outcomes are comparable across different demographic groups (e.g., similar loan approval rates).

Hallucinations (AI)
Instances where generative AI models produce confident but factually incorrect, nonsensical, or fabricated information not grounded in their training data or provided context.

High-Risk AI Systems (AI Act)
AI systems identified under the EU AI Act as posing significant potential risks to health, safety, or fundamental rights. Subject to stringent requirements regarding risk management, data quality, documentation, transparency, human oversight, and cybersecurity. Includes specific financial applications like credit

scoring and insurance risk assessment.

Historical Bias
Bias embedded in training data that reflects past societal prejudices or discriminatory practices present when the data was generated.

Human Bias
Biases originating from human actions, assumptions, or interpretations throughout the AI lifecycle, including cognitive biases of developers or evaluation biases of users.

Human Oversight
The principle and practice of ensuring meaningful human involvement in the monitoring, understanding, intervention, and potential overriding of AI system operations and decisions, particularly crucial for high-risk systems.

Human-in-the-loop
An approach where humans actively participate in the operational loop of an AI system, often reviewing predictions, providing feedback, or making final decisions based on AI recommendations.

Identity Verification
Processes used to confirm the identity of an individual, often required for KYC and AML compliance. AI techniques like facial recognition are sometimes used.

IHREC (Irish Human Rights and Equality Commission)
Ireland's national human rights and equality body, designated as an authority under the EU AI Act concerning fundamental rights.

Implementation Framework
A structured plan or roadmap outlining the phases, steps, roles, and responsibilities for deploying a system or initiative, such as AI governance or a specific AI tool like Copilot.

Inclusiveness
A principle of responsible AI aiming to ensure systems are designed and deployed in ways that empower and engage people from all backgrounds and abilities.

Individual Fairness
A category of fairness metrics aiming to ensure that similar individuals are treated similarly by an AI model, regardless of their group membership.

Information Retrieval (AI)
The use of AI techniques to find and extract relevant

information from large datasets or document repositories based on user queries or prompts.

Infrastructure (for AI)
The underlying technological resources required to support AI development and deployment, including computing power (e.g., GPUs), data storage, and network connectivity.

Innovation
The introduction of new methods, ideas, or products. AI is seen as a major driver of innovation in financial services, balanced by the need for responsible governance.

Insight Research Centre (University of Limerick)
An Irish research centre collaborating with the Central Bank of Ireland on AI-related research.

Insurance Pricing
The process of determining the premium to be charged for an insurance policy. AI use in this area for life and health insurance is considered high-risk under the EU AI Act.

Insurance Underwriting
The process of evaluating the risk associated with insuring a person or asset to decide whether to offer coverage and at what price.

Integrity and Confidentiality (GDPR)
A GDPR principle requiring personal data to be processed securely, protecting against unauthorised or unlawful processing and against accidental loss, destruction, or damage.

Intellectual Property
Intangible creations of the human intellect, such as inventions, literary and artistic works, designs, symbols, names, and images used in commerce. Protection of AI models as intellectual property can sometimes conflict with transparency goals.

Interaction Bias
Bias introduced into an AI system through the way users interact with it over time, potentially reinforcing certain patterns or skewed feedback.

Interpretable AI
AI models whose internal workings and decision-making logic are inherently easier for humans to understand (e.g., decision trees, linear models). Often contrasted with 'black box' models.

Investment Advice

Recommendations provided to clients regarding investment strategies or specific financial products. AI-powered 'robo-advisory' is an emerging application.

IOB (Institute of Banking)
An Irish professional body providing education and qualifications for the banking and financial services sector, offering courses on responsible AI.

Ireland's National AI Strategy
The Irish government's strategic plan outlining its vision and objectives for the development and adoption of AI in Ireland, emphasizing a human-centric and trustworthy approach.

Irish Banking Culture Board
An independent body established to promote cultural change within the Irish banking sector. Provided an anonymized case study on AI in credit decision-making.

ISO/IEC 42001 (AIMS)
The first international management system standard specifically for Artificial Intelligence (AI), providing a framework for organisations to establish, implement, maintain, and improve AI governance responsibly and ethically.

KYC (Know Your Customer)
Regulatory requirements for financial institutions to verify the identity of their clients and assess potential risks for illegal intentions for the business relationship. AI is sometimes used to automate parts of the KYC process.

Large Language Models (LLMs)
(See LLMs).

Lawful Basis (GDPR)
A valid legal justification required under GDPR Article 6 for processing personal data (e.g., consent, contract necessity, legal obligation, legitimate interests).

Least Privilege (Principle of)
A security concept restricting access rights for users, accounts, and computing processes to only those resources absolutely required to perform routine, legitimate activities. Crucial for M365 governance before Copilot deployment.

Legacy Systems
Older IT systems, hardware, or software applications that continue to be used by an organisation, potentially posing challenges for

integration with new AI technologies.

Legal Liability
Legal responsibility for harm or damages caused. Determining liability for outcomes involving complex AI systems can be challenging.

Legitimate Interests (GDPR)
One of the lawful bases for processing personal data under GDPR, requiring the controller to balance their legitimate interests against the rights and freedoms of the data subject. Requires a documented balancing test (LIA).

Lifecycle (AI)
(See AI Lifecycle).

LIME (Local Interpretable Model-Agnostic Explanations)
A specific XAI technique that explains individual predictions of any machine learning model by approximating it locally with a simpler, interpretable model.

Limited Risk AI Systems (AI Act)
AI systems under the EU AI Act that primarily pose risks related to transparency (e.g., chatbots, deepfakes), subject mainly to disclosure obligations.

LLMs (Large Language Models)
Advanced AI models trained on massive text datasets (like GPT-4) capable of understanding context, generating human-like text, translating languages, and performing various language-based tasks. They power tools like Copilot.

Loan Approvals
The process by which a financial institution decides whether to grant a loan to an applicant. AI is increasingly used to automate or assist in this process.

Logging (AI Systems)
The automatic recording of events related to an AI system's operation, including inputs, decisions, and interactions. Required for high-risk systems under the EU AI Act for traceability and monitoring.

Machine Learning (ML)
A subset of AI where systems learn patterns and make predictions from data without being explicitly programmed for the task.

Market Surveillance Authority (AI Act)
National authorities

designated under the EU AI Act responsible for monitoring the market for AI systems and enforcing the Act's requirements. The CBI is expected to fulfil this role for financial services in Ireland.

Measurement Bias
Bias arising from inaccuracies or inconsistencies in how data is measured or collected, or from using flawed proxies for the intended variable.

Microsoft Graph
The API gateway providing access to data and intelligence within the Microsoft 365 ecosystem (emails, files, calendars, etc.). Used by Copilot for Microsoft 365 to access organisational context securely, respecting user permissions.

Microsoft Purview
Microsoft's suite of data governance, risk, and compliance solutions, including tools for data discovery, classification, sensitivity labelling, data loss prevention (DLP), and audit logging relevant for governing Copilot.

Microsoft Responsible AI Standard
Microsoft's internal framework and set of principles (Fairness, Reliability & Safety, Privacy & Security, Inclusiveness, Transparency, Accountability) guiding its development and deployment of AI technologies.

Minimal Risk AI Systems (AI Act)
AI systems posing little or no risk under the EU AI Act's classification, subject to minimal or no mandatory obligations beyond potential voluntary codes.

Mitigation Strategies (Bias)
Techniques and procedures implemented to reduce or eliminate unfair bias in AI systems, applied across the AI lifecycle (data preparation, model training, testing, monitoring).

Model Drift
The degradation of an AI model's performance over time as the statistical properties of the input data change, requiring ongoing monitoring and potential retraining.

Model Inventory
A catalogue maintained by an organisation listing all AI models in use or development, typically including details on purpose,

data, risk level, validation status, and ownership.

Model Risk
The potential for adverse consequences resulting from decisions based on incorrect or misused models. Includes risks from flawed design, data issues, incorrect implementation, or inappropriate use.

Model Validation
The process of confirming that an AI model performs as intended, meets specified requirements, and is suitable for its purpose. Includes testing for accuracy, robustness, and fairness.

Monitoring (AI Systems)
The continuous observation and checking of an AI system's performance, behaviour, and compliance after deployment to detect issues like model drift, emerging biases, or security threats.

Multi-Factor Authentication (MFA)
A security process requiring users to provide two or more verification factors to gain access to a resource, enhancing account security.

National AI Strategy (Ireland)
(See Ireland's National AI Strategy).

Natural Language Processing (NLP)
A field of AI focused on enabling computers to understand, interpret, and generate human language. Used extensively in chatbots and LLMs.

Neural Networks (Artificial)
Computing systems inspired by the biological neural networks that constitute animal brains. They form the basis for deep learning models.

NIST AI Risk Management Framework (AI RMF)
(See AI Risk Management Framework (AI RMF) (NIST)).

Non-Compliance Penalties
Fines or other sanctions imposed by regulatory authorities for failure to adhere to legal requirements, such as those under the EU AI Act or GDPR.

Non-Discrimination
(See Discrimination).

Notified Bodies (AI Act)
Independent third-party organisations designated by EU member states to conduct conformity assessments for certain high-risk AI systems before they can be placed on the market.

Objective Function (AI)
The mathematical function that an AI algorithm aims to optimise (minimise or maximise) during the training process. The choice of objective function can influence model behaviour and potential biases.

Open Banking
A system allowing third-party financial service providers secure access to consumer banking, transaction, and other financial data from banks and non-bank financial institutions, often via APIs. Raises data privacy considerations when combined with AI.

Operational Resilience
The ability of an organisation to prevent, adapt to, respond to, recover from, and learn from operational disruptions. A key focus for financial regulators (e.g., DORA), with AI introducing new resilience considerations.

Operational Risk
The risk of loss resulting from inadequate or failed internal processes, people, and systems or from external events. AI deployment introduces new operational risks.

Outcome Transparency
Ensuring that the results and impacts of AI decisions are clear and understandable to those affected.

Oversight (Human)
(See Human Oversight).

Overreliance (on AI)
The tendency for users to place excessive trust in AI outputs without sufficient critical evaluation, potentially leading to the adoption of errors or a decline in human expertise.

Ownership (AI)
Clearly defined responsibility for an AI system, including its development, performance, maintenance, and outcomes.

Partner Ecosystem
The network of third-party companies (e.g., IT consultants, system integrators, software vendors) that collaborate with major technology providers like Microsoft to sell, implement, and support their products, playing a key role in Copilot adoption.

Permissions (M365)
Access rights granted to users or groups within the Microsoft 365 environment, controlling what data (e.g., SharePoint sites, files, mailboxes) they

can view or modify. Copilot respects these permissions.

Personal Data
Any information relating to an identified or identifiable natural person ('data subject'), as defined under GDPR. Processing of personal data by AI is subject to GDPR rules.

Personalisation
Tailoring services, products, or communications to individual users based on their data, preferences, or behaviour. AI enables enhanced personalisation but raises privacy and fairness concerns.

Phased Rollout
An implementation strategy where a new system or technology (like Copilot) is deployed gradually to specific groups or departments over time, rather than all at once ('big bang'). Allows for testing and refinement.

Phishing
A type of cyberattack where attackers impersonate legitimate entities to trick individuals into revealing sensitive information (e.g., login credentials, financial details). AI can be used to create more convincing phishing attacks.

Pilot Programs
Controlled, small-scale implementations of a new system or process conducted before full deployment to test feasibility, gather feedback, identify issues, and refine the approach.

Plugins (Copilot)
Third-party extensions that can be added to Copilot to connect it to external data sources or services, expanding its capabilities but also introducing potential data sharing risks that require governance.

Policies (AI Usage)
Formal guidelines established by an organisation outlining the acceptable and prohibited uses of AI tools like Copilot, data handling rules, verification requirements, and ethical expectations for employees.

Portfolio Management
The professional management of investment portfolios, including asset allocation and investment decisions. AI is used to assist in analysis and strategy development.

Post-Market Monitoring (AI Act)
Obligations under the EU AI

Act for providers of high-risk AI systems to continuously monitor the system's performance and compliance after it has been placed on the market or put into service.

Power Platform (Microsoft)
Microsoft's suite of low-code tools for building applications, automating workflows, and analysing data, including Power BI and Power Automate. Copilot Studio is part of this platform.

Predictive Analytics
The use of data, statistical algorithms, and machine learning techniques to identify the likelihood of future outcomes based on historical data.

Pre-processing (Fairness Technique)
Bias mitigation techniques applied to the training data before model training begins (e.g., re-weighting, data balancing).

Principle of Least Privilege
(See Least Privilege).

Privacy
The right of individuals to control the collection, use, and disclosure of their personal information. A core principle in AI governance and central to GDPR.

Privacy by Design
An approach to system development where privacy considerations are embedded into the design and architecture from the outset, rather than being added later.

Privacy Enhancing Techniques (PETs)
Technologies and methods designed to protect personal data privacy, such as anonymisation, pseudonymisation, encryption, and differential privacy.

Problem Formulation (AI Lifecycle)
The initial stage of AI development involving defining the business problem to be solved and translating it into a specific task suitable for an AI system. Choices made here can influence downstream bias.

Procedural Fairness
Ensuring that the processes used by an AI system to arrive at decisions are fair, transparent, and consistently applied.

Process Automation
The use of technology, including AI, to automate business processes previously performed by

humans.

Process Transparency
Clarity regarding how AI models are developed, deployed, monitored, and governed within an organisation.

Profiling (GDPR)
Any form of automated processing of personal data consisting of the use of personal data to evaluate certain personal aspects relating to a natural person, in particular to analyse or predict aspects concerning that natural person's performance at work, economic situation, health, personal preferences, interests, reliability, behaviour, location or movements. Subject to specific rules under GDPR.

Prompt Engineering
The process of designing and refining the text inputs (prompts) given to generative AI models to elicit desired, accurate, and relevant outputs.

Protected Characteristics
Attributes of individuals legally protected from discrimination, such as race, gender, age, disability, religion, sexual orientation. AI fairness aims to prevent bias based on these characteristics or their proxies.

Providers (AI Act)
Entities that develop an AI system or have an AI system developed with a view to placing it on the EU market or putting it into service under their own name or trademark. Subject to specific obligations under the AI Act.

Proxies (Data)
Variables used in AI models that are not explicitly sensitive but are statistically correlated with protected characteristics, potentially leading to indirect discrimination if not handled carefully (e.g., postcode correlating with race).

Pseudonymisation
Processing personal data in such a manner that it can no longer be attributed to a specific data subject without the use of additional information, provided that such additional information is kept separately and subject to technical and organisational measures to ensure non-attribution. Still considered personal data under GDPR.

Psychological Safety

A shared belief held by members of a team that the team is safe for interpersonal risk-taking, allowing individuals to speak up with ideas, questions, concerns, or mistakes without fear of negative consequences. Important for raising ethical concerns about AI.

Public Trust
The confidence that the public has in the fairness, reliability, transparency, security, and ethical use of AI systems deployed by organisations.

Purpose Limitation (GDPR)
A GDPR principle requiring that personal data be collected for specified, explicit, and legitimate purposes and not further processed in a manner that is incompatible with those purposes.

Quality (Data)
(See Data Quality).

Readiness (AI)
An organisation's state of preparedness for adopting and implementing AI technologies effectively and responsibly, encompassing technical infrastructure, data maturity, skills, governance, and culture.

Record-Keeping (AI Act)
Obligations under the EU AI Act for high-risk systems to maintain logs and documentation necessary for traceability, monitoring, and demonstrating compliance.

Recruitment (AI Bias)
The potential for AI tools used in hiring processes (e.g., CV screening) to unfairly favour or disadvantage candidates based on demographic factors rather than qualifications.

Redress Mechanisms
Processes allowing individuals negatively affected by an AI decision to seek review, appeal, correction, or compensation.

RegTech (Regulatory Compliance Technology)
The use of technology, often including AI, to enhance and automate regulatory compliance processes within the financial services industry.

Regulatory Compliance
(See Compliance).

Regulatory Landscape
The complex environment of laws, regulations, guidelines, and supervisory practices governing a particular sector or technology, such as AI in Irish finance.

Reliability (AI)
The ability of an AI system to perform its intended function consistently and accurately under specified conditions for a specified period. A core principle of responsible AI.

Remediation (Access Control)
The process of identifying and correcting overly broad or inappropriate user permissions within IT systems like Microsoft 365.

Representation Bias
Bias occurring when the data used to train an AI model does not accurately reflect the diversity of the population it will be applied to in the real world.

Reputational Risk
The risk of damage to an organisation's reputation resulting from negative events, public perception, or unethical behaviour, such as deploying biased AI systems.

Responsible AI
An approach to developing, deploying, and using AI systems in a way that aligns with ethical principles, societal values, and human rights, aiming to maximise benefits while minimising harm. Encompasses fairness, transparency, accountability, privacy, security, reliability, and inclusiveness.

Responsible AI Standard (Microsoft)
(See Microsoft Responsible AI Standard).

Responsibility (AI)
A broad ethical duty for organisations and individuals involved with AI to act proactively to ensure systems are designed, developed, and used safely, fairly, ethically, and beneficially, going beyond mere legal accountability for outcomes.

Retention Policies (Data)
Organisational rules defining how long different types of data should be kept before being securely deleted, essential for GDPR compliance (storage limitation) and managing data volume for AI.

Risk Appetite
The amount and type of risk that an organisation is willing to pursue or retain in pursuit of its objectives. Should be defined for AI adoption.

Risk Assessment
The process of identifying potential risks, analysing their likelihood and potential impact, and evaluating their

significance. Crucial for AI governance and required under the EU AI Act (including FRIAs).

Risk Management
(See AI Risk Management).

Risk Management System (AI Act)
A mandatory, documented system required for high-risk AI systems under the EU AI Act, covering the identification, analysis, evaluation, and mitigation of risks throughout the AI lifecycle.

Roadmap (Implementation)
A strategic plan outlining the sequence of steps, milestones, timelines, and resources required to achieve a specific goal, such as implementing AI governance or deploying Copilot.

Robo-Advisory
Automated financial advice and portfolio management services provided through digital platforms using algorithms and AI, with minimal human intervention.

Robustness (AI)
The ability of an AI system to maintain its level of performance under adversarial conditions, such as noisy or unexpected inputs, or changes in the operating environment. A requirement for high-risk systems under the EU AI Act.

ROT Data (Redundant, Obsolete, Trivial)
Data that is no longer useful, accurate, or necessary for business or legal purposes. Managing ROT data improves data quality and reduces risks associated with AI accessing irrelevant information.

Safety (AI)
A core principle of responsible AI ensuring that systems operate without causing unintended harm to individuals or property.

Sampling Bias
Bias introduced when the method used to select a data sample results in a sample that is not representative of the overall population.

Scalability
The ability of a system, network, or process to handle a growing amount of work or its potential to be enlarged to accommodate that growth.

Security (AI)
Measures taken to protect AI systems and the data they process from unauthorised access, cyberattacks, manipulation, theft, or

disruption. A core principle of responsible AI and GDPR.

Selection Bias
A type of sampling bias where the process used to select data for training an AI model introduces bias (e.g., training a loan model only on approved applicants).

Sensitivity Labels (Microsoft Purview)
Labels applied to documents and emails within Microsoft 365 to classify their sensitivity (e.g., Public, Confidential), enabling the application of protection policies like encryption or access restrictions.

Sentiment Analysis
The use of NLP and AI techniques to identify and extract subjective information, such as opinions or attitudes, from text data (e.g., customer reviews, social media).

Service Boundary (M365)
The defined logical perimeter for Microsoft 365 services, within which customer data is processed and protected according to Microsoft's security and compliance commitments. Copilot for M365 operates within this boundary.

Shadow AI
The use of AI tools and applications by employees within an organisation without official approval, knowledge, or oversight from the IT department or management, potentially introducing security and compliance risks.

SHAP (Shapley Additive exPlanations)
A popular XAI technique based on game theory that assigns an importance value to each feature for a particular prediction, helping to explain model output.

Shared Responsibility Model (AI Act)
The concept under the EU AI Act where both the provider (developer) and the deployer (user) of a high-risk AI system have distinct but overlapping compliance obligations.

SharePoint Online
Microsoft's cloud-based service for document management and collaboration, a key data source for Copilot for Microsoft 365.

Single Supervisory Mechanism (SSM)
The system of banking supervision in the Eurozone,

comprising the European Central Bank (ECB) and national supervisory authorities. Relevant for how AI regulation might be overseen for major banks.

Skills Gaps
A lack of necessary skills and expertise within the workforce required to perform certain tasks or adopt new technologies, identified as a challenge for AI adoption in Ireland.

Social Scoring
The practice of evaluating individuals based on their social behaviour, trustworthiness, or characteristics using data analysis. Prohibited for public authorities under the EU AI Act.

Socio-technical Perspective
An approach that considers the interplay between social factors (people, culture, organisations, ethics) and technical factors (algorithms, data, infrastructure) when analysing or designing systems like AI.

Solvency II
An EU directive codifying and harmonising insurance regulation, establishing capital requirements and risk management standards relevant for insurers using AI.

Special Categories of Personal Data (GDPR)
Sensitive personal data defined under GDPR Article 9 (e.g., race, ethnicity, political opinions, health data, biometric data) subject to stricter processing conditions. The EU AI Act allows processing for bias mitigation under specific safeguards.

Staff Training
Educational programs designed to equip employees with the knowledge, skills, and awareness needed for their roles, crucial for responsible AI use.

Stakeholder Engagement
The process of involving individuals or groups who may be affected by or have an interest in an organisation's activities (e.g., customers, employees, regulators, community) in dialogue and decision-making.

Standards (AI)
Formal documents establishing requirements, specifications, guidelines, or characteristics for AI systems or processes (e.g., ISO/IEC 42001).

Statistical Parity (Demographic Parity)
A fairness metric requiring that an AI model's positive outcome rate (e.g., loan approval) is approximately equal across different demographic groups.
Storage Limitation (GDPR)
A GDPR principle requiring that personal data be kept in a form which permits identification of data subjects for no longer than is necessary for the purposes for which the data are processed.
Stress Testing (Models)
Evaluating an AI model's performance and stability under extreme or unusual conditions to understand its limitations and potential failure points.
Structured Approach
A methodical and organised way of tackling a problem or implementing a project, such as using a phased framework for AI governance rollout.
Subject Matter Expertise
Deep knowledge and understanding of a specific field or domain, essential for humans verifying AI outputs or providing effective oversight.
Summarisation (AI)
The use of AI, particularly LLMs, to automatically generate concise summaries of longer texts, documents, emails, or meetings.
Supervisory Expectations (CBI)
Guidance and requirements communicated by the Central Bank of Ireland to the financial institutions it regulates regarding specific practices, risks, or areas of focus, such as the use of AI.
Supply Chain Security
Measures taken to protect the integrity and security of products, services, and data throughout the supply chain, relevant for managing risks associated with third-party AI providers.
Synthetic Data
Artificially generated data created algorithmically, often used to augment limited datasets, improve model robustness, or test AI systems without using real personal data. Can be used for bias mitigation (data balancing).
Systemic Risk
The risk of disruption or collapse affecting an entire system (e.g., the financial system) rather than just individual components, potentially arising from

correlated behaviour of AI systems or concentration in AI providers.

Taxonomy of Bias
A classification system organising the different types and sources of bias that can affect AI systems (e.g., data bias, algorithmic bias, human bias).

Technical Documentation (AI Act)
Comprehensive documentation required for high-risk AI systems under the EU AI Act, detailing the system's design, development, capabilities, limitations, data usage, testing, and compliance measures.

Testing (AI Models)
The process of evaluating an AI model's performance, accuracy, robustness, fairness, and security using specific datasets and metrics before and after deployment.

Third-Party AI Providers
External companies or vendors that supply AI models, platforms, tools, data, or related services to organisations. Managing risks associated with these providers is crucial.

Third-Party Risk Management
Processes within an organisation for identifying, assessing, monitoring, and mitigating risks arising from relationships with external third-party vendors and suppliers. Mandated under DORA and critical for AI governance.

Traceability
The ability to track the origin, processing history, and usage of data and the decision-making steps within an AI system, often enabled by logging. Essential for accountability and debugging.

Training (AI Models)
The process by which machine learning models learn patterns and relationships from data to perform a specific task.

Training Data
The dataset used to train an AI model. The quality, representativeness, and potential biases within training data significantly impact the resulting model's performance and fairness.

Transparency
The principle that AI systems and their operations should be understandable. Encompasses transparency of

data used, model processes (explainability), development and governance processes, and decision outcomes. A core principle of responsible AI and a requirement under the EU AI Act.

Transparency Obligations (AI Act)
Specific requirements under the EU AI Act for certain AI systems (e.g., chatbots, deepfakes) to disclose their AI nature to users.

Trust
Confidence in the reliability, integrity, fairness, security, and competence of a person, organisation, or system. Building and maintaining trust is paramount for AI adoption, especially in financial services.

Trustworthy AI
AI systems that are lawful, ethical, and robust, encompassing principles like fairness, transparency, accountability, privacy, security, and human oversight. The overarching goal of AI governance and regulation.

Unacceptable Risk AI Systems (AI Act)
AI practices deemed under the EU AI Act to pose a clear threat to fundamental rights or safety, which are consequently prohibited within the EU (e.g., social scoring by public authorities).

Undersampling
A data balancing technique used in bias mitigation where instances from the majority class in a dataset are removed to create a more balanced representation relative to minority classes.

Underwriting (Insurance)
(See Insurance Underwriting).

Unfairness
Lack of impartiality or equity; outcomes or processes that disadvantage certain individuals or groups without justification. AI bias can lead to unfairness.

Unintended Consequences
Unexpected and often negative outcomes resulting from the deployment or interaction of systems, including AI, which were not foreseen during design or development.

Upskilling
Training employees to acquire new or more advanced skills, necessary for adapting to technological changes like the introduction of AI.

Usability Testing

Evaluating how easy and effective an AI system or tool is to use from the perspective of end-users.

Use Cases (AI)
Specific applications or scenarios where AI technology is employed to solve a business problem or achieve a particular objective.

Validation (AI Models)
(See Model Validation).

Values (Organisational)
The core principles and beliefs that guide an organisation's behaviour and decision-making. AI deployment should align with these values.

Vendor Lock-in
A situation where an organisation becomes dependent on a specific vendor's products or services, making it difficult or costly to switch to an alternative provider. A potential risk with third-party AI solutions.

Vendor Management
(See Third-Party Risk Management).

Verification (Output)
The process of checking AI-generated outputs for accuracy, plausibility, fairness, and appropriateness before relying on them, typically involving human review.

Virtual Assistants
AI-powered applications (like chatbots or voice assistants) designed to perform tasks or provide information for users based on commands or questions.

Vulnerabilities (Security)
Weaknesses in IT systems, software, or processes that could be exploited by attackers. AI systems introduce new potential vulnerabilities.

XAI (Explainable AI)

11 Index

A

Accountability .. 6, 7, 9, 11, 83, 142, 144, 147, 150, 151, 156, 157, 166, 169, 173, 174, 177, 181, 188, 190, 210, 252, 328, 336, 351, 374, 376, 377, 378, 390, 398, 402
Adversarial Attacks.................. 228
AI Advisory Council...............19, 21
AI Compliance 175
AI Governance.... 1, 3, 5, 7, 76, 115, 175, 186, 188, 190, 237, 241, 265, 272, 273, 276, 279, 282, 283, 398, 402, 415, 419, 435
AI Governance Frameworks 5, 7, 115, 237
AI Governance Principles ..265, 279
AI Inventory......................333, 337
AI Lifecycle 8, 76, 292, 318, 331, 337
AI Readiness 42
AI Standards and Assurance Roadmap............................. 179
AI Usage Policy (AUP)........393, 415
Algorithmic Bias5, 7, 111, 223, 244, 290
Algorithmic Consumer 21
Algorithmic Trading.......5, 102, 219
Allied Irish Banks (AIB) 321
An Post Money.....6, 123, 130, 139, 140
Anti-Money Laundering (AML) 104, 218
Artificial Intelligence (AI) 21, 85, 86, 135, 178, 180, 182
Auditability............................. 157
Azure AI Content Safety 366, 378

B

Bank of America.......................101
Bank of Ireland. 6, 7, 35, 46, 48, 63, 83, 126, 137, 138, 142, 143, 145, 152, 154, 160, 163, 166, 169, 173, 175, 183, 188, 195, 197, 199, 207, 209, 248, 249, 262, 268, 269, 274, 280, 286, 323, 325, 346, 353, 433
Bias Detection..................311, 315
BondGPT 68, 80
Broadridge 80
Bytes Technology Group...409, 438

C

Capacity Building.......301, 332, 338
Capital Requirements Directive (CRD)..................................208
Case Studies... 5, 6, 10, 43, 80, 123, 281, 404
Central Bank of Ireland (CBI) 61, 95, 97, 152, 160, 209, 299, 355, 374, 375
Change Management..........10, 418
Chartered Accountants Ireland.434
Chatbots...............5, 101, 219, 296
ChatGPT 12
Chief Data Officer (CDO) 335
Chief Risk Officer (CRO) 335
Cognitive Bias...........................291
Cognizant 123, 139
Compliance 1, 3, 55, 68, 73, 133, 137, 151, 195, 218, 245, 279, 335, 336, 337, 338, 340, 378, 398, 400, 402, 415, 419, 429, 431, 432, 436
Compliance Officer 73, 335, 340
Concentration Risk...................234

Confirmation Bias 291
Consent Management 5, 106
Consumer Protection... 7, 8, 48, 97, 138, 173, 209, 249, 273, 300, 304, 305, 335, 352, 376
Consumer Protection Code . 8, 300, 304, 305, 335, 352
Copilot Chat..... 360, 362, 368, 369, 389, 427
Copilot Copyright Commitment 378
Copilot for Finance 358, 382
Copilot for Microsoft 365 .... 9, 358, 362, 364, 366, 367, 373, 379, 386, 404, 405, 409, 412, 421, 424, 425, 428
Copilot for Sales................ 358, 380
Copilot for Service 358, 384
Copilot Pro... 9, 358, 361, 367, 427, 429
Copilot Studio 9, 358, 364, 367, 368, 378, 381, 383, 384, 411, 423, 426, 430, 434
Counterfactual Fairness.............. 21
Credit Scoring .. 5, 31, 66, 100, 138, 203, 204, 205, 218, 295
Customer Service..... 5, 66, 73, 101, 219, 296, 383, 410, 436
Cybersecurity... 5, 7, 112, 132, 138, 219, 232, 303

D

DALL-E....................... 360, 366, 368
Data Bias.................................. 289
Data Classification 415
Data Collection 292, 318
Data Discovery.................. 395, 400
Data Ethics 274
Data Governance..... 8, 9, 189, 191, 203, 241, 300, 302, 310, 312, 318, 322, 331, 335, 336, 337, 395, 400, 415, 422, 432, 436, 437
Data Handling...360, 361, 363, 365, 394
Data Literacy 132, 172, 283
Data Management 7, 259
Data Minimisation.................... 373
Data Poisoning 228
Data Protection 5, 6, 63, 85, 86, 89, 95, 97, 106, 117, 123, 128, 133, 137, 140, 183, 212, 214, 216, 262, 271, 275, 278, 280, 281, 355, 374, 375, 413, 425, 428, 429, 432
Data Protection Act 2018......... 212
Data Protection Commission (DPC) ..95, 97, 117, 216, 355, 374, 375
Data Protection Impact Assessments (DPIAs) 5, 117, 214, 374
Data Quality 244, 311
Data Residency......................... 387
Data Transparency 53
Dataverse 364
Decision Support 221
Demographic Parity.................. 313
Department of Enterprise, Trade and Employment (DETE) 36
Digital Literacy............................ 21
Digital Operational Resilience Act (DORA) 207, 330
Dimensions of Transparency.. 4, 53
Discriminatory Outcomes........... 21
Disparate Impact 313
Disparate Impact Analysis 313
Document Summarisation.......... 68
Dogpatch Labs 325
Dr. Patricia Scanlon 19, 21

E

Employee Training................ 9, 397
Enterprise Digital Advisory Forum

.... 36
Enterprise Ireland...................... 36
Enterprise Risk Management (ERM) 329
Ethical AI Framework 415
Ethical Considerations......6, 7, 159, 190, 192, 249, 394
Ethical Culture 332
Ethical Guidelines......241, 317, 400
Ethics 174, 175, 300, 328, 336, 349, 397, 400, 437
EU Data Boundary.............363, 387
Executive Sponsorship 321
Explainability (XAI) 8, 316, 331
Explainable AI (XAI) 22, 31, 49, 227, 316

F

Fair Housing Act 30
Fairness .. 4, 7, 8, 11, 22, 25, 27, 48, 55, 188, 191, 223, 251, 299, 300, 312, 313, 315, 319, 321, 337, 339, 373, 377, 378, 413
Fairness Metrics 8, 313, 315
Fairness Testing........................ 337
Fairness-Aware Algorithms 312
Feature Engineering.............8, 310
Feature Selection 311
Feedzai 99
Fexco 325
FICO Platform 99
Financial Consumer Protection . 22, 268, 349
Financial Inclusion 250
Financial Institutions 4, 7, 8, 41, 66, 73, 135, 170, 194, 217, 268, 277, 307
Financial Services and Pensions Ombudsman (FSPO).95, 97, 154, 287
Financial Stability 172, 222, 266, 276
Financial Stability Board (FSB) ..222
Finclude................. 6, 126, 130, 141
Fintech 179, 325, 347
Fraud Detection . 5, 32, 66, 99, 203, 218, 296
Fundamental Rights ... 84, 135, 177, 303, 329, 350
Fundamental Rights Impact Assessment (FRIA) 303

G

Gap Analysis..............................333
General Data Protection Regulation (GDPR) . 5, 9, 89, 133, 212, 286, 355, 372
General-Purpose AI (GPAI) 200, 371
Generative AI (GenAI)...............218
GitHub Copilot . 358, 382, 393, 409, 411, 435
Glossary of Terms 4, 10, 21, 441
Governance.. 7, 9, 10, 11, 173, 181, 182, 210, 241, 243, 244, 254, 256, 258, 259, 273, 300, 322, 328, 336, 364, 367, 369, 376, 392, 393, 398, 411, 415, 417, 421
Group Fairness............................22

H

Historical Bias............................289
Human Bias...............................291
Human Oversight ... 5, 8, 9, 60, 113, 189, 192, 205, 300, 303, 316, 318, 331, 337, 396, 401, 422
Human Rights............................136
Human-in-the-loop 319

I

IBM...... 48, 126, 141, 313, 326, 351
IBM AI Fairness 360 313

IFS Skillnet................................326
Implementation Framework.... 4, 8, 10, 76, 328, 336, 412
Inclusiveness............................377
Index............................ 10, 11, 442
Individual Fairness......................22
Innovation ..1, 3, 84, 197, 211, 260, 325, 346, 376, 433
Innovation Hubs 325
Innovative teaching with AI: Creative approaches to enhancing learning in education 15
Inscribe 325
Insurance Ireland. 8, 134, 178, 295, 324
Insurance Link..........................324
Insurance Pricing 203, 204
Insurance Underwriting.... 205, 295
Interaction Bias.........................291
Internal Audit...........................336
Investment Advice.....................67
Investment Management.........219
Ireland...3, 4, 7, 8, 9, 14, 20, 21, 33, 35, 38, 39, 40, 45, 46, 49, 50, 61, 63, 69, 83, 84, 86, 88, 89, 95, 100, 103, 111, 121, 126, 129, 130, 132, 133, 134, 135, 136, 137, 138, 140, 142, 143, 145, 152, 154, 171, 172, 174, 175, 176, 177, 179, 180, 183, 194, 195, 199, 207, 211, 212, 216, 217, 218, 221, 256, 262, 268, 269, 270, 271, 272, 274, 275, 278, 279, 280, 281, 283, 286, 298, 303, 306, 307, 323, 325, 326, 347, 349, 350, 351, 354, 357, 370, 382, 383, 384, 404, 407, 409, 410, 411, 421, 432, 434, 438
Ireland's National AI Strategy...323
Irish Banking Culture Board..... 125, 141, 177
Irish Data Protection Law..... 7, 212
Irish Human Rights and Equality Commission (IHREC)..... 154, 286
ISO/IEC 27001.......................... 238
Itaú Bank 383

K

KPMG Ireland .10, 42, 49, 180, 272, 281, 349, 407, 433

L

Label Bias................................ 292
Large Language Models (LLMs) 357, 365
Leadership Commitment.......... 328
Legal Counsel........................... 335
LIME (Local Interpretable Model-Agnostic Explanations)........... 58
Loan Approvals.................. 31, 295

M

MacBook Air.............................. 12
Machine Learning............. 136, 354
Measurement Bias 290
Microsoft..9, 10, 12, 355, 357, 358, 360, 361, 362, 363, 364, 365, 366, 367, 368, 370, 373, 377, 378, 379, 386, 387, 388, 393, 395, 404, 405, 407, 409, 410, 412, 420, 421, 422, 423, 424, 425, 426, 427, 428, 429, 430, 433, 434, 435, 436, 438, 439, 440
Microsoft 365...355, 357, 361, 362, 363, 366, 379, 421, 422, 424, 426, 427, 428, 436
Microsoft Edge 360
Microsoft Graph...... 357, 362, 364, 366, 368, 386, 395, 421

Microsoft Power Platform........ 365
Microsoft Purview.....363, 364, 395
Microsoft Word.......................... 12
MiFID II..............................208, 376
Mitigation Strategies....9, 388, 393, 425
Model Inventory....................... 329
Model Risk.....7, 229, 246, 336, 337
Model Risk Management......... 336
Model Transparency 53
Multidisciplinary Approach 321
Multi-Factor Authentication (MFA) 401
Musgrave Group 10, 405

N

National AI Research Nexus ..38, 40
Natural Language Processing (NLP) 218
Neon Bank.........................383, 436
NIST AI Risk Management Framework (AI RMF)............ 239
Non-Discrimination 4, 7, 25, 30, 188, 191, 251
Numerai 103

O

OneNote............................361, 362
Ongoing Monitoring 315
Open Banking............4, 72, 84, 140
Open Culture............................ 321
OpenAI 384, 430, 440
Operational Efficiency.............. 218
Operational Resilience 210, 330
Operational Risk....................... 308
Organisational Readiness......... 414
Outcome Transparency............. 54

P

Partner Ecosystem 411, 423
Permanent TSB..287, 325, 326, 351
Personalisation 219
Phased Rollout..........................322
Picture perfect............................17
Pilot Programs.....................10, 416
Plus One Education series...........15
Policy Development............10, 415
PorterShed 325
Portfolio Management 220
Power BI...................................382
Power Platform.................364, 369
PowerPoint 361, 362
Predictive Analytics...................221
Privacy...... 5, 6, 7, 9, 11, 85, 86, 99, 103, 106, 123, 133, 139, 140, 189, 191, 227, 245, 250, 377, 378, 386, 397, 413, 424, 427
Privacy by Design 5, 103
Privacy Risks............................5, 99
Process Transparency 53
Professional Services 10, 407
Project management made easy 15
Prompt Engineering..................397
Public Trust 22
PwC Ireland 83, 139, 176, 272, 281, 282, 409

R

Raiffeisen Bank International...383, 435
Regulatory Compliance.... 5, 43, 60, 119, 218, 286
Regulatory Environment...........422
Regulatory Guidance.....9, 239, 374
Regulatory Interpretation.....7, 258
Regulatory Landscape. 5, 6, 89, 152
Regulatory Penalties.................307
Representation Bias..................289
Representative Data 310
Reputational Damage 308
Reputational Risk......................287
Requests for Proposals (RFPs) ..380

Research and Innovation........ 4, 38
Resource Constraints........... 7, 256
Responsibility... 6, 8, 130, 142, 144, 147, 148, 150, 151, 158, 159, 166, 169, 174, 273, 299, 336, 396
Responsible AI 5, 7, 8, 9, 10, 49, 106, 134, 139, 174, 176, 178, 253, 254, 255, 269, 270, 274, 275, 277, 281, 282, 322, 323, 328, 333, 343, 346, 351, 366, 377, 378, 390, 400, 405, 408, 415, 432, 433, 436
Risk Assessment5, 32, 76, 100, 218, 244, 337, 413
Risk Management 5, 50, 55, 78, 83, 132, 139, 177, 203, 210, 218, 246, 273, 281, 300, 302, 329, 335, 337, 376, 398
Risk Management Lifecycle 5, 78
Risk Mitigation...................... 7, 244
Robo-Advisory 204, 220
Role-Based Training................. 402

S

Salesforce 380
Sampling Bias........................... 290
SAS.. 180
Security Controls 245
Selection Bias........................... 290
SHAP (Shapley Additive exPlanations).......................... 58
SharePoint Online.................... 395
Single Supervisory Mechanism (SSM).................................. 207
Skills Development 326
Skills Gaps........................... 7, 256
Solvency II........................ 376, 382
Staff Training 5, 119, 338
Stakeholder Engagement 332
Statistical Parity....................... 313
Streets of Dublin 17
Stripe 325, 346
Supply Chain Security............... 234

T

Take your time – the art and craft of long exposure photography17
Taxonomy of Bias 8, 289
Technical Integration.......... 10, 417
Third-Party AI Providers 5, 79
Third-Party Risk Management.. 246
Traceability.............................. 389
Training Data 216
TransferMate........................... 325
Transparency.... 4, 5, 7, 8, 9, 11, 51, 52, 53, 54, 55, 71, 73, 77, 81, 83, 109, 126, 161, 166, 173, 174, 188, 190, 204, 214, 226, 244, 249, 300, 302, 304, 306, 316, 318, 331, 337, 371, 373, 377, 378, 389, 394
Trust 6, 54, 130, 195, 287, 307, 437
Trustworthy AI........................... 24
Tungsten Intelligent Automation Platform 41, 42

U

Ulster Bank 325
Unintended Consequences 24
University of Limerick 83, 211, 268, 280, 301, 323
User Support 418

V

Vendor Lock-in 234
Vendor Management ... 5, 121, 259
Virtual Assistants.......... 5, 101, 219

W

Walkers Global 176, 274, 426

www.ingramcontent.com/pod-product-compliance
Lightning Source LLC
Chambersburg PA
CBHW052103230326
41599CB00054B/3620